OF WOODS & WATERS

Of Woods
& Waters

A KENTUCKY
OUTDOORS
READER

EDITED BY Ron Ellis

FOREWORD BY Nick Lyons

THE UNIVERSITY PRESS
OF KENTUCKY

Publication of this volume was made possible in part by
a grant from the National Endowment for the Humanities.

Scholarly publisher for the Commonwealth,
serving Bellarmine University, Berea College, Centre
College of Kentucky, Eastern Kentucky University,
The Filson Historical Society, Georgetown College,
Kentucky Historical Society, Kentucky State University,
Morehead State University, Murray State University,
Northern Kentucky University, Transylvania University,
University of Kentucky, University of Louisville,
and Western Kentucky University.
All rights reserved.

Editorial and Sales Offices: The University Press of Kentucky
663 South Limestone Street, Lexington, Kentucky 40508-4008
www.kentuckypress.com

09 08 07 06 05 5 4 3 2 1

Library of Congress Cataloging-in-Publication Data
Of woods and waters : a Kentucky outdoors reader /
edited by Ron Ellis ; foreword by Nick Lyons.
     p. cm.
A collection of reprints of writings and poems originally
published from 1889 to 2005.
Includes bibliographical references (p.   ) and index.
ISBN 0-8131-2373-9 (hardcover : alk. paper)
 1. Natural history—Kentucky. 2. Outdoor life—Kentucky—
Anecdotes. 3. Outdoor life—Kentucky—Fiction.
I. Ellis, Ron, 1949–
QH105.K4034 2005
508.769—dc22   2005015813

This book is printed on acid-free recycled paper meeting
the requirements of the American National Standard for
Permanence of Paper for Printed Library Materials.

Design and typesetting by Julie Allred, BW&A Books, Inc.
Manufactured in the United States of America.

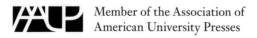

Member of the Association of
American University Presses

For Jim Pruett
   who believed in the dream
   and opened the door

In Memoriam
Adolph Leo Thelen (1910–2005)
   Father-in-law, friend, fisherman
Margery Thomas Rouse (1920–2005)
   Teacher, colleague, friend

He'd lived for woods and waters in those days, he and his buddies, passionate hunters and fishermen . . . Unable to say it, still he'd known that certain things were beautiful.

—Jim Wayne Miller, *His First, Best Country*

CONTENTS

FOREWORD

WHAT AN EARTHY and eclectic cornucopia this is—essays, fiction, and poetry that celebrate the wide-ranging sporting life of Kentucky. It is also a special revelation to me, a passionate fisherman who once spent seven months in the state without once fishing.

Ron Ellis—whose introduction to this unique volume is itself wonderfully full, wise, and personal—has done a fine job of ferreting out and collecting immensely different approaches to the state's world of spirited contrasts. There are pieces by and about such historical figures as Daniel Boone and John J. Audubon (who finds the better part of a suckling pig in the belly of a catfish); a fine selection from James A. Henshall, the father of bass fishing; and there are stories, poems, and articles that present the disparate group of activities that limn the unique character of the state, including trotline fishing, tickling, fox hunting

(in essay and story), frog hunting, bass fishing, carp fishing with a fly rod; hunting deer, ducks, turkey, grouse, and squirrels; recipes for barbecuing groundhog and baking possum; close looks at deer camps, a dove hunt, some hilarious profiteering with the carcass of a gigantic catfish, and much more. There is a memorable profile of a great old muskie fisherman; historical reports on the Kentucky long rifle and those first great bait-casting reels made by George Snyder (as early as 1810) and then Ben Meek and Ben Milam. Legendary men pursue legendary bass, the catfish grow to one hundred pounds, and an old Cherokee can persuade a hunter not to take a certain black buck, a "spirit deer" of high consequence to his people.

Folded into this ample portrait are works by authors of national importance: Robert Penn Warren, Barbara Kingsolver, Elizabeth Madox Roberts, Wendell Berry (always one of the world's finest writers on the natural world and our relationship to it), Bobbie Ann Mason (whose story of an older woman's struggle, to her own near-death, after catching a huge catfish, you won't forget), a selection from Caroline Gordon's classic *Aleck Maury, Sportsman*, which I've admired for more than forty years, and Ron Ellis's own vignette of Christmas in the hills, grouse hunting, from his superb *Cogan's Woods*.

MY OWN EXPERIENCES with Kentucky sport are slender but perhaps worth recording. An old friend, then in his eighties, once pointed to a large painting of an austere old fellow above his piano in Long Island, New York, and said that it was "Great Grandfather Milam"; and I later learned that his grandfather was the famous Kentucky bourbon distiller, George T. Stagg, whose name he bore. George was a passionate fly fisherman and the closest fishing companion of the pioneer angling entomologist Preston Jennings. Along with the painting, he had an exquisite German silver bait-casting reel produced by Meek & Milam, and a bronze medal from the 1893 Columbian Exposition honoring B.C. Milam & Sons. I arranged for the Kentucky Historical Society in Frankfort to take both items as gifts. George also showed me a large drawer in his basement full of thousands of loose parts for reels and I assumed at the time that this was the last resting place of the famous reel company. Some years later, after George had died, his son-in-law—his last surviving relative—sent me a brief notice announcing a tag sale to be held at George's house. I went, bought a few items as keepsakes, and asked the fellow about the reel parts. "Oh," he said, "we threw all that stuff out last week with a lot of other trash." Only recently did I learn, from Michael Hudson at the Kentucky Historical Society, that they had in fact been given, many years earlier, a full complement of tools and parts from the company. Fortunately, I guess, what I had been shown, what had been thrown away as junk, was less than the final resting place of a great firm.

In June 1954, after completing basic training at Ft. Dix in New Jersey, I was sent to Ft. Knox in Louisville, Kentucky. I had studied business in college, graduated, and then something unsettling had begun to happen to me, tugging me away from the fishing that had been so much a part of my life from before memory . . . and from what I had studied. I only vaguely knew what "tooth" was "nibbling" at my soul—as Emily Dickinson has it—but I could not resist its effects.

In the mornings I was the battalion morning-report checker, so my work was essentially over by one o'clock. I was required to be in the headquarters office for another few hours but had no job other than to look busy. I was reading Steinbeck then and can remember typing out whole chapters of *East of Eden* and all of *Of Mice and Men*, reading as I went, trying to type as fast as I could on a big Underwood Standard Model "S," a model I continued to write on for forty years, only recently graduating to a Royal standard. I wanted to throw over a life I had taken a degree for, change one hundred and eighty degrees, and I knew only that reading and writing were somehow connected to where I wanted to go. So I did not fish all that hot summer of 1954, did not explore the waters near Ft. Knox for the largemouth bass I'd always loved to fish for with plugs, but instead read, with increasing intensity, either in my barracks or under a certain massive live oak.

At a rummage sale in July I found *The Portable Hemingway*— an anthology edited by Malcolm Cowley. It had a red flexible binding and fit comfortably into one of the top pockets of my olive-drab field jacket, so I carried it there, always. I carried it for a week before finding "Big Two-Hearted River," which I read at one sitting beneath my tree. It had a stunning effect on me, not least because it showed me that something great and important could be written with fishing as its central subject. I sat there all that hot Kentucky afternoon, read the story twice more, took out a notebook, and, my head flooded with Hemingway's river and a dozen of my own, became so absorbed that a patch of skin that had been exposed between sock and pants' cuff to the sun had developed a bright red welt. The welt was painful and distended, like proud flesh, but it spoke of a new intensity, a new concentration—and it has been since then an emblem I can never forget.

How I wish, though, that I had read Stephen Wrinn's "A Connecticut Yankee in a Kentucky Trout Stream" then, so I might have driven the few hours to what sounds like a remarkable trout stream, the Cumberland, or had explored the nearby farm ponds for bass. But who is to say I didn't "fish" in Kentucky, even if it was an Upper Peninsula Michigan river?

A RECURRENT THEME in *Of Woods and Waters* is the persistence of the past—both the rich fullness of what happened before and the need to return to it not merely as an excursion from the present but as a source of renewal in wilderness. Returns to old places figure repeatedly in this book—in a large family's returns to camping on an island in the great Dale Hollow Lake, in the nostalgia imbued in old hunting gear, in memories so deeply ingrained that they only become sharper with age, in portraits of legendary hunters and fishermen who remain near at hand. Wilderness changes, this book notes over and over, but we can cling to the older values it engendered.

Another cluster of images address the question of why we hunt and fish to begin with, the spirit and ethics of good sport, and why and how the outdoor life in a state as rich in sport as Kentucky can build character better than, say, sitting on a couch, and the inescapable pleasures of woods and waters. Such elemental values are manifest in fine essays like Gary Garth's "When the Cork Goes Under," which proposes, wisely, that "fishing sometimes seems to be overdosing on itself," and that we ought to return to simpler ways. For myself, I still find that moment electric when a bobber lunges beneath the surface.

Of Woods and Waters is first a textured look at sport in Kentucky—one full of unparalleled diversity; but in its values and its human stories, its uses of the sights and sounds of the natural world, it is not only Kentucky but radiates out to touch the heart of all sportsmen. It proves again that the universal is always best found in the local, if we know how to look for it. Graced by the woodcuts of Harlan Hubbard and the superb pen-and-ink drawings of Rick Hill, this book is a treasure.

—Nick Lyons
Woodstock, New York
July 2005

ACKNOWLEDGMENTS

Of Woods and Waters came together because of the hard work and dedication of many minds and hearts, and so there are many people I wish to thank:

First and foremost, I am grateful to the writers and artists who contributed their work; to Bill Coffey of Frankfort, Kentucky, for providing the front cover painting "The Fisherman" by Paul Sawyier; and to Bill Caddell of Franklin, Indiana, for providing the Harlan Hubbard woodcuts used throughout the collection.

Special thanks are also due the Kentucky Department of Fish and Wildlife Resources (KDFWR); Dave Baker, editor of *Kentucky Afield*, who was enthusiastic about this collection from the beginning; and the department's wildlife artist Rick Hill for his beautiful back cover painting "Pitching Down" and his pen and ink drawings illustrating the text. Thanks also to KDFWR's John A. Boone for scanning those drawings and paintings, Nancy McIver for research assistance, and Lee McClellan and Norm Minch for providing and updating the lists of Kentucky's record fish and white-tailed deer, respectively.

My warm thanks and gratitude go to Nick Lyons for his continued support, friendship, and encouragement and for his wonderful foreword, which happily reveals his own important connections to Kentucky. He has taught me many things, especially about books, art, writing, and, of course, fishing.

The research needed to assemble this collection required the assistance and counsel of colleagues located at libraries, universities, and organizations throughout the region. Let me begin

by thanking my friends and colleagues at Northern Kentucky University: Steely Library's Jennifer Gregory, Ann Harding, Rebecca Kelm, and especially Cynthia Valletta, without whom the content of this collection would not be nearly as complete; Dr. James C. Claypool, emeritus professor of history; and Dr. Danny Miller, chair, Department of Literature and Language.

Thanks also to Steve Albert of the Kenton County Public Library, Albert Pyle and Mark Pierce at Cincinnati's Mercantile Library, Beth Cunningham at Eastern Kentucky University's Crabbe Library, and Sharon Bidwell, librarian for the *Louisville Courier-Journal*.

For additional assistance and counsel, many thanks to teacher-author-bookseller Richard Taylor for his early belief in this collection; the *Kentucky Post*'s Mark Neikirk, Jim Reis, and Tim Stein; Laurie Risch, executive director of the Behringer-Crawford Museum in Covington; Mike Embry, editor of *Kentucky Monthly*; Lisa McDowell Snuggs, executive director of the Southeastern Outdoor Press Association; Joel Vance, historian for the Outdoor Writers Association of America; Mary Ellen Miller, co-ordinator of Western Kentucky University's Center for Robert Penn Warren Studies; Jonathan Greene, publisher of Gnomon Press; and Jeanie Thompson, poet, teacher, friend, and executive director of the Alabama Writers' Forum.

I am also grateful to those colleagues who worked so hard behind the scenes: Linda Lotz for the meticulous copyediting, Julie Allred for the book's perfect design, and Merrill Gilfillan for his counsel and careful proofreading.

I am extremely grateful to Stephen Wrinn, director of the University Press of Kentucky, for the opportunity to edit the collection, and to the Press's Anne Dean Watkins, Gena Henry, Lin Wirkus, Leila Salisbury, Wyn Morris, Mack McCormick, and Allison Webster.

Special thanks to my friend and colleague Mary Ellen Elsbernd for her support of my dream of "living the writing life" and for understanding my insatiable love of "woods and waters," which served as an inspiration, as did the writings of Jim Wayne Miller, in naming this collection. Thanks also to my friend John A. Ruthven and to Anne Caudill.

And, as always, my love and gratitude to my wife, Debbie, who is my best friend and who makes this writing dream possible.

The following sources were invaluable in preparing *Of Woods and Waters*:

"Chronology of the Kentucky Department of Fish and Wild-life Resources" (Spring–Summer 1995), compiled by Kimberly M. Hermes; *Conversations with Kentucky Writers I* and *II*, edited by L. Elizabeth Beattie; *Fishing Reel Makers of Kentucky* by Steven K. Vernon and Frank M. Stewart III; *Happy Hunting Ground; Home and Beyond: An Anthology of Kentucky Short Stories*, edited by Morris Allen Grubbs; *Kentucky Afield; A Kentucky Christmas,* edited by George Ella Lyon; *The Kentucky Encyclopedia*, edited by John E. Kleber; *Kentucky in American Letters 1784–1912* (volumes 1 and 2) by John Wilson Townsend; *Kentucky Renaissance: An Anthology of Contemporary Writing*, edited by Jonathan Greene; KLIT (a Web site devoted to Kentucky writers), maintained by the English Department of Eastern Kentucky University (www. eku.edu); *A Literary History of Kentucky* by William S. Ward; and *Poets Laureate of Kentucky* by Betty J. Sparks.

INTRODUCTION

WHEN STEPHEN WRINN and I first discussed the University Press of Kentucky's interest in publishing a collection of some of the best writing by Kentuckians about their outdoor experiences, he suggested that I put together a "dream" table of contents to prepare for our next round of conversations. I didn't need a lot of time to think about Stephen's proposal and committed to the quest right there in his office.

In the weeks ahead, I wandered through every bookstore I could find and often found myself happily lost in the stacks of libraries—both old sentinels with their well-thumbed card catalogs and modern structures with highly efficient computerized indexes. I leafed through ancient first editions with blackened leather covers that smudged my fingers and contemporary volumes with protective wrappings of acetate. I spent hours asking librarians and booksellers to suggest authors whose work might belong in such a collection. I also spent wonderful unstructured hours wandering in and out of the "Regional Literature" and "Kentucky Authors" sections in bookstores and libraries, fast-forwarding through years of newspapers cataloged on reels of microfilm, and searching through stacks of musty magazines. It was the feel and the smell of those magazines that started me thinking about how I had been unknowingly preparing for this quest for quite some time.

I WAS BORN in the historical river town of Maysville, Kentucky, but I grew up in Latonia, some fifty miles downstream in northern Kenton County, a land famous for expeditions mounted by such legendary hunters and explorers as Daniel Boone, Simon Kenton (the county's namesake), and Christopher Gist. This area had also attracted the attention of renowned wildlife artist John James Audubon (he served for a time as taxidermist at the Western Museum in nearby Cincinnati), and it was also the boyhood home of Daniel Carter Beard, the founder of the Boy Scouts of America. My friends and I were not unaware of this outdoor legacy as we fished for catfish, carp, and bass in the Licking River and Banklick Creek and built camps and set rabbit snares in nearby hollows. We were consumed by the outdoors— of course, this was *before* girls—and when we were not fishing or camping, we sat around on cinder blocks behind the corner grocery store and carved on sticks with our Barlow pocketknives (every boy owned one back then) and fantasized about the hunting and fishing expeditions we would take when we were older.

These fantasies were fueled by my father's monthly issues of *Outdoor Life, Sports Afield, Field & Stream*, and Kentucky Fish and Wildlife's *Happy Hunting Ground*, which I read, from cover to wonderful cover, as he passed them along to me. Every issue carried notes inscribed by my father in the margins of his favorite stories, printed there in his distinctive hand in the red ink he favored, which makes me think that he may have been an editor at heart. Most every story also carried a rating, with "AAA" being the best; he often defended this rating by adding comments in the margins that explained why a certain story or passage had earned his highest ranking. Clearly, he was passionate about good writing and anxious to

show me what stories could teach us about the outdoors. We read mostly magazines, with just a few books about the outdoors finding their way onto the shelves in my mother's secretary. Most of those were "how-to" books from the Outdoor Life Book Club, and they were primarily about hunting, since my father did not fish.

It was not until 1971, when I read Ernest Hemingway's "Big Two-Hearted River" in an English class at Northern Kentucky State College taught by my early mentor, the late Margery Thomas Rouse, that I noticed that serious writing—the kind I was beginning to be attracted to in books and literary journals—often celebrated nature and hunting and fishing. (Years later, we were again discussing Hemingway, and when I told Mrs. Rouse about one of my recent trout fishing trips, she smiled and asked, "Do you remember what Hemingway taught us about trout?" Before I could answer, she said, "He told us to always wet our hands before handling them so as not to harm their protective mucus," referring, of course, to the fisherman's caution offered by Nick Adams in "Big Two-Hearted River.") Before Mrs. Rouse celebrated that tale in her class, all the great stories we read in our school anthologies took place in cities and explored city themes, or so it seemed to me. Hemingway made me a reader with that famous short story, fanned the embers until they glowed white-hot, and sent me on what has become a lifelong hunt for more and more books and stories that explored similar themes. I found them in William Faulkner's work, especially his story "The Bear," from *Big Woods* (The Hunting Stories); Robert Ruark's *The Old Man and the Boy*; Ivan Turgenev's *Sketches from a Hunter's Album*; Dana Lamb's *Where the Pools Are Bright and Deep*; Harry Middleton's *The Earth Is Enough*; and in anything by Thomas McGuane, Jim Harrison, Rick Bass, Gretel Ehrlich, Wendell Berry, Guy de la Valdene, Nick Lyons, Howard Frank Mosher, and, most recently, Jim Wayne Miller and many more of the writers represented in this collection.

And so when my father died in March 1998, just days after I had completed the early pages of my first book, the fictionalized memoir *Cogan's Woods*—my paean to him and to a place on earth we both dearly loved—I inherited three boxes of back issues of one of his favorite magazines, *Happy Hunting Ground*, which would later become *Kentucky Afield*. I stored those boxes in my garage for more than two years before I could find the courage to sort through them. I knew I would find those notes in the margins, penned in that familiar red ink, and I would remember.

And I did remember, but instead of the pain I feared, I found great joy in returning to so many favorite articles and being transported again to many of the outdoor haunts I had first discovered in those pages. And so for several days I spent hours sitting on a camp stool out in the garage, clipping favorite articles and covers and incorporating them into my own growing files of stories and art that celebrated Kentucky's wild heritage, never suspecting that they would serve me well when the opportunity was presented to edit this collection.

FROM THE MOMENT Daniel Boone first "gained the summit of a commanding ridge, and, beheld the ample plains, the beauteous tracts below," Kentuckians have been tightly connected to the wild beauty of this place, first as subsistence hunters following streams and traces in search of fish and game—primarily buffalo, wild turkey, small game, and white-tailed deer (Kentucky had 315,000 to 435,000 white-tailed deer around the time Columbus discovered America and some 166,000 to 375,000 animals by 1800, according to the best estimates of the Department of Fish and Wildlife Resources, compared with the current deer herd, which is estimated at 900,000). Later, the harvesting of wild game shifted in its emphasis from primarily providing fish and meat for the table to providing *sport* in contemporary times, although that is not a word my father used when teaching me to hunt, since he considered hunting to be a deadly serious activity that bordered on the sacred. Art Lander's essay "Partners in the Web of Life" is as fine a musing on the subject as I have read, along with the excerpt from Jim Wayne Miller's novel *His First, Best Country*, which is a poet's celebration of the joy of being outdoors, in the woods and on the waters, "so close to something amazing and beautiful."

Although *Of Woods and Waters* does not claim to be the definitive collection of works by Kentuckians writing about their outdoor experiences, it offers a wide and diverse selection of personal essays, fiction, and poems—mostly set in Kentucky—by both established and emerging writers, native sons and daughters from all regions of the state and a few adopted Kentuckians as well.

In all the writings gathered here, each author, or so it seems to me, has "fallen under the spell of the land and its penetrating environmental influence," as Dr. Thomas D. Clark describes the influence of the Kentucky landscape in his foreword to William S. Ward's *A Literary History of Kentucky*. Or, as Chris Offutt describes that "influence" in an essay in the University of Kentucky Art Museum's *A Place Not Forgotten: Landscapes of the South*: "Kentuckians are the land—whether the taciturn people living so far in the woods they have to go toward town to hunt, or the quick moving apartment dwellers in cities. The image on our state flag reflects the dual nature of Kentucky's landscape—a pioneer wearing buckskins shakes hands with a man wearing a fancy suit. They are the land and the land is us." Indeed.

Readers will find the work of seven of Kentucky's twenty-two poet laureates appointed since 1926: Jesse Stuart (1954), a short story from *Come Gentle Spring*, set in the country near his beloved W-Hollow; Soc Clay (1984), an essay about Lewis County's legendary fisherman Muskie Joe Stamper, from *Happy Hunting Ground*; four poems by Jim Wayne Miller (1986) and an excerpt from his second novel, *His First, Best Country*; James

Still (1995), two poems from his new and collected work in *From the Mountain, From the Valley*; Richard Taylor (1999), four poems from *Bluegrass* and *Earth Bones* and an excerpt from his novel *Girty*; two poems by James Baker Hall (2001) from *The Mother on the Other Side of the World*; and from Joe Survant (2003), a poem from *Anne & Alpheus, 1842–1882*, which won the Arkansas Poetry Prize, and a new poem that first appeared in the *Louisville Review* in May 2005.

Stories by other distinguished novelists and essayists include "An Entrance to the Woods," an essay about a solitary hiking and camping trip in Red River Gorge by Wendell Berry, from *Recollected Essays 1965–1980*, and an excerpt on duck hunting from his first novel *Nathan Coulter*; a family hiking story from George Ella Lyon's novel *Gina. Jamie. Father. Bear.*; two short stories from Billy Clark's classic *Sourwood Tales*; a tale of fireworks, black powder, and "rabbit killers of high order" from Dr. Thomas D. Clark's *Pills, Petticoats and Plows: The Southern Country Store*; a hunting and fishing excerpt from Janice Holt Giles's *40 Acres and No Mule*; a remembrance of roaming the fields and creeks around Nicholas County from Barbara Kingsolver's *High Tide in Tucson*; a fond look at chasing "the little red-coated aristocrat" from *Blue-grass and Rhododendron* by John Fox Jr.; and a wonderful profile of a solo fishing trip to catch "old big one" from Bobbie Ann Mason's memoir *Clear Springs*. Included, too, is a tale of witches and deer hunting from Harry Caudill's *The Mountain, the Miner, and the Lord*; a testament to "heaven on earth" while canoeing on the Licking River, from David and Eulalie Dick's *Rivers of Kentucky*; an excerpt from Harriette Arnow's 1949 classic novel *Hunter's Horn*; and a profile of a beloved bird gun, a fourteen-gauge Greener, from Caroline Gordon's *Aleck Maury, Sportsman*.

I included excerpts from two books by Dr. James A. Henshall, the celebrated author of *The Book of the Black Bass*, in which he famously describes the black bass as "inch for inch and pound for pound the gamest fish that swims." Also included are recipes from Stoney Fork, Kentucky's, Sidney Saylor Farr; Elkhorn Creek memories by Scott County's George Lusby; and a poignant tale of a last quail hunt near Kentucky's Green River from Chad Mason's *Voices in the Wind*. From Maysville, Kentucky, natives Frank Mathias and myself, there are excerpts from two memoirs, *The GI Generation* and *Cogan's Woods*, respectively.

Catfish, I discovered, hold a special place in many of the stories I read while assembling this collection. I included four (in addition to Bobbie Ann Mason's "old big one"), beginning with John James Audubon's early account of trotline fishing for "Catfish" in the Ohio River near Henderson, Kentucky; an excerpt from Harlan Hubbard's *Shantyboat* about "staging" hooks to a trotline intended for catching catfish in the Ohio River near his beloved Payne Hollow; and two humorous short stories: William Ellis's "Big Boy," an excerpt from his Kentucky River collection *River Bends and Meanders*, and Gaylord Cooper's "The Great Ohio River Catfish Hunting Expedition," from *Down the River: A Collection of Ohio Valley Fiction & Poetry*.

Contributions from newspapers and magazines include essays on fly-fishing in northern Kentucky by the late John Murphy, award-winning outdoor columnist for the *Kentucky Post*, and by renowned wildlife artist and Ludlow, Kentucky, native W. D. "Bill" Gaither; Art Lander's song of praise to the "king of the spring woods," from his *Lexington Herald-Leader* outdoor column, and his previously unpublished "Partners in the Web of Life"; "Spirit Deer," a fiction from *Sporting Classics* by the Lexington-based outfitter Fredrick Pfister; Joe Tom Erwin's humorous column on frog hunting from the *Louisville Courier-Journal*; and turkey- and dove-hunting stories by Stephen Vest and Garnett C. Brown Jr., respectively, from *Kentucky Monthly*. There are two poems from Owen County farmer and writer James Gash, one of which recently appeared in *Gray's Sporting Journal*; adopted Kentuckian Stephen Wrinn's praise for the

Cumberland River and its trophy brown trout in "A Connecticut Yankee in a Kentucky Trout Stream," from the *Kentucky Fishing Journal;* Sam Bevard's tender " A Special Incident," from the *Maysville Ledger-Independent;* and "When the Cork Goes Under," an expanded version of a story that originally appeared in *Field & Stream,* by Gary Garth, outdoor columnist for the *Louisville Courier-Journal.*

Three more stories are included from the pages of Kentucky Fish and Wildlife's *Happy Hunting Ground:* John Wilson's informative essay on the "practical art" of the Bluegrass reel makers; Walter Cato's tribute to coffee as an unforgettable staple in the outdoorsman's larder; and Dick Farmer's humorous account of a unique form of Kentucky fishing in "Tickling, Noodling, etc."

The poetry section includes, in addition to the works of the poet laureates previously mentioned, three classics by Robert Penn Warren, the first poet laureate of the United States and a three-time winner of the Pulitzer Prize (the only writer to win the prize for both poetry and fiction); two by Gnomon Press publisher Jonathan Greene; "a gurgling mystery" from Wind Publications publisher Charlie Hughes; and, by Elizabeth Madox Roberts, "Woodcock of the Ivory Beak," which I first learned about while reading Roberts's novel *The Great Meadow,* characterized by the *New York Times Book Review* in 1930 as "the stuff of which enduring literature is made."

Stories and poems commissioned for this collection include "A Place of Noble Trees," an essay by novelist Silas House about his family's wonderful tradition of camping and fishing at Dale Hollow Lake; an admiration for the prowess and efficiency of the Kentucky longrifle by Thomas Schiffer, former president of the National Muzzle Loading Rifle Association and the Corps of Kentucky Longriflemen; a look at Kentucky deer camps through the eyes of Dave Baker, editor of *Kentucky Afield,* who, by his own admission, "consumed approximately 137.5 cans of Spam, barbecue Vienna Sausages, and Beanie Weenies before taking his first deer nearly two decades ago"; two lyrical poems from northeastern Kentucky's Stephen Holt, recipient of the 2002 James Still Award for Poetry; a daughter's tender portrait of learning to fish at her father's side in "Fishing with My Father in the Middle Field Pond" by Leatha Kendrick; a poem about hunting of another kind from Linda Caldwell in "Predator and Prey"; and an essay about the renewal of the father-son connection, courtesy of Green River smallmouths, by Dave "Mudcat" Shuffett, host of Kentucky Educational Television's Emmy-winning *Kentucky Life*.

From cover to cover, *Of Woods and Waters* is wrapped in a rich tapestry of art, beginning with the front cover painting, "The Fisherman," by Kentucky impressionist Paul Sawyier (1865–1917). The painting, provided courtesy of William Coffey (owner of Paul Sawyier Galleries and publisher of Sawyier art prints), is from the original watercolor in the King Collection and was, according to Coffey, "probably done in Sawyier's 1895–1908 period, when he changed from portraits to impressionistic landscapes [and] riverscapes." Coffey confirms that the painting has a Kentucky-era signature (Sawyier painted in both New York and Kentucky) and that it is one of Sawyier's "few vertical paintings —maybe 50 out of 2,500-plus originals"—and is likely an Elkhorn Creek scene, with its "typical sycamore trees."

The title page, epigraph, and section dividers carry selected woodcuts by celebrated writer and artist Harlan Hubbard (1900–1988), a Bellevue, Kentucky, native son. For many years, Hubbard lived a Thoreau-like existence and worked at his life and art beside his beloved wife, Anna, in Payne Hollow in Trimble County, along the Kentucky shore of the Ohio River. The woodcuts are graciously provided from the collection of Bill Caddell, Hubbard's artistic executor, and each first appeared in *The Woodcuts of Harlan Hubbard* (University Press of Kentucky).

The back cover features the painting "Pitching Down," a stunningly real depiction of wild turkeys leaving their roost at dawn, by Jeffersontown, Kentucky, native Rick Hill. A mostly self-taught painter and sculptor, he works as a wildlife artist for the Kentucky Department of Fish and Wildlife Resources, which has generously allowed his work to appear in this collection, and illustrates the department's official magazine, *Kentucky Afield*. Hill's precise renderings in pen and ink can also be found throughout, illustrating the text.

A FAVORITE PASSAGE of mine comes from native Ohioan Merrill Gilfillan's *Chokecherry Places: Essays from the High Plains:* "What you bring home from a hunt or a fishing trip is sometimes not what you went after, most everyone knows that. I have traditional links to the school that claims bagging game doesn't ultimately matter, compared to the blue of the sky and the sun on the sumac up the hill."

It occurs to me that Gilfillan's "blue of the sky" and "sun on the sumac," coupled with a passionate sense of place and an equally strong love of storytelling, are central to the writings offered in this collection. Bag limits and full creels are but a very small part of these woodland songs. They are more about celebrating the gathering of family and friends in special outdoor places and creating good memories, such as the sound of the whistling wings of ducks overhead just before they land on a slough in the dark, the startling flight of a ruffed grouse flushing from beneath the nose of a pointing dog, the thrill of watching a daughter or son catch that first fish, the familiarity of driving around in an old pickup truck with a favorite dog asleep on the seat, the heart-pounding excitement when a white-tailed buck appears at first light in a gray November woods, or the acrobatic jumps and tuggings of a lunker bass, catfish, or trout.

Or sometimes, if we are very lucky, we find wonder in our outdoor experiences, as did my best hunting buddy and his grandson this past November. While on their way to hunt deer, they witnessed a pair of shooting stars streaking across the night sky. Then, just after dawn, within minutes of each other, they took a pair of white-tailed bucks as they waited together in the same deer stand where my friend and his twin boys had taken so many fine bucks over the years. And so there will be venison chili for lunch next season, just as there has always been, courtesy of this annual hunt, but this batch will have a burst of magic stirred in for the friends who will gather to hunt yet again in those beloved November woods.

It is my hope readers will agree that *Of Woods and Waters* contains some of the truest "songs" ever composed in celebration of Kentucky and its wild bounty. They are good reading all, I believe, with each piece worthy of my father's "AAA" rating, without further comment from his son.

—Ron Ellis
Lakeside Park, Kentucky
February 2005

The Adventures of Col. Daniel Boon; Containing a Narrative of the Wars of Kentucke (An Excerpt)

From *The Discovery, Settlement and present State of Kentucke* by John Filson (1784)

IT WAS ON the first of May, in the year 1769, that I resigned my domestic happiness for a time, and left my family and peaceable habitation on the Yadkin River, in North-Carolina, to wander through the wilderness of America, in quest of the country of Kentucke, in company with John Finley, John Stewart, Joseph Holden, James Monay, and William Cool. We proceeded successfully, and after a long and fatiguing journey through a mountainous wilderness, in a westward direction, on the seventh day of June following, we found ourselves on Red-River, where John Finley had formerly been trading with the Indians, and, from the top of an eminence, saw with pleasure the beautiful level of Kentucke. Here let me observe, that for some time we had experienced the most uncomfortable weather as a prelibation of our future sufferings. At this place we encamped, and made a shelter to defend us from the inclement season, and began to hunt and reconnoitre the country. We found every where abundance of wild beasts of all sorts, through this vast forest. The buffaloes were more frequent than I have seen cattle in the settlements, browzing on the leaves of the cane, or croping the herbage on those extensive plains, fearless, because ignorant, of the violence of man. Sometimes we saw hundreds in a drove, and the numbers about the salt springs were amazing. In this forest, the habitation of beasts of every kind natural to America, we practiced hunting with great success . . . .

One day I undertook a tour through the country, and the diversity and beauties of nature I met with in this charming season, expelled every gloomy and vexatious thought. Just at the close of day the gentle gales retired, and left the place to the disposal of a profound calm. Not a breeze shook the most tremulous leaf. I had gained the summit of a commanding ridge, and, looking round with astonishing delight, beheld the ample plains, the beauteous tracts below. On the other hand, I surveyed the famous river Ohio, that rolled in silent dignity, marking the western boundary of Kentucke with inconceivable grandeur. At a vast distance I beheld the mountains lift their venerable brows, and penetrate the clouds. All things were still. I kindled a fire near a fountain of sweet water, and feasted on the loin of a buck, which a few hours before I had killed. The sullen shades of night soon overspread the whole hemisphere, and the earth seemed to gasp after the hovering moisture. My roving excursion this day had fatigued my body, and diverted my imagination. I laid me down to sleep, and I awoke not until the sun had chased away the night.

ESSAYS

At the river's edge I begin tracking a deer.
The prints are coming my way, which means
I'm not following the deer but trailing it in
reverse, going where it came from. The snow
inside each print is compacted but loose, a
fresh trail. I find where the animal ducked a
low branch, knocking snow from the bough.
I duck under it too. The tree limb brushes my
back as it brushed the deer. The tracks end
on a slight rise forty yards from the river at
a spot that is protected from wind. An oval
swatch of earth is imprinted in the snow. The
deer slept here last night, melting the snow
beneath it. I've found where it sleeps, giving
me a power as ancient as knowing a wizard's
name.

—Chris Offutt, *The Same River Twice*

JOHN JAMES AUDUBON

Fishing in the Ohio

From *Delineations of American Scenery and Character* (1926)

IT IS WITH mingled feelings of pleasure and regret that I recall to my mind the many pleasant days I have spent on the shores of the Ohio. The visions of former years crowd on my view, as I picture to myself the fertile soil and genial atmosphere of our great western garden, Kentucky, and view the placid waters of the fair stream that flows along its western boundary. Methinks I am now on the banks of the noble river. Twenty years of my life have returned to me; my sinews are strong, and the "bow-string of my spirit is not slack"; bright visions of the future float before me, as I sit on a grassy bank, gazing on the glittering waters. Around me are dense forests of lofty trees and thickly tangled undergrowth, amid which are heard the songs of feathered choristers, and from whose boughs hang clusters of glowing fruits and beautiful flowers. Reader, I am very happy. But now the dream has vanished, and here I am in the British Athens, penning an episode for my *Ornithological Biography*, and having before me sundry well-thumbed and weather-beaten folios, from which I expect to be able to extract some interesting particulars respecting the methods employed in those days in catching Cat-fish.

But, before entering on my subject, I will present you with a brief description of the place of my residence on the banks of the Ohio. When I first landed at Henderson in Kentucky, my family, like the village, was quite small. The latter consisted of six or eight houses; the former of my wife, myself, and a young child. Few as the houses were, we fortunately found one empty. It was a log-*cabin*, not a log-*house;* but as better could not be had, we were pleased. Well, then, we were located. The country around was thinly peopled, and all purchasable provisions rather scarce; but our neighbours were friendly, and we had brought with us flour and bacon-hams. Our pleasures were those of young people not long married, and full of life and merriment; a single smile from our infant was, I assure you, more valued by us than all the treasures of a modern Crœsus would have been. The woods were amply stocked with game, the river with fish; and now and then the hoarded sweets of the industrious bees were brought from some hollow tree to our little table. Our child's cradle was our richest piece of furniture, our guns and fishing-lines our most serviceable implements, for although we began to cultivate a garden, the rankness of the soil kept the seeds we planted far beneath the tall weeds that sprung up the first year. I had then a partner, a "man of business," and there was also with me a Kentucky youth, who much preferred the sports of the forest and river to either day-book or ledger. He was naturally, as I may say, a good woodsman, hunter, and angler, and, like me, thought chiefly of procuring supplies of fish and fowl. To the task accordingly we directed all our energies.

Quantity as well as quality was an object with us, and although we well knew that three species of Cat-fish existed in the Ohio, and that all were sufficiently good, we were not sure as to the best method of securing them. We determined, however, to work on a large scale, and immediately commenced making a famous

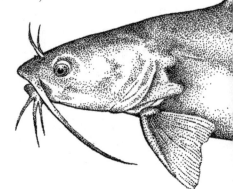

"trot-line." Now, reader, as you may probably know nothing about this engine, I shall describe it to you.

A trot-line is one of considerable length and thickness, both qualities, however, varying according to the extent of water, and the size of the fish you expect to catch. As the Ohio, at Henderson, is rather more than half a mile in breadth, and as Cat-fishes weigh from one to an hundred pounds, we manufactured a line which measured about two hundred yards in length, as thick as the little finger of some fair one yet in her teens, and as white as the damsel's finger well could be, for it was wholly of Kentucky cotton, just, let me tell you, because that substance stands the water better than either hemp or flax. The main line finished, we made a hundred smaller ones, about five feet in length, to each of which we fastened a capital hook of Kirby and Co.'s manufacture. Now for the bait!

It was the month of May. Nature had brought abroad myriads of living beings: they covered the earth, glided through the water, and swarmed in the air. The Cat-fish is a voracious creature, not at all nice in feeding, but one who, like the vulture, contents himself with carrion when nothing better can be had. A few experiments proved to us that, of the dainties with which we tried to allure them to our hooks, they gave a decided preference, at that season, to *live toads*. These animals were very abundant about Henderson. They ramble or feed, whether by instinct or reason, during early or late twilight more than at any other time, especially after a shower, and are unable to bear the heat of the sun's rays for several hours before and after noon. We have a good number of these crawling things in America, particularly in the western and southern parts of the Union, and are very well supplied with frogs, snakes, lizards, and even crocodiles, which we call alligators; but there is enough of food for them all, and we generally suffer them to creep about, to leap or to flounder as they please, or in accordance with the habits which have been given them by the great Conductor of all.

During the month of May, and indeed until autumn, we found an abundant supply of toads. Many "fine ladies," no doubt, would have swooned, or at least screamed and gone into hysterics, had they seen one of our baskets filled with these animals, all alive and plump. Fortunately we had no tragedy queen or sentimental spinster at Henderson. Our Kentucky ladies mind their own affairs, and seldom meddle with those of others farther than to do all they can for their comfort. The toads, collected one by one, and brought home in baskets, were deposited in a barrel for use. And now that night is over, and as it is the first trial we are going to give our trot-line, just watch our movements from that high bank beside the stream. There sit down under the large cotton-wood tree. You are in no danger of catching cold at this season.

My assistant follows me with a gaff hook, while I carry the paddle of our canoe; a boy bears on his back a hundred toads as good as ever hopped. Our line—oh, I forgot to inform you that we had set it last night, but without the small ones you now see on my arm. Fastening one end to yon sycamore, we paddled our canoe, with the rest nicely coiled in the stern, and soon reached its extremity, when I threw over the side the heavy stone fastened to it as a sinker. All this was done that it might be thoroughly soaked, and without kinks or snarls in the morning. Now, you observe, we launch our light bark, the toads in the basket are placed next to my feet in the bow; I have the small lines across my knees all ready looped at the end. Nat, with the paddle, and assisted by the current, keeps the stern of our boat directly down stream; and David fixes, by the skin of the back and hind parts, the living bait to the hook. I hold the main line all the while, and now, having fixed one linelet to it, over goes the latter. Can you see the poor toad kicking and flouncing in the water? "No"—well, I do. You observe at length that all the lines, one after another, have been fixed, baited, and dropped. We now return swiftly to the shore.

"What a delightful thing is fishing!" have I more than once heard some knowing angler exclaim, who, with "the patience of Job," stands or slowly moves along some rivulet twenty feet wide, and three or four feet deep, with a sham fly to allure a trout, which, when at length caught, weighs half a pound. Reader, I never had such patience. Although I have waited ten years, and yet seen only three-fourths of the *Birds of America* engraved, although some of the drawings of that work were patiently made so long ago as 1805, and although I have to wait with patience two years more before I see the end of it, I never could hold a line or a rod for many minutes, unless I had—not a "nibble," but a hearty bite, and could throw the fish at once over my head on the ground. No, no—if I fish for trout, I must soon give up, or catch, as I have done in Pennsylvania's Lehigh, or the streams of Maine, fifty or more in a couple of hours. But the trot-line is in the river, and there *it* may patiently wait, until I visit it toward night. Now I take up my gun and note-book, and, accompanied by my dog, intend to ramble through the woods until breakfast. Who knows but I may shoot a turkey or a deer? It is barely four o'clock; and see what delightful mornings we have at this season in Kentucky!

Evening has returned. The heavens have already opened their

twinkling eyes, although the orb of day has yet scarcely withdrawn itself from our view. How calm is the air! The nocturnal insects and quadrupeds are abroad; the bear is moving through the dark cane-brake, the land crows are flying towards their roosts, their aquatic brethren towards the interior of the forests, the squirrel is barking his adieu, and the Barred Owl glides silently and swiftly from his retreat, to seize upon the gay and noisy animal. The boat is pushed off from the shore; the main-line is in my hands; now it shakes; surely some fish have been hooked. Hand over hand I proceed to the first hook. Nothing there! But now I feel several jerks stronger and more frequent than before. Several hooks I pass; but see, what a fine Cat-fish is twisting round and round the little line to which he is fast! Nat, look to your gaff—hook him close to the tail. Keep it up, my dear fellow!—there now, we have him. More are on, and we proceed. When we have reached the end many goodly fishes are lying in the bottom of our skiff. New bait has been put on, and, as we return, I congratulate myself and my companions on the success of our efforts; for there lies fish enough for ourselves and our neighbours.

A trot-line at this period was perfectly safe at Henderson, should I have allowed it to remain for weeks at a time. The navigation was mostly performed by flat-bottomed boats, which during calm nights floated in the middle current of the river, so that the people on board could not observe the fish that had been hooked. Not a single steamer had as yet ever gone down the Ohio; now and then, it is true, a barge or a keel-boat was propelled by poles and oars; but the nature of the river is such at that place, that these boats when ascending were obliged to keep near the Indian shore, until above the landing of the village (below which I always fixed my lines), when they pulled across the stream.

Several species or varieties of Cat-fish are found in the Ohio, namely the Blue, the White, and the Mud Cats, which differ considerably in their form and colour, as well as in their habits. The Mud Cat is the best, although it seldom attains so great a size as the rest. The Blue Cat is the coarsest, but when not exceeding from four to six pounds, it affords tolerable eating. The White Cat is preferable to the last, but not so common; and the Yellow Mud Cat is the best and rarest. Of the blue kind some have been caught that weighed a hundred pounds. Such fishes, however, are looked upon as monsters.

The form in all the varieties inclines to the conical, the head being disproportionately large, while the body tapers away to the root of the tail. The eyes, which are small, are placed far apart, and situated as it were on the top of the forehead, but laterally. Their mouth is wide, and armed with numerous small and very sharp teeth, while it is defended by single-sided spines, which, when the fish is in the agonies of death, stand out at right angles, and are so firmly fixed as sometimes to break before you can loosen them. The Cat-fish has also feelers of proportionate length, apparently intended to guide its motions over the bottom, whilst its eyes are watching the objects passing above.

Trot-lines cannot be used with much success unless during the middle stages of the water. When very low, it is too clear, and the fish, although extremely voracious, will rarely risk its life for a toad. When the waters are rising rapidly, your trot-lines are likely to be carried away by one of the numerous trees that float in the stream. A "happy medium" is therefore best.

When the waters are rising fast and have become muddy, a single line is used for catching Cat-fish. It is fastened to the elastic branch of some willow several feet above the water, and must be twenty or thirty feet in length. The entrails of a Wild Turkey, or a piece of fresh venison, furnish good bait; and if, when you visit your line the next morning after you have set it, the water has not risen too much, the swinging of the willow indicates that a fish has been hooked, and you have only to haul the prize ashore.

One evening I saw that the river was rising at a great rate, although it was still within its banks. I knew that the White Perch were running, that is, ascending the river from the sea, and, anxious to have a tasting of that fine fish, I baited a line with a crayfish, and fastened it to the bough of a tree. Next morning as I pulled in the line, it felt as if fast at the bottom, yet on drawing it slowly I found that it came. Presently I felt a strong pull, the line slipped through my fingers, and next instant a large Cat-fish leaped out of the water. I played it for a while, until it became exhausted, when I drew it ashore. It had swallowed the hook, and I cut off the line close to its head. Then passing a stick through one of the gills, I and a servant tugged the fish home. On cutting it open, we, to our surprise, found in its stomach a fine White Perch, dead, but not in the least injured. The Perch had been lightly hooked, and the Cat-fish, after swallowing it, had been hooked in the stomach, so that, although the instrument was small, the torture caused by it no doubt tended to disable the Cat-fish. The Perch we ate, and the Cat, which was fine, we divided into four parts, and distributed among our neighbours. My most worthy friend and relative, Nicholas Berthoud, Esq., who formerly resided at Shippingport in Kentucky, but now in New York, a better fisher than whom I never knew, once placed a trot-line in "the basin" below "Tarascon's Mills," at the foot of the Rapids of the Ohio. I cannot recollect the bait which was used; but on taking up the line we obtained a remarkably fine Cat-fish, in which was found the greater part of a sucking pig!

DAVE BAKER

Deer Camp (2004)

MY HIGHLY PAID lawyer says I have to issue a disclaimer before you read any further. I say "highly paid" because he always ends up in the dove field with a new shotgun after I pay him a visit (and his fee). I know he's a good lawyer because his motto is: "Never let the facts stand in the way of a good story."

Case in point: the buck he's got hanging on his office wall. It's a big rack. A trophy. Some client gave it to him as partial payment. I guess the poor guy didn't have a shotgun. My lawyer wasn't quite sure what to do with it. He brought it home, but his wife told him, "It's either me or *that*." I should point out that my lawyer married before he got to the prenuptial class in law school. So he did the next best thing with the buck: He hung it above his desk at work.

A few days after he put up the deer, a guy comes in with a case. A top-of-the-line Benelli (shotgun) kind of case. The only problem is, he doesn't trust lawyers. Well, the guy is pretty suspicious when he shuffles into my lawyer's office. He keeps his hand on his wallet like it's a rabbit about to flush. Then he spots that big buck. "Do you deer hunt?" he asks.

My lawyer has never deer hunted a day in his life. But if he's got a big fee standing broadside in his sights, he's not going to pass on the shot. "Sure do," he replies, then spins a tale that would make Hemingway proud. Needless to say, my lawyer gets the case, and soon word gets around that here's a suit that hunts deer. His case-load among the four-wheel-drive crowd skyrockets.

However, I digress. My Latin's a little rusty, but I think my lawyer says that I'm supposed to tell readers not to try any of what I'm about to tell you at home. Also, some animals were harmed in the creation of this story, but you've got to expect that when you're writing about deer hunting.

Anyway, here's the moral of my story: Don't make your deer camp in the back of a dynamite van. You'll wake up with one of those Sunday morning "never again" headaches, and you won't be good for anything else the rest of the day.

Chances are that you've got a place to stay if you've hunted the same property for a number of years. Perhaps you've got a battered old mobile home in which to sleep, or you've pulled a camper onto the farm and have the conveniences of home on hand, such as a stove and shower. Regardless, deer camps in Kentucky aren't quite what you see on television.

My wife thinks deer hunting is easy. She also thinks deer camps are like vacations. She's been brainwashed by those Saturday morning television shows where the hunters sleep on feather mattresses and enjoy meals prepared by a four-star chef. These are the same shows where the hunter-personality climbs into a plywood box built atop a tower, then selects the buck he wants to shoot from among a group of deer standing next to a feeder. Afterward, he tries to make it sound like a real hunt. "Thanks to (insert name of product here), I was able to take this trophy from inside a pen," the hunter–sponsor–paid spokesman gushes for the camera.

Not everybody has it so good. When you've got no place to go, you become a hunting hobo. Hunting hobos don't beg for spare change. They panhandle for hunting access. They're the kind of people who go into a country store and buy the dustiest can on the shelf, hoping the grateful owner will give them leads on hunting areas in return. You know you're standing in line with a hobo if you hear him tell the cashier, "I've looked *every-*

where for pickled sardines and ground brussels sprouts packed in beef hearts! I'd buy every can if you had more than one!"

Hunting hobos are careful not to reveal the whereabouts of a softhearted landowner. As a result, they'll settle for setting up camp inside any building that's dry. That's because nothing brings others knocking at the door like a herd of tents or pop-up campers sitting within sight of the road in prime deer country.

Joe, Brian, and I were hobos by default. Our families didn't have farms to hunt. We didn't have a camper, a tent, or a truck with a shell over the bed. Joe didn't even own a sleeping bag. He just draped his army-surplus coat over his shoulders and slept wherever he could stretch out. "We didn't have much," Joe recalled years later, "except the will to hunt."

Our camps included that dynamite van, an old school bus we nicknamed "Frigidaire," tobacco barns, and, finally, an abandoned farmhouse that doubled as a hayloft. The critters living inside that house weren't too pleased about their new squatters. Brian tried to evict them one night with a .44-magnum pistol, but more on that later.

I should have been a little worried the night Joe called me about a new place he had found to hunt. It was in Owen County, in overgrown hill country without a barn, shed, or building on the place.

"Where are we going to sleep?" I asked.

"Don't worry," he replied. "I've got it covered."

I arrived at Joe's house on Friday afternoon. A white Ford van was parked in his driveway, its back doors open and a cloud of white dust pulsing from the interior. Joe appeared at the opening with a broom in his hand. "We're camping in style this time," he said with a grin. "I borrowed it from work."

Joe installed sewer lines for a contractor in Lexington. His company used the van to carry the cases of dynamite and bags of ammonium nitrate needed to blast through limestone. Farmers

use ammonium nitrate to kick-start the growth of tobacco plants; blasters use it to turbocharge the dynamite. It's potent stuff. Despite Joe's best efforts, chunks of the chemical still nested in every nook and cranny of the cargo area. The van bore no markings on the outside, save for a removable orange sign on the back that read "EXPLOSIVES." I asked Joe if we should take off the sign. "Let's leave it on," he replied. "It'll scare off the root hoggers." (Experienced hunters know that setting up camp in remote areas involves certain risks, including the chance that thieves will visit your site while you're away and take everything you've got. It's called "root hogging.")

I realized Joe was on to something when we reached the interstate. Nobody tailgated us, and the drivers who pulled alongside the van quickly sped away once they got a look at us. Joe and I are both big guys who sported bushy, Civil War–style beards at the time. Joe helped push things along by occasionally turning to look at passing cars with his eyes wide and a crazed smile on his face.

A light rain started falling as we arrived at the Owen County farm—a good sign, because the wet leaves would muffle the sound of our footsteps. We rolled up the windows of the van and stayed up late that night, telling lies and bragging about the next day's hunt before falling asleep with our noses to the floor.

We found religion the next morning. All night we'd been breathing chemical fumes in an enclosed area. We awoke with headaches registering 6.5 or better on the Richter scale. "Please God, just let me live," I chanted softly to myself as I sat in the woods. We drove back home at lunchtime—with the windows down all the way.

Tobacco barns make much better deer camps. The smell of tobacco aging in the rafters is certainly more pleasant than sniffing fertilizer all night. Barns are plentiful in deer country, and most farmers don't mind if you camp in them, as long as you don't build a campfire anywhere nearby. That can make for some cold nights.

Joe and I were prepared to do some barn camping after we received an invitation to hunt a farm in Butler County. That western Kentucky county has thousands of acres of corn and soybeans. It's also home to one of the highest concentrations of deer in the state. We were ecstatic. With that many deer, we figured it ought to be easy to bring home some venison.

The trip came about after I helped my boss move his wife's piano down a flight of stairs without snapping the legs off the instrument or my boss. He was so grateful that he granted permission for us to hunt at his dad's farm in Butler County.

Compton, my boss's dad, greeted us warmly when we arrived shortly before dark. The barn where we would be staying was right by his house, so he gave us a tour of the place. He even showed us a pile of scrap plywood we could use to cover the groundhog holes in the driest corner of the barn. We would be sleeping on the floor because we didn't have any cots.

We prepared a simple dinner that night on the tailgate of Joe's truck. We took the lids off a can of beans and a can of beef stew, peeled off the labels, then put the cans directly on the burner of my Coleman stove. Supper was ready when the cans boiled over and the smoke started rolling. We hadn't thought to bring any pot holders, so I covered each hand with a tube sock, lifted the cans, and split the contents between our army-surplus mess kits.

Joe and I were sopping up the last of the gravy with slices of white bread when Compton appeared out of the darkness. We figured he was going to have some words with us about the smoke, but that wasn't the reason for his visit. Compton was about to share his secret with us.

He walked into a tool shed built alongside the barn and emerged with a fifth of Old Granddad in his hand. "Friends, I'll give you a nip, but you can't tell my wife," he said in a low voice. "She don't like me drinking. She'd pour out this whole bottle if she figured out where I was keepin' it." Compton took a slash and then handed the bottle to me. Being guests and all, Joe and I felt obligated to join him. Compton visited twice more that night. It made sleeping on the dirt a little easier.

A pneumonia rain—too warm to freeze but just this side of ice—settled in the next morning. My clothes soaked through to the skin, and we saw no deer. Some days you wonder why you hunt, and this was one of them. It showed on our faces. Then the improbable happened. Two other hunters had driven in before daylight to hunt Compton's farm that day. We met them during our lunch break. One had a doe just barely out of its spots lying in the bed of his pickup truck. "You guys can have it," he offered. "I've already got one in the freezer."

Hunters killed 417 deer in Butler County that year. And although we weren't among them, we had our venison. We took the doe back to the barn to skin and quarter it, but we couldn't find a water hose to wash the meat. Joe then noticed a 55-gallon barrel brimming with water at the corner of Compton's house. Perfect. We were dunking the hams and backstraps in the barrel when Compton's wife came out of the house with a strange look on her face. She wasn't happy. "Boys," she said, "that's our good water."

We were used to the conveniences of the city. It never occurred to us that some folks got their drinking water out of a rain barrel. Shamed by our naivete, we apologized and left Butler County, never to return.

By that time, I had stopped working for Compton's son anyway. Joe, however, still worked for a contractor who just happened to own a 365-acre farm in Carroll County. We not only got permission to hunt there, but Joe's boss gave him the keys to an old school bus that had been converted into a camper, beds and all.

Joe's boss had given the bus new life with a fresh coat of maroon and white paint to conceal its old identity. It became a rugby team's bus, then served as temporary living quarters while Joe's boss built his house. Now that the house was finished, Joe's boss wanted the bus driven to his farm for retirement. We were glad to help. The old bus, in its third reincarnation, became our Carroll County deer camp.

School buses aren't exactly off-road vehicles. They have a tendency to hang up at steep creek crossings and on the humps of rutted roads. That means you have to jack up the stuck bus, insert some flat rocks underneath the wheels, and then gun it past the obstruction. You might even have to cut some trees to wiggle it through the woods. Sometimes it's best to throw away the keys once you've reached the final destination.

Some folks in coal country use old school buses as houses. They'll rent a wide spot in the road and have the bus towed to the location, since the engine has usually long since been removed for salvage. All these buses have coal stoves in them; often you'll see their chimneys belching black smoke even on Indian summer days. Now I know why.

School buses are nothing but meat lockers without the need of refrigeration units. Our new camp was an oversized Frigidaire. The bare metal walls absorbed the chill like a sponge, then dripped cold on us throughout the night. Frost grew so heavy on the windows that you could write your name prisoner-style on the glass. We always awoke tired from a night of shivering when camping in the bus. We abandoned it after a few trips.

Brian and another hunting buddy reverted to the old standby on their next trip: a tobacco barn located on a nearby ridge. They built a fire some five feet away from the main doors the first night to stave off the cold, breaking a cardinal rule in the process. They returned for lunch the next day to discover all their belongings missing from the barn. In their place was a note from the tenant farmer, telling them to see him if they wanted everything back. That barn, which was full of tobacco, represented a year's worth of work, the mortgage payment, and Christmas for the farmer's family. A stray ember from the campfire could risk it all. It wasn't a pleasant scene when the hunters went to ask for their gear back.

Joe's boss should have banned the lot of us from his farm after that. Instead, he suggested that we set up camp in an abandoned two-room house near the back of the farm. The old frame house had no glass in the windows, its floors sagged, and hay bales were strewn throughout. But it was dry and put us within short walking distance of the best hunting on the farm. We moved the hay to one room and nailed sheets of plywood to the window frames. A rock propped against the weather-beaten door kept it closed. It was now relatively weather tight, and the lanterns helped keep the room reasonably warm. We brought lawn chair loungers so we no longer had to sleep on the floor.

There was, however, a slight problem with critters. The raccoons did not intend to give up the house without a fight. All night long you'd hear them in the ceiling, underneath the floor, and rooting around in the next room. Brian's irritation at the ruckus boiled over one night. I was on the verge of sleep, but Brian and Joe had stayed up talking. I remember a clap of thunder and a ringing in my ears; Brian had pulled out his .44-magnum pistol and fired a shot through the wall. I don't know whether it worked or not—my hearing didn't come back until the next morning.

Despite some inconveniences, the hunting was phenomenal. Joe took seven deer over the years from an oak he called the "doe tree." If college classes kept me in town Friday night, Brian usually had a deer field-dressed and hanging in a nearby tree by the time I arrived on Saturday afternoon. My first buck ever was an eight-pointer taken from the bottom of a hollow. We hunted the farm for a decade.

The great deer hunting couldn't last. One summer, Joe's boss decided to lease the farm to a bunch of doctors at a price we couldn't afford. I can't really blame him. The lease paid his property taxes.

Joe grew tired of being a hobo and bought his own place in Anderson County. It's a wonderful little farm with cleared, rolling ridgetops, wooded ravines, and enough oak and hickory trees to keep everything and everybody happy. The only thing it lacks is a tobacco barn.

Joe's son has it made. He rolls out of his comfortable bed before dawn, walks out the back door, and usually returns home dragging a deer by 8:30 A.M.

Sometimes I wonder if he knows what he's missing.

WENDELL BERRY

An Entrance to the Woods

From *Recollected Essays 1965–1980* (1981)

ON A FINE sunny afternoon at the end of September I leave my
work in Lexington and drive east on I-64 and the Mountain
Parkway. When I leave the Parkway at the little town of Pine
Ridge I am in the watershed of the Red River in the Daniel
Boone National Forest. From Pine Ridge I take Highway 715 out
along the narrow ridgetops, a winding tunnel through the trees.
And then I turn off on a Forest Service Road and follow it to the
head of a foot trail that goes down the steep valley wall of one of
the tributary creeks. I pull my car off the road and lock it, and
lift on my pack.

It is nearly five o'clock when I start walking. The afternoon
is brilliant and warm, absolutely still, not enough air stirring to
move a leaf. There is only the steady somnolent trilling of insects, and now and again in the woods below me the cry of a pileated woodpecker. Those, and my footsteps on the path, are the
only sounds.

From the dry oak woods of the ridge I pass down into the
rock. The foot trails of the Red River Gorge all seek these stony
notches that little streams have cut back through the cliffs. I pass
a ledge overhanging a sheer drop of the rock, where in a wetter
time there would be a waterfall. The ledge is dry and mute now,
but on the face of the rock below are the characteristic mosses,
ferns, liverwort, meadow rue. And here where the ravine suddenly steepens and narrows, where the shadows are long-lived

and the dampness stays, the trees are different. Here are beech and hemlock and poplar, straight and tall, reaching way up into the light. Under them are evergreen thickets of rhododendron. And wherever the dampness is there are mosses and ferns. The faces of the rock are intricately scalloped with veins of ironstone, scooped and carved by the wind.

Finally from the crease of the ravine I am following there begins to come the trickling and splashing of water. There is a great restfulness in the sounds these small streams make; they are going down as fast as they can, but their sounds seem leisurely and idle, as if produced like gemstones with the greatest patience and care.

A little later, stopping, I hear not far away the more voluble flowing of the creek. I go on down to where the trail crosses and begin to look for a camping place. The little bottoms along the creek here are thickety and weedy, probably having been kept clear and cropped or pastured not so long ago. In the more open places are little lavender asters, and the even smaller-flowered white ones that some people call beeweed or farewell-summer. And in low wet places are the richly flowered spikes of great lobelia, the blooms an intense startling blue, exquisitely shaped.

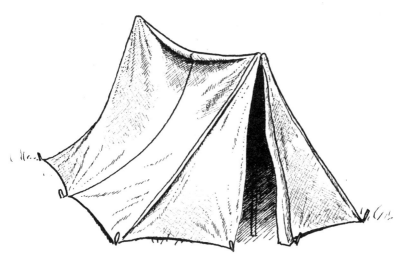

I choose a place in an open thicket near the stream, and make camp.

It is a simple matter to make camp. I string up a shelter and put my air mattress and sleeping bag in it, and I am ready for the night. And supper is even simpler, for I have brought sandwiches for this first meal. In less than an hour all my chores are done. It will still be light for a good while, and I go over and sit down on a rock at the edge of the stream.

And then a heavy feeling of melancholy and lonesomeness comes over me. This does not surprise me, for I have felt it before when I have been alone at evening in wilderness places that I am not familiar with. But here it has a quality that I recognize as peculiar to the narrow hollows of the Red River Gorge. These are deeply shaded by the trees and by the valley walls, the sun rising on them late and setting early; they are more dark than light. And there will often be little rapids in the stream that will sound, at a certain distance, exactly like people talking. As I sit on my rock by the stream now, I could swear that there is a party of campers coming up the trail toward me, and for several minutes I stay alert, listening for them, their voices seeming to rise and fall, fade out and lift again, in happy conversation. When I finally realize that it is only a sound the creek is making, though I have not come here for company and do not want any, I am inexplicably sad.

These are haunted places, or at least it is easy to feel haunted in them, alone at nightfall. As the air darkens and the cool of the night rises, one feels the immanence of the wraiths of the ancient tribesmen who used to inhabit the rock houses of the cliffs; of the white hunters from east of the mountains; of the farmers who accepted the isolation of these nearly inaccessible valleys to crop the narrow bottoms and ridges and pasture their cattle and hogs in the woods; of the seekers of quick wealth in timber and ore. For though this is a wilderness place, it bears its part of the burden of human history. If one spends much time here and feels much liking for the place, it is hard to escape the sense of one's predecessors. If one has read of the prehistoric Indians whose flint arrowpoints and pottery and hominy holes and petroglyphs have been found here, then every rock shelter and clifty spring will suggest the presence of those dim people who have disappeared into the earth. Walking along the ridges and the stream bottoms, one will come upon the heaped stones of a chimney, or the slowly filling depression of an old cellar, or will find in the spring a japonica bush or periwinkles or a few jonquils blooming in a thicket that used to be a dooryard. Wherever the land is level enough there are abandoned fields and pastures. And nearly always there is the evidence that one follows in the steps of the loggers.

That sense of the past is probably one reason for the melancholy that I feel. But I know that there are other reasons.

One is that, though I am here in body, my mind and my nerves too are not yet altogether here. We seem to grant to our high-speed roads and our airlines the rather thoughtless assumption that people can change places as rapidly as their bodies can be transported. That, as my own experience keeps proving to me, is not true. In the middle of the afternoon I left off being busy at work, and drove through traffic to the freeway, and then for a solid hour or more I drove sixty or seventy miles an hour, hardly aware of the country I was passing through, because on the freeway one does not have to be. The landscape has been subdued so that one may drive over it at seventy miles per hour without any concession whatsoever to one's whereabouts. One might as well be flying. Though one is in Kentucky one is not experiencing Kentucky; one is experiencing the highway, which might be in nearly any hill country east of the Mississippi.

Once off the freeway, my pace gradually slowed, as the roads became progressively more primitive, from seventy miles an hour to a walk. And now, here at my camping place, I have stopped altogether. But my mind is still keyed to seventy miles an hour. And having come here so fast, it is still busy with the work I am usually doing. Having come here by the freeway, my mind is not so fully here as it would have been if I had come by the crookeder, slower state roads; it is incalculably farther away than it would have been if I had come all the way on foot, as my earliest predecessors came. When the Indians and the first white hunters entered this country they were altogether here as soon as they arrived, for they had seen and experienced fully everything between here and their starting place, and so the transition was gradual and articulate in their consciousness. Our senses, after all, were developed to function at foot speeds; and the transition from foot travel to motor travel, in terms of evolutionary time, has been abrupt. The faster one goes, the more strain there is on the senses, the more they fail to take in, the more confusion they must tolerate or gloss over—and the longer it takes to bring the mind to a stop in the presence of anything. Though the freeway passes through the very heart of this forest, the motorist remains several hours' journey by foot from what is living at the edge of the right-of-way.

BUT I HAVE NOT only come to this strangely haunted place in a short time and too fast. I have in that move made an enormous change: I have departed from my life as I am used to living it, and have come into the wilderness. It is not fear that I feel; I have learned to fear the everyday events of human history much more than I fear the everyday occurrences of the woods; in general, I would rather trust myself to the woods than to any government that I know of. I feel, instead, an uneasy awareness of severed connections, of being cut off from all familiar places and of being a stranger where I am. What is happening at home? I wonder, and I know I can't find out very easily or very soon.

Even more discomforting is a pervasive sense of unfamiliarity. In the places I am most familiar with—my house, or my garden, or even the woods near home that I have walked in for years —I am surrounded by associations; everywhere I look I am reminded of my history and my hopes; even unconsciously I am comforted by any number of proofs that my life on the earth is an established and a going thing. But I am in this hollow for the first time in my life. I see nothing that I recognize. Everything looks as it did before I came, as it will when I am gone. When I look over at my little camp I see how tentative and insignificant it is. Lying there in my bed in the dark tonight, I will be absorbed in the being of this place, invisible as a squirrel in his nest.

Uneasy as this feeling is, I know it will pass. Its passing will produce a deep pleasure in being here. And I have felt it often enough before that I have begun to understand something of what it means:

Nobody knows where I am. I don't know what is happening to anybody else in the world. While I am here I will not speak, and will have no reason or need for speech. It is only beyond this lonesomeness for the places I have come from that I can reach the vital reality of a place such as this. Turning toward this place, I confront a presence that none of my schooling and none of my usual assumptions have prepared me for: the wilderness, mostly unknowable and mostly alien, that is the universe. Perhaps the most difficult labor for my species is to accept its limits, its weakness and ignorance. But here I am. This wild place where I have camped lies within an enormous cone widening from the center of the earth out across the universe, nearly all of it a mysterious wilderness in which the power and the knowledge of men count for nothing. As long as its instruments are correct and its engines run, the airplane now flying through this great cone is safely within the human freehold; its behavior is as familiar and predictable to those concerned as the inside of a man's living room. But let its instruments or its engines fail, and at once it enters the wilderness where nothing is foreseeable. And these steep narrow hollows, these cliffs and forested ridges that lie below, are the antithesis of flight.

Wilderness is the element in which we live encased in civilization, as a mollusk lives in his shell in the sea. It is a wilderness that is beautiful, dangerous, abundant, oblivious of us, mysterious, never to be conquered or controlled or second-guessed, or known more than a little. It is a wilderness that for most of us most of the time is kept out of sight, camouflaged, by the edifices and the busyness and the bothers of human society.

And so, coming here, what I have done is strip away the human facade that usually stands between me and the universe, and I see more clearly where I am. What I am able to ignore much of the time, but find undeniable here, is that all wildernesses are one: there is a profound joining between this wild stream deep in one of the folds of my native country and the tropical jungles, the tundras of the north, the oceans and the deserts. Alone here, among the rocks and the trees, I see that I am alone also among the stars. A stranger here, unfamiliar with my surroundings, I am aware also that I know only in the most relative terms my whereabouts within the black reaches of the universe. And because the natural processes are here so little qualified by anything human, this fragment of the wilderness is also joined to other times; there flows over it a nonhuman time to be told by the growth and death of the forest and the wearing of the stream. I feel drawing out beyond my comprehension perspectives from which the growth and the death of a large poplar would seem as continuous and sudden as the raising and the lowering of a man's hand, from which men's history in the world, their brief clearing of the ground, will seem no more than the opening and shutting of an eye.

And so I have come here to enact—not because I want to but because, once here, I cannot help it—the loneliness and the humbleness of my kind. I must see in my flimsy shelter, pitched here for two nights, the transience of capitols and cathedrals. In growing used to being in this place, I will have to accept a humbler and a truer view of myself than I usually have.

A man enters and leaves the world naked. And it is only naked—or nearly so—that he can enter and leave the wilderness. If he walks, that is; and if he doesn't walk it can hardly be said that he has entered. He can bring only what he can carry—the little that it takes to replace for a few hours or a few days an animal's fur and teeth and claws and functioning instincts. In comparison to the usual traveler with his dependence on machines and highways and restaurants and motels—on the economy and the government, in short—the man who walks into the wilderness is naked indeed. He leaves behind his work, his household, his duties, his comforts—even, if he comes alone, his words. He immerses himself in what he is not. It is a kind of death.

THE DAWN COMES slow and cold. Only occasionally, somewhere along the creek or on the slopes above, a bird sings. I have not slept well, and I waken without much interest in the day. I set the camp to rights, and fix breakfast, and eat. The day is clear, and high up on the points and ridges to the west of my camp I can see the sun shining on the woods. And suddenly I am full of an ambition: I want to get up where the sun is; I want to sit in the sun up there among the high rocks until I can feel its warmth in my bones.

I put some lunch into a little canvas bag, and start out, leaving my jacket so as not to have to carry it after the day gets warm. Without my jacket, even climbing, it is cold in the shadow of the hollow, and I have a long way to go to get to the sun. I climb the steep path up the valley wall, walking rapidly, thinking only of the sunlight above me. It is as though I have entered into a deep sympathy with those tulip poplars that grow so straight and tall out of the shady ravines, not growing a branch worth the name until their heads are in the sun. I am so concentrated on the sun that when some grouse flush from the undergrowth ahead of me, I am thunderstruck; they are already planing down into the underbrush again before I can get my wits together and realize what they are.

The path zigzags up the last steepness of the bluff and then slowly levels out. For some distance it follows the backbone of a ridge, and then where the ridge is narrowest there is a great slab of bare rock lying full in the sun. This is what I have been looking for. I walk out into the center of the rock and sit, the clear warm light falling unobstructed all around. As the sun warms me I begin to grow comfortable not only in my clothes, but in the place and the day. And like those light-seeking poplars of the ravines, my mind begins to branch out.

Southward, I can hear the traffic on the Mountain Parkway, a steady continuous roar—the corporate voice of twentieth-century humanity, sustained above the transient voices of its members. Last night, except for an occasional airplane passing over, I camped out of reach of the sounds of engines. For long stretches of time I heard no sounds but the sounds of the woods.

Near where I am sitting there is an inscription cut into the rock:

A • J • SARGENT
fEB • 2ᵻ • 1903

Those letters were carved there more than sixty-six years ago. As I look around me I realize that I can see no evidence of the lapse of so much time. In every direction I can see only narrow ridges and narrow deep hollows, all covered with trees. For all that can be told from this height by looking, it might still be 1903—or, for that matter, 1803 or 1703, or 1003. Indians no doubt sat here and looked over the country as I am doing now; the visual impression is so pure and strong that I can almost imagine myself one of them. But the insistent, the overwhelming, evidence of the time of my own arrival is in what I can hear—that roar of the highway off there in the distance. In 1903 the continent was still covered by a great ocean of silence, in which the sounds of machinery were scattered at wide intervals of time and space. Here, in 1903, there were only the natural sounds of the place. On a day like this, at the end of September, there would have been only the sounds of a few faint crickets, a woodpecker now and then, now and then the wind. But today, two-thirds of a century later, the continent is covered by an ocean of engine noise, in which silences occur only sporadically and at wide intervals.

From where I am sitting in the midst of this island of wilderness, it is as though I am listening to the machine of human history—a huge flywheel building speed until finally the force of its whirling will break it in pieces, and the world with it. That is not an attractive thought, and yet I find it impossible to escape, for it has seemed to me for years now that the doings of men no longer occur within nature, but that the natural places which the human economy has so far spared now survive almost accidentally within the doings of men. This wilderness of the Red River now carries on its ancient processes *within* the human climate of war and waste and confusion. And I know that the distant roar of engines, though it may *seem* only to be passing through this wilderness, is really bearing down upon it. The machine is running now with a speed that produces blindness—as to the driver of a speeding automobile the only thing stable, the only thing not a mere blur on the edge of the retina, is the automobile itself—and the blindness of a thing with power promises the destruction of what cannot be seen. That roar of the highway is the voice of the American economy; it is sounding also wherever strip mines are being cut in the steep slopes of Appalachia, and wherever cropland is being destroyed to make roads and suburbs, and wherever rivers and marshes and bays and forests are being destroyed for the sake of industry or commerce.

No. Even here where the economy of life is really an economy

—where the creation is yet fully alive and continuous and self-enriching, where whatever dies enters directly into the life of the living—even here one cannot fully escape the sense of an impending human catastrophe. One cannot come here without the awareness that this is an island surrounded by the machinery and the workings of an insane greed, hungering for the world's end—that ours is a "civilization" of which the work of no builder or artist is symbol, nor the life of any good man, but rather the bulldozer, the poison spray, the hugging fire of napalm, the cloud of Hiroshima.

THOUGH FROM the high vantage point of this stony ridge I see little hope that I will ever live a day as an optimist, still I am not desperate. In fact, with the sun warming me now, and with the whole day before me to wander in this beautiful country, I am happy. A man cannot despair if he can imagine a better life, and if he can enact something of its possibility. It is only when I am ensnarled in the meaningless ordeals and the ordeals of mean-inglessness, of which our public and political life is now so productive, that I lose the awareness of something better, and feel the despair of having come to the dead end of possibility.

Today, as always when I am afoot in the woods, I feel the possibility, the reasonableness, the practicability of living in the world in a way that would enlarge rather than diminish the hope of life. I feel the possibility of a frugal and protective love for the creation that would be unimaginably more meaningful and joyful than our present destructive and wasteful economy. The absence of human society, that made me so uneasy last night, now begins to be a comfort to me. I am afoot in the woods. I am alive in the world, this moment, without the help or the interference of any machine. I can move without reference to anything except the lay of the land and the capabilities of my own body. The necessities of foot travel in this steep country have stripped away all superfluities. I simply could not enter into this place and assume its quiet with all the belongings of a family man, property holder, etc. For the time, I am reduced to my irreducible self. I feel the lightness of body that a man must feel who has just lost fifty pounds of fat. As I leave the bare expanse of the rock and go in under the trees again, I am aware that I move in the landscape as one of its details.

WALKING THROUGH the woods, you can never see far, either ahead or behind, so you move without much of a sense of getting anywhere or of moving at any certain speed. You burrow through the foliage in the air much as a mole burrows through the roots in the ground. The views that open out occasionally from the ridges afford a relief, a recovery of orientation, that they could never give as mere "scenery," looked at from a turnout at the edge of a highway.

The trail leaves the ridge and goes down a ravine into the valley of a creek where the night chill has stayed. I pause only long enough to drink the cold clean water. The trail climbs up onto the next ridge.

It is the ebb of the year. Though the slopes have not yet taken on the bright colors of the autumn maples and oaks, some of the duller trees are already shedding. The foliage has begun to flow down the cliff faces and the slopes like a tide pulling back. The woods is mostly quiet, subdued, as if the pressure of survival has grown heavy upon it, as if above the growing warmth of the day the cold of winter can be felt waiting to descend.

At my approach a big hawk flies off the low branch of an oak and out over the treetops. Now and again a nut-hatch hoots, off somewhere in the woods. Twice I stop and watch an ovenbird. A few feet ahead of me there is a sudden movement in the leaves, and then quiet. When I slip up and examine the spot there is nothing to be found. Whatever passed there has disappeared, quicker than the hand that is quicker than the eye, a shadow fallen into a shadow.

In the afternoon I leave the trail. My walk so far has come perhaps three-quarters of the way around a long zigzagging loop that will eventually bring me back to my starting place. I turn down a small unnamed branch of the creek where I am camped, and I begin the loveliest part of the day. There is nothing here resembling a trail. The best way is nearly always to follow the edge of the stream, stepping from one stone to another. Crossing back and forth over the water, stepping on or over rocks and logs, the way ahead is never clear for more than a few feet. The stream accompanies me down, threading its way under boulders and logs and over little falls and rapids. The rhododendron overhangs it so closely in places that I can go only by stooping. Over the rhododendron are the great dark heads of the hemlocks. The streambanks are ferny and mossy. And through this green tunnel the voice of the stream changes from rock to rock; subdued like all the other autumn voices of the woods, it seems sunk in a deep contented meditation on the sounds of *l*.

The water in the pools is absolutely clear. If it weren't for the shadows and ripples you would hardly notice that it is water; the fish would seem to swim in the air. As it is, where there is no leaf floating, it is impossible to tell exactly where the plane of the surface lies. As I walk up on a pool the little fish dart every which way out of sight. And then after I sit still a while, watching, they come out again. Their shadows flow over the rocks and leaves on the bottom. Now I have come into the heart of the woods. I am far from the highway and can hear no sound of it. All around there is a grand deep autumn quiet, in which a few insects dream their summer songs. Suddenly a wren sings way off in the underbrush. A redbreasted nuthatch walks, hooting, headfirst down the trunk of a walnut. An ovenbird walks out along the limb of a hemlock and looks at me, curious. The little fish soar in the pool, turning their clean quick angles, their shadows seeming barely to keep up. As I lean and dip my cup in the water, they scatter. I drink, and go on.

WHEN I GET BACK to camp it is only the middle of the afternoon or a little after. Since I left in the morning I have walked something like eight miles. I haven't hurried—have mostly poked along, stopping often and looking around. But I am tired, and coming down the creek I have got both feet wet. I find a sunny place, and take off my shoes and socks and set them to dry. For a long time then, lying propped against the trunk of a tree, I read and rest and watch the evening come.

All day I have moved through the woods, making as little noise as possible. Slowly my mind and my nerves have slowed to a walk. The quiet of the woods has ceased to be something that I observe; now it is something that I am a part of. I have joined it with my own quiet. As the twilight draws on I no longer feel the strangeness and uneasiness of the evening before. The sounds of the creek move through my mind as they move through the valley, unimpeded and clear.

When the time comes I prepare supper and eat, and then wash kettle and cup and spoon and put them away. As far as possible I get things ready for an early start in the morning. Soon after dark I go to bed, and I sleep well.

I WAKE long before dawn. The air is warm and I feel rested and wide awake. By the light of a small candle lantern I break camp and pack. And then I begin the steep climb back to the car.

The moon is bright and high. The woods stands in deep shadow, the light falling soft through the openings of the foliage. The trees appear immensely tall, and black, gravely looming over the path. It is windless and still; the moonlight pouring over the country seems more potent than the air. All around me there is still that constant low singing of the insects. For days now it has continued without letup or inflection, like ripples on water under a steady breeze. While I slept it went on through the night, a shimmer on my mind. My shoulder brushes a low tree overhanging the path and a bird that was asleep on one of the branches startles awake and flies off into the shadows, and I go on with the sense that I am passing near to the sleep of things.

In a way this is the best part of the trip. Stopping now and again to rest, I linger over it, sorry to be going. It seems to me that if I were to stay on, today would be better than yesterday, and I realize it was to renew the life of that possibility that I came here. What I am leaving is something to look forward to.

GARNETT C. BROWN JR.

Dove Autumn

From *Kentucky Monthly* (November 2000)

YOU COULDN'T have asked for a better opening day of dove season in Kentucky. The weather was mild and dry, with a light breeze blowing thin wisps of clouds high overhead.

Sunshine flooded still-green fields bordered with black rail fences, and nearby you could hear an occasional "Mooooo" from within a bovine herd on the graze. The air smelled good and clean, offering a pure sensual pleasure to be out. As a friend once observed, "Ya gotta get out and git the house-smell off."

Dove hunts, particularly in the South, are often a matter of ritual. In some places they are more formal, more structured than in other places, but there is always some ritual to observe.

For me, the ritual is pretty simple. Old, comfortable clothes, a scatter-gun and shells, the boots I wore in Vietnam. I carry a whistle, a bird-hunter's knife, a small compass, and an ancient metal match safe my father-in-law gave me long ago. My hunting vest was brand new 20 or so years ago, and in its pocket I keep some Chap Stick and an old pair of flying gloves that do well in the field if the weather turns cool.

Some hunters swear by a particular shotgun: a new expensive model that cost more than my house payment, or a favorite old beat-up hand-me-down, with the cracked wrist wrapped with tape. The guns are as different as the owners. You will hear debates on gauge and shot size, and on techniques of lead and

follow-through. A dove
hunt is as much a social
outing as a sporting event.

You'll find just about every type
of person you can imagine at a dove
hunt if you go to them long enough. You
might be surprised to find the preacher, a
professor, local shopkeepers and landowners,
politicians, blue-collar workers, policemen, wives
and sweethearts, and possibly even a smattering of rogues and
ne'er-do-wells among the lawyers, bankers, and doctors.

The landowner who has set up the hunt may not hunt at all if
the years are becoming a burden. One who may have come riding up on a horse in years past may now arrive in a car or a late-
model sport utility vehicle to say "howdy" to the boys. If he is
lucky, he has sons to join the hunt and to carry on the tradition.

While the cars and clothes and shotguns may sometimes an-
nounce the economic status of the shooters—"shooters" usually being a more accurate term than "hunters"—they may have
nothing to do with how well or poorly a person may shoot. Regardless of what is said, the end of the day tells the tale.

The dove itself, contrary to what you might think, is not the centerpiece of a dove hunt. To my mind that honor goes to the tradition, to the renewal of an ancient part of man's heritage. It's an acknowledgement that, despite our technological brilliance, a part of us still needs to be afield, still needs to reaffirm that we are hunters—no matter how foolish and shallow or out of place we appear. Yes, the need is deeper than some macho thing.

Tradition does not matter a whit to the dove. With his bright brown eyes and beautiful plumage, he is a fearless fighter pilot speeding to a graceful landing to pluck a tasty seed from a bit of grass. Amidst the roar of guns, he twists and turns and gives a whole line of shooters a chance to hit him before darting behind a grove of trees. His only crime is that his flesh is sweet and tasty, and when properly prepared by carefully browning in a great iron skillet, basted with wine and herbs and spices, he is moist and wonderful to the palate.

To start the hunt, mid-afternoon, you will usually find a truck or a wagon that takes each shooter to a spot adjacent to an open field where doves have been spotted. The distance between shooters is judged to be the effective range of a shotgun, to avoid an unpleasant mishap in the heat of tracking a bird that dives between shooters.

Some carry a stool to sit on, or a cooler that doubles as a chair, for dove hunting does not require walking till you fetch a bird you've downed.

There is fun and genuine sport in shooting at a small, fast-moving target. And the only time you will ever see a dove over your gunsight that is not moving is if you aim at one sitting in a tree or on a fence rail or an overhead line. Shooting at a still bird, unless it has been crippled, is considered bad form and poor sportsmanship by all but a few bird hunters.

A half hour before sunset the shooting is over. But not the tradition. You can hear the stories as the shooters gather together again. "How many did you get?" "Well, I shot 15, but I could only find these three...."

"How many boxes of shells did you use?" "Let's see, five boxes, that's 125 shots, and five birds in the bag. Helluva shot, eh?"

Then there is the crack shot who, instead of quietly saying, "I got the limit today," can't resist the urge to brag.

"Look at this, man," he'll say. "Fifteen birds on one box of shells. That's not bragging; that's fact! I mean, am I a good shot or what?"

The only thing worse than a poor loser is a poor winner.

You'll find all kinds at a dove shoot. Old. Young. Brand new at the game and seasoned heads working down to that last season, and hoping this isn't the one, hoping fate will be kind enough to let there be just one more good hunt. You'll see wealthy men with name-brand hunting togs and accessories, and you'll see somebody wearing a torn T-shirt, with a ball cap turned backward on his head.

But they all are part of something larger, something special. For both the right and wrong reasons they each have a need to commune with a part of our collective past and to carry it to our future.

Finally, there is the tired pleasure of getting home, letting the family and the dog look in your game bag, and to begin putting things away and cleaning the birds. Later, when everything is done, the smell of spent shotgun shells is still in your nostrils. Your tired feeling is a good feeling.

I'm already looking forward to next season.

WALTER L. CATO JR.

An Essential Ingredient

From *Happy Hunting Ground* (September–October 1991)

MY 14-FOOT Grumman boat floated in calm water in the Ohio River at the Westport ramp. A pretty picture, I thought, as I walked down the slope. The dull, grass-colored painted boat in the deep green late summer river was framed by bank-side sandbar willows and cottonwood. The cottonwood leaves were beginning to bleach out before changing to the autumn gray-brown hue that reminds me of the color of a whitetail's coat.

The boat was piled high, gunwale to gunwale, with a cargo which included tent, sleeping bags, cooking gear, groceries, my Browning automatic, my friend Moose's Ithaca pump, spinning rods, fly rods, trotlines, bait, buckets, cameras, and cooler. On top of the load, the heads of Moose's duck decoys peeked from their open-topped burlap sack. Next to the decoy sack was my smoke-blackened enamelware coffee pot.

Heading upstream in the late afternoon sun on the eve of opening day of early wood duck season, I thought about how Moose and I had anticipated this trip for months. Our plans included camping out Friday night, hunting ducks over decoys Saturday morning, then a trotline run on lines set Friday evening, bass fishing, dove shooting along a sandbar and finally back to the ramp in obedience to inflexible schedules which prohibited a longer expedition. We had put together a list of gear to take and groceries to buy. I bought the groceries in a hurry the evening before our departure, but was fairly confident I had not over-looked buying any of the listed items.

Before an hour had passed, we beached my boat downstream from the mouth of Camp Creek at a campsite we had used before. It must have been attractive to prehistoric men too, judging from the occasional chert (flint-like rock) shards and points we found along that stretch of riverbank. We pitched our version of a Whelen lean-to, built a rock fireplace and stowed our gear out of reach of the wash of passing tows. By the time we set two trot-lines, evening shadows were lengthening and we were hungry.

Dinner preparations began. While I set up a grill over the driftwood fire and unwrapped the rib eyes, the setting sun glinted off the clip blade of Moose's stockman's knife as he peeled and diced potatoes and sliced onions and bell peppers. The vegetables would be sauteed in lard in an iron skillet. The end product was standard fare on our cookouts. We called it "Potatoes Moose." The remainder of the dinner included the steaks, homegrown bib lettuce and tomato salad with store-bought fried pies and coffee for dessert.

When I set the skillet on the grill, I discovered that I had forgotten to bring the lard. No matter. "Potatoes Moose," we decided, could be brought off by the addition of a little water in lieu of lard if we covered the skillet.

As I mentally retraced my steps through the familiar grocery store aisles, trying to reconstruct how I could have forgotten to buy a one-pound container of lard, a chilling question popped into my mind. Did I remember to buy the coffee? I frantically searched the cardboard grocery boxes and was shocked to discover that I had, in fact, forgotten the coffee!

Moose noticed my agitated state as he looked up from his vegetable chopping.

"What's the matter?"

"I forgot the coffee."

"Oh, no! Not that."

"I don't want to abort this trip, Moose, but as much as I enjoy your company, I'm not going to enjoy my dinner knowing I can't have coffee afterward. Moreover, I refuse to get up in the morning and spend the day on the river without coffee."

"You're right, of course. We could run back to Westport and try our luck at finding the general store operator and persuading him to reopen to sell us a can of coffee, but that's chancy and it would be a long round trip."

I stared at the river in desperation. Dusk was coming on.

A string of summer cabins across the deserted river about a half-mile upstream offered some hope of finding someone who would sell us some coffee. We decided to try.

We put dinner on hold and within minutes were on a plane heading upstream, cutting the warm, humid river atmosphere. Under different circumstances, the boat ride would have been fun.

About 10 cabins lined the riverbank. All seemed unoccupied except possibly one. A 10-year-old Chevrolet pickup truck was parked in front of it. Looking through a pane in the cabin's front door, I anxiously noticed no light or sign of life in the living room. I knocked on the door.

Somewhere in the back of the cabin a chair leg scraped the floor. A woman clad in slacks, blouse, and apron appeared and moved toward the front door. Moose and I introduced ourselves and explained our plight. The explanation must have sounded plausible because she invited us into a kitchen filled with the aroma of cooking tomatoes. A man, who appeared to be in his late 60s and wearing a sleeveless tee shirt, khaki pants, and about a two days' growth of beard, was seated at the table peeling big scalded tomatoes with a paring knife. He greeted us and told us that he and his wife had driven to Bray's orchard in Trimble County and bought several bushels of tomatoes to can. The kitchen was filled with new tomatoes, cooked tomatoes, jars, and lids. The people were obviously enjoying their canning project.

My face broke into a broad grin as I watched the woman take from her cupboard two vacuum-packed foil bags marked "Churchill Downs Coffee." The labels indicated each package contained enough coffee to make an eight-cup pot.

I restrained myself from falling to my knees in gratitude. The woman refused payment but I thrust four dollar bills into her hand, and with profuse thanks we left the couple happily canning their tomatoes.

Back at our camp, cooking dinner, we were exuberant. Moose got out his 35mm camera and took a flash photo of the steaks grilling over coals. Dinner was delicious. With full bellies we lounged on the sandbar drinking coffee from restaurant-type mugs, listening to night sounds. A great blue heron flew close by, croaking intermittently. Sparks blew skyward as Moose added a driftwood log to the fire. I adjusted the position of the coffee pot next to the embers to keep it hot but not boiling. About 11:30, we retired to our sleeping bags, drifting off to sleep with visions of good hunting and fishing come dawn.

Next morning the coffee and sweet rolls tasted especially good. We ate and drank standing at the water's edge peering out in the darkness at a string of barges pushed by the towboat, *Lime Rock*. The string had apparently broken loose and jammed into the bank upstream from our camp sometime during the night. We concluded with satisfaction that the barges would not encroach on our intended duck hunting place.

The wood duck hunting segment of our quest was not blessed with birds in the bag. We saw only a few birds, but they weren't drawn to our decoys. The trotlines yielded five good channel cats, a flathead that weighed about seven pounds and a big eel which I skinned and saved to barbecue back home. We caught no bass on our fly rods and concluded we'd started fishing too late. We should've been popping the stumps and grass beds immediately after daylight. Late that afternoon, we shot seven doves as they came to a sandbar for gravel or water. Not an overwhelming bag, but we were pleased.

The setting sun found us breaking camp to return to our launch site. Standing in knee-deep water next to the gear-laden boat, feeling the osmosis of pleasing coolness from the river water through my hip boots, I remarked to Moose that I had come to a realization the previous evening:

"The main reason I enjoy these river trips is not to hunt or fish, but to drink coffee. I herewith make a solemn vow to never again forget the coffee."

"Amen," intoned Moose.

To this day I have kept that vow.

The Frontier (An Excerpt)

From *The Mountain, the Miner, and the Lord* (1980)

BETTY SEXTON FIELDS was a Melungeon who died at the age of ninety. The origins of the "dark people" are lost in the mists of our country's history. They are found in many parts of the Appalachians and are called by many names. In some places they are known as "Guians," in others as "Red Bones," "Ramps," "Wooly-boogers," and "Portagees." According to lingering traditions they were living deep in the hills long before the Battle of Fallen Timbers in 1794.

In any event, Betty Sexton Fields was a Melungeon whose forebear fought in the Revolution. Betty came to my office because of a neighborhood disagreement, and while she was there she told me about her great-grandmother and how a little band of settlers made their way into the headwaters of the Kentucky River "back in Indian times."

Betty said that several families came together "so they wouldn't be so lonesome" and for protection against the "savages." They left the old settlements too late in the year and passed through Pound Gap in the Pine Mountain after the leaves had turned brilliant with autumn colors. Thus they had to rely on the grain they carried on their mules, the livestock they herded before them, and such wild game as they could slay in the forests.

The families found a dry place under an arching cliff where they sheltered through the winter. They "faced up" the front with upright poles and tough bark peeled from huge chestnut

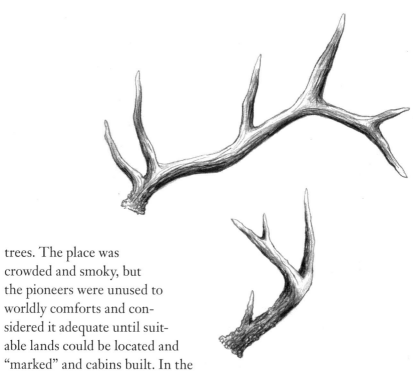

trees. The place was crowded and smoky, but the pioneers were unused to worldly comforts and considered it adequate until suitable lands could be located and "marked" and cabins built. In the spring all these things would be attended to and another fall would find them snugly set up on their own puncheon floors, within chinked walls, and with "rived" white oak boards above their heads.

Then winter came on. In January the snows fell and the creeks froze hard as iron. The ground was flinty and the bitter wind zipped through deerskins and woolens like a razor. The mastfall had been light and game was scarce. The men broke the ice to fish in the water but the black bass lay deep and were not tempted by the bait. The stocks of meal and parched corn dwindled and vanished. The families became desperate. The forest was silent. The dense canebrakes in the bottoms at the creek mouths were traversed time and time again without starting deer, elk, or buffalo. Time after time the hunters returned with nothing more than a few rabbits.

At last one night the men came home beaten and hopeless. There was no game in this vast wild country or, if it existed, it was hidden beyond their ken. Weak and hungry, they sat down around the fire, resigned to starvation. They could think of no way out of their dilemma and supposed that two or three more days of gnawing hunger and piercing cold would bring the end.

While they huddled in despair, Betty's great-grandmother put a chunk of fresh wood on the fire and sat down with the hunters. She told them not to give up, that things would turn out better tomorrow. She said that when they rose the next morning she would be missing from the camp. They must load their rifles with fresh dry powder and go into the forest very early. They would find a sign marked on a beech tree and should wait there in silence. The bark would be cut with an "upside down cross," and she demonstrated in the dust: ⊥ They must not leave the marked tree under any circumstance. In a little while they would see a herd of deer approaching, led by a black doe. Each hunter would aim at a deer and kill it, but they must not aim at the black doe. "No matter what happens, you must not shoot the foremost deer!" she warned them.

Dawn came with calamitous cold. Only glowing embers remained of the fire but it was stoked to desultory life with a few fallen branches from the gigantic oaks and chestnuts that encircled the "rock house." Mrs. Sexton was nowhere to be seen, and everything went as she had predicted. By the first light of dawn they found the huge regal beech, the inverted cross carved deep into its silvery bark. They waited with gnawing bellies under the twisted branches and amid the gnarled roots. About two hours after sunrise they heard a faint sound and there, moving in their direction, was a herd of a dozen deer, their heads high, their dainty hooves clicking against the crusted snow. At the head of the procession was a black doe which even the antlered bucks followed. On they came, closer and closer, wholly oblivious to the long-barreled rifles now aimed in their direction. Suddenly the black doe stopped and the others passed behind her. The black doe lowered her head as if sniffing the snow, and the rifles boomed. The black doe dashed into the forest and the others scattered amid a flurry of sharp hooves and white tails. They left behind them on the snow three carcasses—two bucks and a doe. As the men carried the heavy bodies to the half-starved camp they marveled that the herd could have escaped their relentless search during the preceding days.

The women and children were jubilant. They ran to meet the hunters and there among them was Mrs. Sexton, safely returned from her mysterious foray into the frozen forest.

The ravenous people filled their stomachs with the fresh venison and drank the fat rendered out of the intestines and other "soft parts." Their strength and spirits revived and they looked forward to spring. But the snow and bitter cold lingered and within a week the last of the meat was gone. Again they scoured the forest for game but found nothing. When they were worn out and sick with exhaustion and frustration Mrs. Sexton came again to their fire. The next morning all went precisely as before, and the hunters returned a second time laden with venison. At the camp they were greeted by the woman whose assistance had saved them from starvation. But the snow lay deep through February and the arctic winds blew with such terrible effect that the men could scarcely stir from the flames. Then came the night when the men returned empty-handed and the last morsel of the meat was gone.

Mrs. Sexton told them a third time that when they awakened she would be gone from the camp, and they must do as she had instructed them before. "Take good aim, and do not shoot the foremost deer!"

The next morning the men waited at the giant beech, puzzled by the strange happenings that had kept them alive through seven terrible weeks. One of them was named Gibson, a tall muscular man who feared nothing. His rifle carried a heavy charge of powder and two balls. When the black doe came into view he aimed at her chest and when she dipped her head he fired. The two balls struck close together and penetrated her lungs. When Gibson rushed up with his butcher knife in hand the men shivered because her dying eyes glared at him with the hatred they had seen in cornered wolves. The others berated Gibson for disobeying the instructions that had brought them so much good fortune, but he laughed at them.

This time Mrs. Sexton did not meet them at the camp. They searched far and wide for her and called her name many times. They fired their rifles and listened for some answering cry, but none came. She was never found, and no trace of her footprint was seen in the snow.

When Gibson cut up the carcass of the black doe, it gave off a foul, sickening smell. The meat could not be eaten and was discarded in a sinkhole where it was covered with brush and rocks. Eventually warm weather softened the soil, and Betty's great-grandfather buried the carcass.

Betty watched me to make sure I was listening to her story. "You see," she explained, "my great-grandmother followed the dark ways and had many powers people nowadays know nothing about. The dark ways were brought from the yon side of the waters, and my people brought them to the new settlements. People who followed the dark ways were healthy and strong and lived long lives. They was never sick a day of their lives."

She went on with her tale. Her great-grandfather had learned many things from his wife and now he tried hard to remember all that he had heard her say and seen her do concerning her mysterious practices. He was not a witch himself but had lived with his wife for a dozen or so years, and she had told him much that he took lightly at the time but now recalled as important. He too could follow the dark ways.

Spring days melted the snow. The streams ran high with sparkling water, and wild flowers peeped up where the sun touched the forest loam. The people under the "rock house" scattered in search of lands suitable for farming, and Sexton was left with a motherless brood and grief for his vanished wife.

He went deep into the wilderness in search of things he had heard her mention. At last he found them high in a hillside cove. A gigantic poplar had fallen, leaving a hollow stump about three feet high. Lichens and fungi grew on its rotten sides, and dark, foul-smelling water filled its basin. Toadstools—"the devil's wild flowers"—grew all about, sprouting in profusion out of the prostrate trunk. A dozen yards away a white beech lifted its twisted limbs. The water-filled stump was in a little clearing which the moon could reach on a cloudless night. The setting was satisfactory.

Sexton carved an "image" into the bark of the beech tree. It was a passable outline of the face and features of Gibson, the errant hunter. That night when darkness enveloped the forest, Sexton dipped his hand into the stump water and sprinkled it over the image. Six nights in a row he returned and repeated the ritual. On the seventh night he brought a sharp wooden spike carved from seasoned hickory and hammered the "trunnel" into the living bark and wood of the beech so that it protruded from the forehead of the image. Then he went home.

A day or so later Gibson awoke with a headache. It worsened throughout the day. The next day he was frantic with pain and sent for Sexton. Betty's great-grandfather reached the unfinished cabin to find the man stretched in agony on a bed of moss. He looked at Sexton and grimaced with the agony inside his skull. "You have hexed me for killing your wife," he moaned. He said he felt as if a nail had been driven straight into his forehead. Then he died.

Betty told me things that witches knew and other people did not suspect. For example, God made everything that people eat and "made it perfect." All food should be eaten whole just as it grows out of the ground. "The devil tells us to take the bran from the wheat and the peel from the apple, but the people who believe in the Lord know better." Most of the things people eat these days have been "touched by the devil," and had the best parts taken out. That is why there is so much sickness and so many doctors and hospitals.

Folks talk about vitamins, she said, and think they are something new. The people who followed the dark ways knew about them thousands of years ago and concentrated them in the potions they boiled out of forest plants. "People have to take vitamins out of a bottle," she opined, "because old Satan has been tampering with their grub!"

I asked her about the poplar stump in the clearing, and she explained. When the devil passes through the dark woods he looks for a hollow stump with water in it. He is vain, stops to see himself reflected in the moonlit water, and will come back again and again. That becomes Satan's ground.

She smiled and concluded her lecture. "The next time you go for a walk in the woods look for a hollow stump in a little clear place. If the stump is full of water and has toadstools growing on and around it you may know Satan has been there. If you are there at midnight you may see his old black face in the moonlight."

DR. THOMAS D. CLARK

A Little Bit of Santa Claus (An Excerpt)

From *Pills, Petticoats and Plows: The Southern Country Store* (1944)

UNLIKE THEIR YANKEE brethren, southerners saved their fireworks for Christmas instead of the Fourth of July. There seems to be little fundamental reason for this traditional difference between the sections. Some have explained that because the siege of Vicksburg was ended on the Fourth of July, southerners refused to celebrate the day in any other way than that of going to fish fries and political picnics. This is hardly true. Perhaps the weather conditions were a more vital factor, but whatever the reason, the stores did not stock firecrackers for the July trade. It has always seemed that for a southerner to shoot firecrackers and Roman candles in the summertime was just about as incongruous as killing hogs in August.

The louder the noise the country-store customers could make, the happier they were. When the last firecracker fizzled out, the more adventurous resorted to the use of black powder and anvils for noisemaking. Powder was packed tightly into the round and square holes of one anvil, and a second one was placed securely on top of the charge so that when the powder was ignited both anvils rang out in loud metallic tones which could be heard for miles around. Traditionally, anvil shooting was a part of every Christmas affair. Country stores, school and church grounds boomed with thunderous impacts of these black-powder charges, and evidence of this primitive custom has lingered in many farmyards. Few of the half-drunken celebrants who fired their

steely blasts realized that they would dehorn their anvils in the explosion, and many a "muley-headed" block of steel was carried home to tell its mute tale for years to come of a hilarious country Christmas.

All of the stores kept black powder during the years 1865 to 1900. One entry after another is for the inseparable combination of powder, shot, caps, and sheets of wadding, and it is a remarkable fact that with all of the storekeeper's harum-scarum methods of keeping stock there is no record of powder kegs exploding. Yet many powder barrels and kegs were left as carelessly exposed inside store buildings as were barrels of sugar and coffee.

The Winchester Arms Company along with all the other manufacturers of guns and ammunition were quick to shift manufacturing practices after 1865 to that of supplying ready-prepared ammunition which could be used in the new-type breech-loading guns. But the muzzle-loader remained popular

in the South for forty years after Appomattox. The typical reluctant rural southern attitude toward a change in plow tools
and implements prevailed toward guns. A muzzle-loader would
shoot, and a man could hit birds, rabbits, and squirrels with it;
it took time to load, but time was cheap. Because of this un-
progressive attitude the powder, shot, and cap trade remained
constant in the stores. Not only did merchants sell supplies for
ammunition, but they made some profit from the sale of detach-
able tubes which were screwed into the base of powder chambers
and on which percussion caps were exploded. Literally thousands of entries were made in account books for these outmoded
hunting supplies. The muzzle-loading gun was an institution,
and if not an entirely safe and certain one, at least most people
had learned its weak points. They were slow to accept new and
improved arms which involved such a fundamental change as
that of loading prepared ammunition into the breech.

When at last the primitive weapon of the ante-bellum South was outmoded, orders for shot and powder were changed to demands for boxes of shells, and the South quickly became a land of the single-barreled breech-loading shotgun. Remington, Stevens, Winchester, Iver-Johnson, L. C. Smith, Sears, Roebuck, and Montgomery and Ward distributed thousands of these cheap weapons throughout the South. Rabbit hunters much preferred the light choke-bore, single-barrel twelve- and sixteen-gauge guns. When they were loaded with their characteristic yellow hulls charged with three drams of black powder and one and an eighth ounces of number-six shot they became bush cutters and rabbit killers of a high order.

By December crops were gathered, and it was safe to set the woods and fields afire. For a whole week during the Christmas season hillbilly and cane-cutter rabbits lived in misery. Christmas day was the big day of this season of hunting. Sedge fields and heavily wooded bottomlands rang out with the constant firing of hard-kicking breechloaders. Scarcely a southern community got through the season without some type of casualty. Occasionally accidents were slight; sometimes they were the result of an irresponsible prankster forgetting that shot and powder were wholly devoid of a sense of humor. There were, however, unhappy tragedies which caused many southern families to bemoan Christmas day for many years. Persons were killed or maimed with unhappy regularity in the big hunting sprees. Livestock was killed, and fences and buildings destroyed. Yet these big hunting parties were as characteristic of the holiday season as were coconut cakes, apples, oranges, and raisins.

SOC CLAY

Muskie Joe: The Legend Continues

From *Happy Hunting Ground* (September–October 1984)

Happy Hunting Ground Editor's Note: Muskie Joe Stamper was a
living legend along the tree-lined banks of Kentucky's Kinniconick
Creek for nearly 50 years. That was how long the dedicated angler
pursued the muskies the stream is famed for. He was the first full-
time muskie fisherman anyone could remember in eastern Kentucky and was perhaps the oldest active muskie fisherman in the
country until he died suddenly in March 1981. In his lifetime, he
probably caught as many as 300 legal-size muskies and was considered the champion muskie angler of all time in the rugged hill
country of eastern Kentucky. His fame as a muskie fisherman was
widespread, and few fishermen in the tristate area of Kentucky,
Ohio, and West Virginia had not heard of the legend of Muskie Joe.
Many thought he was just that, a legend, but in truth, he was real,
very real. This is the story of Muskie Joe.

HE WAS BORN Joe Edward Stamper on March 2, 1887, on the
head of Grassy near the headwaters of the Laurel Fork of the
Kinniconick. His father, the late Taylor Stamper, was a barrel
maker and cross-tie drifter. The Stamper family was well known
for conducting huge cross-tie floats each spring when as many
as 150,000 hand-hewn ties were pushed into the flood-swollen
waters of the tributaries of the Kinniconick and herded downstream some 40 miles to the steamboat landing at Garrison.

From their origin deep in the back country of Lewis County, twenty men, teams of mules, a floatboat capable of feeding the entire crew, and a young cook by the name of Joe E. Stamper fought multitudes of run-offs and low water periods during their annual six-week float.

It was on the last great tie run the Stamper family made down the Kinniconick that the young cook and handyman would start a lifelong experience with the fabled six-foot muskies of the stream.

"He was big and a good 72 inches and his sides were the color of polished silver. His eyes were wild, fire-flecked and looked as if they belonged to a demon. It was the first live muskie I ever really seen up close and it was mad enough to snort flames when it came from beneath the tie jam and scooted a good 40 feet on top of the slippery logs before it found an open spot in the creek.

"We were on the last float my folks made down the Kinniconick and I was trying to break a jam of ties that had been caught in the forks of a big laydown maple when I spooked the fish.

"He must have been a-lookin' for a way out of there and when I rammed that spud bar down in the heap, I suspect he seen daylight and made a break for the sky," Joe said.

The year was 1905 and the big silver-sided fish flopping over the piled-up ties was enough to cause Joe to catch a bad case of muskie fever that would stay with him until the fire in his own pale blue eyes flickered and finally died away a week and a half before his 94th birthday.

Joe's recollections of the Kinniconick muskie went back even farther than the last cross-tie float down the stream. "When I was a barefoot boy a-growin' up on the Laurel Fork, pike, as they were known then, came up the little clear-water stream to spawn on top of the clean gravel bars." He remembered that he and his young friends would fashion gig-like devices or borrow pitchforks from the barn to try and spear the big fish.

"That creek was clear and clean to boot," Joe recalled. "Old

Doc Rose had her tested one time and she came back 97% pure. No wonder muskies like to come there to spawn," he said.

Joe called up memories about the way he fished when he was a youngster. "We took 'em anyway we could. There wasn't any such thing as a rod and reel in our part of the country. Couldn't a-had 'em if we'd of known about 'em. No one had any money for such things back in those days," he explained.

"Our tackle was stout lines, willow limbs, a trotline now and then, pitchforks, and rifle bullets. Ever once in a while someone would fashion a big seine or manage to get a few sticks of dynamite. That was when enough fish would be brought home to fill a 90 gallon picklin' barrel."

Joe was getting on towards middle age when he finally settled into serious muskie angling for sport. It was during the years of the Great Depression, and making a living in rural Lewis County was no easy task. Joe and his brother, Commodore Stamper, figured as how a small sawmill operation might be a paying proposition. They owned a tract of timber on the banks of the Kinniconick and there were enough squirrels in the hills and fish in the creek to keep a man alive until the lumber operation became profitable.

It took a while, but eventually the mill was set up and Joe and his brother built a small cabin high enough on the bank to keep the creek out of the door on a rise. Some timber was cut and sawed into boards but Joe and his brother would take time out daily from their duties at the mill to get in a few hours of fishing, or spend early mornings on the ridgetops in search of gray squirrels.

Commodore was a family man and owned a farm back on the Laurel Fork, so he was absent from the mill operations quite a bit. To keep himself busy, Joe turned more and more to fishing the creek.

He enjoyed catching the smallmouth of the Kinniconick, and the rock bass were plump and good eating. But the real fish in

Joe's opinion was the big muskies that often lay in shallow water, sunning themselves on a bright spring day.

It wasn't long until Joe turned his attention to fishing for muskie almost completely.

A few sport fishermen from the Cincinnati area had heard about the muskie and smallmouth of the Kinniconick and made trips to the stream by riding the C & O and the old Kinniconick Railway. Local farmers would then be hired to haul their camping and fishing equipment to a good location on the stream and sometimes a boat could be rented.

Joe saw the need for a guide and boat rental service to accommodate the growing number of fishermen visiting the stream, so he set to work sawing big poplar trees which he later fashioned into a total of 13 wide-bottom johnboats that measured 16 feet long.

"A man needs a big boat, wide and stable to cast for a six-foot muskie," Joe was fond of saying.

Joe charged a dollar a day for renting his boats, but he never hired out as a guide even though he was asked numerous times. "I always told the boys everything I knew about fishing in the creek and couldn't see me taking no money for it. Wouldn't seem right since we were all chums and fishing buddies," he added.

For several years, Joe lived a laid-back lifestyle on the banks of the Kinniconick. He and his brother Commodore continued to saw a little lumber at the mill and Joe found time to raise a garden in between his fishing and lumbering. "Why I'd fish an eddy in the mornin', come home and have a big dinner of cornbread and beans, go back out in the afternoon and fish a big eddy—maybe even catch me a three-footer or two—then go home and have me a big supper of cornbread and beans. I'll tell you feller, I eat an awful lot of cornbread and beans back in those hard times," Joe chuckled.

The title of "Muskie Joe" was hung on him by his sport-fishing friends from the Cincinnati area. That was during the late 1930s and it would stay with him, gaining in stature and reputation, until his death in 1981. Joe was proud of the title and figures as how he was just about as good a fisherman that ever threw a big spoon towards the muskie of the Kinniconick.

A tribute to Joe's fishing ability on his home stream was made a few years ago by Elmer Claxon, dean of east Kentucky muskie men and the Grand Patriarch of the fabled Lost Creek Muskie Clan. When Elmer was asked who he thought the best muskie fisherman was in the state of Kentucky, his reply was "on the Kinniconick, Muskie Joe Stamper's the best. Anywhere else, I am!"

Joe always measured Kinniconick muskies by the foot. "I catched a three-footer or a four-footer," he would say. He told about his late uncle, G. W. Stamper, who brought a sport fishing outfit up from Cincinnati about 1910. "G. W. bought him a rod and reel, some braided silk line and a big brass spoon. Went out on the creek that very afternoon and catched hisself a five-footer," Joe recalled.

Joe was always talking about the legendary "six-footers" he claimed lived in some of the large eddies of the stream. "Why, me and a woman was fishing the Armstrong Eddy one day and a six-footer come up and sunned himself a while. We had plenty of time to measure him against the seven-foot boat oar we had and he was a good six feet if he was an inch," Joe claimed.

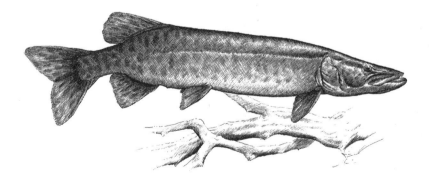

"Christ did better than me. He fed a multitude on five loaves and two fishes, I fed 27 on one fish and had two skillets left over that two preachers from Vanceburg cleaned up the next day," Joe said.

Joe never caught a six-footer. The best he ever did was a four-footer that weighed 32 pounds and set a stream record for the species. The fish was caught in time to feed well-wishers at Joe's 78th birthday party.

Joe claimed he was bested in the number of muskie caught in a single day by his longtime friend and fishing companion, Old Doc Bertram.

"Old Doc Bertram [Doctor Bertram was, in fact, a bit younger than Joe] went down to Cincinnati and bought an outfit and two new muskie lures and came up to the Punchin Eddy and catched eight muskie that went from 12 to 19 pounds in one afternoon," Joe remembered.

No one is sure how many legal-size muskie Joe caught from the Kinniconick in the 60 years he actively fished for them. He lost count himself many years ago. "Me and Charley Rose kept track of the fish we caught while we fished together in the 40s and 50s, but we lost count after we catched one hundred," Joe said.

Joe did all his fishing from the big johnboats he built in the 1930s. He never did like aluminum. "Too damn noisy," Joe complained. "Besides you can't nail brush on the side of a metal boat," he added.

Joe was known to make his boat look like a brush pile during certain times of the year. He claimed that a muskie following a lure will grab it every time if he thinks it's getting away by running into a brush pile.

"Boys I'll tell ye, if the Lord mites for muskie to bite, they bite. If He don't, all hell won't make 'em!"

Joe's tackle box wasn't much to brag about and he never owned more than a dozen lures in his life until some company learned about his preferences for spoons and sent him a box full. "A muskie on the prowl will hit a corncob, but won't hit the best lure in the world if he ain't on the prowl," he said.

Joe thought a muskie and a fat man had a lot in common. Both will lay around in the shade most of the time.

He also noted that muskie are deep water loafers but take two-thirds of their food from the surface. "Ain't much use to throw a bottom-bouncer at a muskie; he ain't even lookin' that way!" Joe exclaimed.

Joe claimed a muskie feeds every nine days and that you could wear a reel out casting for muskie in July and August without catchin' one.

Joe's favorite times for muskie fishing were April and May (number one), September and October (number two) and November and December (number three). "I've catched a muskie on every holiday of the year and had to make up a few besides," Joe would brag.

He enjoyed fishing the big eddies of the Kinniconick during October most of all. "Fishin's good when leaves are floatin' on the water. Minnows stay in the leaves and muskie keep an eye peeled on the open places on the surface. I call it winder watchin' and I'll throw a big plug right smack in the middle of 'em when I get a chance," Joe said.

Another muskie habit Joe noted from his many years of fishing and observing the species was that muskie will hit best during periods when temperatures vary from low degrees at night to warm degrees during the day. A good time to muskie fish is just before a major storm. "Creeks can come up and stay up for several days. A muskie knows that and will feed up to tide him over," Joe explained.

Overcast days are good times to fish muskie, according to Joe, and his advice was to always fish in a shaded area whether the sun is shining or not.

Joe was a conservationist all the way to his very soul and despaired at the lack of attention being paid to his Kinniconick and similar streams across the state and the union.

"If they let the trees grow back, keep the bulldozers out of the creek and allow nature to reclaim it, it will still take a thousand years to undo the damage man has done on these streams."

According to Joe, the U.S. has played Santa Claus to the rest of the world and allowed the streams and rivers of the nation to "go straight to hell!"

"Son, I can remember when we caught bass out of the Laurel Fork that were as big as a ham of meat. Not so anymore. Bass are scattered and the rock bass have all but disappeared. All the big holes are fillin' up with silt and my old Kinniconick muskies are going to have lot worse 'fore it starts gettin' better," was his prediction.

"I'll fish right on as long as I'm able, and I'm a-goin' catch that six-footer this spring. I know just the log he's a-layin' under."

If Joe would have lived 11 days longer, he would have spent a grand total of 94 years on earth—and much of that time on the clear waters of the Kinniconick. "You know boys, it's the winter that kills us old folks. If I can make it through March, I'll catch that big 'en this year."

Ironically, Joe never made it through March. He died while visiting his daughter in Indiana on one of the rare times he ever left his warm little cabin during winter.

For nearly 60 years, the muskie fisherman who lived on the banks of the Kinniconick was a living legend. He's gone now, but the spirit he instilled in the hearts of anglers who fish the creeks of Kentucky will live on as long as stout-hearted muskie men float the twisting waters, searching for the fabled six-footers that Joe knew lived in the Kinniconick.

"You know boys, I've got a sweet water spring in my front yard, a good warm cabin, plenty of fishing tackle and muskie in my back yard. What else in the world could an old fisherman want in his lifetime?"

DAVID DICK AND EULALIE C. DICK

An Excerpt from *Rivers of Kentucky* (2001)

THERE ARE TWO THINGS as good as food. One is making love, the other is canoeing on Licking. The three combined make an afternoon in June seem like heaven on earth, mindful that around each bend there can be a message from hell, when gravity and flow get together on the proposition. All the food on the most sumptuous of Tom Jones table spreads, all the love in the most feathery of beds, or buck naked beneath the pawpaw trees, cannot match the thrill of floating from slack water into rapids on Middle Fork of Licking.

We turn onto MouthofCedar Road and put in downstream from the mouth of Cedar Creek southwest of Mt. Olivet, eight of us in four canoes. Michael and Miranda lead the way, followed by Barry and Lalie, William and Ravy, and Bill and David. In each canoe, more experienced river rats paddle aft of the unschooled, untried first-timers, fine-tuning the direction of the needle bow with pinpoint precision, canoes being as willowy and vain as they are vulnerable. The authors of *Rivers of Kentucky* and their daughter ride separately on the slicing edge where the water curls back with a pleasant, deceptively innocent, rippling sound. Bringing up the rear, seventy-year-old David and eighty-six-year-old Bill are wise and noble, somber chieftains content to allow younger braves to read the river.

With each sound of approaching rapids, Michael, Barry, and Willie stand upright, perfectly balanced in the cool breeze. They calmly study the unpredictable current ahead, looking for the deepest "V" on the water's surface, deciding whether to take the port or starboard side, lay in close to the bank or shoot down the middle where rocks the size of cannonballs lie beneath the surface. Submerged boulders, slick as deer gut on a doorknob, are primed to capsize canoes and disgorge their human contents, young or old, fed or unfed, loved or unloved. The slippery, larger rocks usually don't move. They wait for the moment when the bow of the canoe strikes, lifts, and pivots. The current is constant, pressure insistent.

No two rapids, as no two days, are alike. The fallen tree trunk that was not here yesterday could be a threat today, could be swept away tomorrow. Even a slender limb of a fallen silver maple or sycamore acts like a lowered limbo bar.

Miranda, Lalie, and Ravy drop their heads as Michael, Barry, and Willie maneuver their canoes through the narrow passage. They come about in the new slack water and look back to watch Bill and David make their approach. David's hand goes up to take the small limb and push it up as he ducks under, as if he were on a riding mower on a lazy Sunday afternoon. This limb on this day does not move. The canoe responds by tipping, water pouring in, David and Bill pouring out. They are like pieces of moon sliding beyond the horizon. Not a pretty sight.

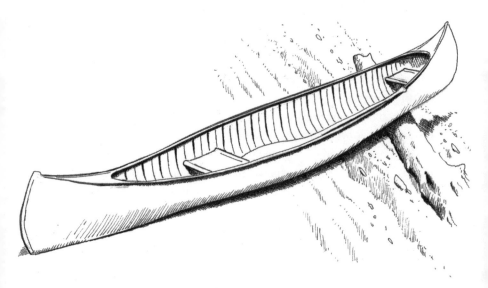

Feet seek the bottom of the shallow rapids. Lungs hold on tightly, windpipes automatically slam to the off-position. Knees strike rocks worn as smooth as the Western Wall by millions of kisses. When faces reappear they are drawn, peevish, wrinkled with amazement. Hands claw for the nearest thing to cling to. Swimming is a redundancy. The upside-down canoe is jammed. David's new tape recorder squeaks pitifully as it drowns, the elements of oral history as lost as baby ducks fluttering and failing to follow their warning mother. The reporter's notebook is waterlogged, pages melded, words wiped away as if nothing had ever been written. Wrist watch ticking? It is. John Cameron Swayze'd be proud. (Old-time newsman who saw nothing wrong with selling waterproof watches at the same time he was commentating.) Billfold in hip pocket? Yes. Hen and Rooster whittler's knife? Yes, but rust is on the way and fused blades can't be far behind. And how is Bill? He's standing in the rapids, water dripping from his face, wondering how in hell he ever got hooked up with a feller who doesn't know a canoe from a riding mower. For a moment the octogenarian seems dazed, but then he speaks, clearly: "I'm all right. A little excitement is good!" Bill is the Chief Sitting Bull of Licking.

The braves come back to help their senior Hunkpapas empty water from their canoe, steady it while gingerly they regain their seats, and grandly push them off again for the rest of the seventeen-mile, five-hour trip from mouth of Cedar, past the mouths of Beaver Creek and Greasy Creek, under the Claysville Bridge to Bill's getaway in Harrison County. His wife, Martha, is waiting there with real food and knowing looks.

"How many more rapids are there?" frets David.

"Several," says Bill, remorsefully.

Canoeing on lower Licking is like being in a primitive world, devoid of menacing civilization. Trees rise up, roots exposed by natural erosion, limbs extended toward the center of the winding stream. Overhead, parallel jet trails are wispy reminders of the other sphere of commerce and urgency. The river is as silent as the jet trails except for the distant reverberation of the turbulence in the next rapids.

The sound begins as a whisper, a murmur, a susurration increasing in intensity until whiteness appears, water bubbling like a rapid boil in a stovetop pan. The intensity is not as great as white water in a "wild river," but the rapids on lower Licking are a training ground where injuries do occur. Solo treks involving anything fewer than two canoes can spell disaster. To be thrown and dashed against a large rock, to be trapped beneath a canoe, to be tumbled through a rapids, can be fatal if there's no immediate help. The river stretches ahead, pressured by the current, a ceaseless, demanding force. Human life sits astride the narrow spine of the canoe wherein balance is precariously paramount. Paddles provide a measure of control, but the will of the water will not be denied. It need not be flood time to see such a fundamental truth.

Even in the calmest of times, hunger enters the picture of aching shoulders and soiled, sticky underwear. It's time for a midday rest stop on the Robertson County side of Licking, where there are several large flat boulders upon which to spread picnic lunches. The only sounds are the occasional pileated woodpeckers at work on a tall sycamore, the hum of insects on the young leaves of approaching summer. Miranda, Lalie, and Ravy have water-splashed, sunbaked faces where cosmetics are swept away like words in a reporter's drowned notebook. Femininity has been brought to a new reckoning in shoulders, arms, hands, legs, ankles, and feet, coordinating strength to countervail the river. The power of the hydrologic cycle has dulled eroticism.

Michael, Barry, and Willie are confident in their competence to shoot most any rapids, but at every bend of the river their manhood has been sounded out and carried to a sobering brink. In the depths of their testosterone they know there are certain limits imposed by the flow of the river. There's neither dread nor paranoia about helplessness, only quiet acceptance that the day will come when no amount of potency or ingenuity will satisfy or compromise the Water Carrier.

Bill and David look like old beavers emerging from underwater dwellings. They rub the backs of their wrists against their mouths as if to confirm that their lips have not been sacrificed to the clever rocks in the rapids. The septuagenarian and the octogenarian reach out for younger hands to help with the first and trickiest step from the canoe to the riverbank. Age has its uncertainties as well as its prerogatives. When seated or stretched upon the ground there's an illusion of youth with remembrances of pleasurable tumbles in stinkweeds along the water's edge. The remembrance of fantasies fulfilled on hot summer days before the indulgence of canoes was in a time when it was blood-pumping joyful to walk through ripened clover to the water's edge, sit and stare at the muddy water for a time, strip down and take a plunge to the bottom where the water was cooler and sweeter.

The conversation turns to the most recent tumble from the canoe. "You've been baptized," says Barry.

"Didn't hear a blessing," replies David, glumly.

After sandwiches, cookies, and lemonade, it's time to push off again. There's no hurry, but nobody wants to be in darkness on the river. Nor would a storm be a welcomed event. Lightning searching for a home, wind bending eroded tree giants, and flash floods descending from upstream would be hellish. The canoe represents stability spinning on the head of a pin.

The rapids come and are left behind until there's a widening expanse of frothing spray where the stream is dotted with so many rocks the "deepest V" is difficult to discern. Michael and Miranda shoot through at midstream, the canoe rising and falling as if it were designed especially for them. Barry and Lalie follow more to the port side, and Willie and Ravy traverse slightly closer to the Harrison County side. They wait in the slack water to watch the descent of Bill and David.

"We're going in closer to the bank," says Bill. The water seems a little quieter there. David places his paddle alongside his right leg and takes a firm grip on the opposite edges of the canoe. He sees the partially submerged tree trunk and watches the narrowing gap as plummeting speed becomes a new factor. A clean hit might be tolerable. Then again, might not. Thoughts come in microseconds. To those watching in slack water it may seem like hideous slow motion.

The bow strikes the tree trunk. The sound is a hard thud. The canoe rises, twists, and spins. David is thrown like a weatherworn rodeo clown on a penis-pinched maverick. Bill, too. The water is slightly deeper but both Hunkpapas bounce from the rocky bottom and burst through the surface as grinning warriors appear to help and comment. "Baptized again," shouts Barry.

"Still no blessing," mutters David, sourly.

The safe arrival at Bill's camp comes none too soon. Bodies ache for dry clothes, but spirits address the possibility of more outings on the rivers of Kentucky. "How about Red next time? How about Green? Hell *far*, how about a trip all the way down to New Orleans?"

JOE TOM ERWIN

Frog Fever

From the *Louisville Courier-Journal* (Summer 1975)

EVERY JUNE WHEN Mike Voyles of Owensboro visits for a week, I relive some of my best boyhood days by taking him frog hunting. And every time we creep up a pond bank on our bellies to survey a pond studded with fist-sized bullfrog heads, eleven-year-old Mike rewards me by shaking slightly when he draws a bead on his first target.

In fact, if the game is especially plentiful and large, he may take the rifle from his shoulder for a couple of deep breaths to steady his aim. And I'm under standing orders not to comment on the bigness of a frog when pointing one out to Mike.

"When you say he's a big one, I get so nervous I almost drop the gun," he tells me.

Despite his frog fever, Mike packs a mean gun and returns to Owensboro after each visit with a mess of frogs for his grandfather, Logan Leonard.

We scheduled our hunt this year for late in the afternoon, as temperatures all last week had been near ninety and we figured the big ones left the water during the hottest hours for shady places on the bank. Mike had spent the day helping my brother Bill and his son Bucky of Hazel haul hay, so we invited them and Jerry White, another young member of the haying crew, to go along. The last bale was in the barn at 5:30 P.M., and thirty minutes later we were slipping up to our first pond.

While Bill and I stood back and watched, the three boys

climbed a levy, scanned the pond, and let loose a barrage that would have compared with Little Big Horn. When they returned with only three of the two dozen or so frogs that had lined the banks, Bill and I sat them down for a lecture on "one bullet, one piece of game" and "sharing and shooting."

In the meantime, several of the big croakers had reappeared at the surface. When we released the properly restrained boys, they chose their shots well, took careful aim, and bagged eleven more frogs.

We hunted three more ponds before dark and ended the day with twenty-six frogs. Bill and I then lectured the boys on the hunter's duty to clean his own game, supplied them with pocketknives, lay back in the pasture grass that surrounded the pond, and listened to the chuck-will's-widow tune up for a serenade.

DICK FARMER

Tickling, Noodling, etc.

From *Happy Hunting Ground* (November–December 1979)

"EXCUSE ME," I said, "but people have been committed to mental institutions for doing saner things than sticking their hands
under rocks like these and I don't think I'm going to do it!" That
comment drew a grin from Kerry Prather, Eastern Fishery District biologist, while Letcher County conservation officer (CO)
Jerry Coots spit another stream of tobacco juice, Bill Braswell,
Perry County CO, looked on with apprehension, and Seventh
District supervisor Tommy Cantrell shuffled along beside the
small eastern Kentucky stream we were about to start wading.

I'd like to return to this pregnant moment in my life, but first
let's go back a few weeks to a sunny day in Frankfort when the
editor called out my name and I knew another story assignment
was on its way. "I want you to write a story about tickling, noodling, and grabbing," I remember Martha saying. "Do it in the
Seventh Wildlife District [far eastern Kentucky]."

The idea sounded fine to me. After all, not knowing what
"tickling, noodling, and grabbing" was, it sounded like fun. I
hadn't done any serious tickling and grabbing since my high
school days at the dive (or is it drive-in?) and don't remember
that I ever noodled, but I'm game for anything. Then the suspi-
cions began to mount that Martha wasn't talking about the same
sort of sport I had in mind. "You better set it up quick since the
season closes the last day of August," she'd said.

Well, all the tickling etc. I'd seen had no season, per se, so I de-

71

cided I'd better check out the situation and immediately dashed to the department's law enforcement offices.

I figured if anyone could set me straight on all this tickling and grabbing business it had to be the assistant director of law enforcement, Steve Yontz, who not only grew up in eastern Kentucky but had worked there several years. If anybody would know about the tickling, noodling, and grabbing that goes on up in the mountains only until the end of August, Steve would.

"Well," chuckled Steve. "I think you have the wrong idea about all this tickling business—what it is, is a method of taking fish, a method that has proved downright controversial in the last few years, as a matter of fact."

Yontz continued his dissertation as I listened in stunned silence. Finally it began to sink in that what Martha had in mind was a diabolical scheme to have me reach under submerged rocks and treelaps in a remote mountain stream, wiggle my fingers around until I touched something clammy and scaly, then jerk a fish out of the water.

"Of course, I should point out one modification," Yontz continued. "They tickle, noodle, and grab fish in streams all over the state, but in some sections, and eastern Kentucky's one of them, you could be working a submerged car body or an old refrigerator instead of a rock or a stump." Needless to say, the assignment sounded more tantalizing by the minute.

So it was with great trepidation that I shuffled back to my office and began dialing the phone to speak with Cantrell, wondering if this would be one of the last times that finger would ever dial a telephone. Soon Cantrell understood what I needed and put himself at my disposal.

Taking the bull by the horns, Tommy told me to exercise my fingers and he'd set up the trip. Sure enough, he waited just long enough to spawn hope that the deal was off before his voice crackled over the long-distance line to let me know the big show

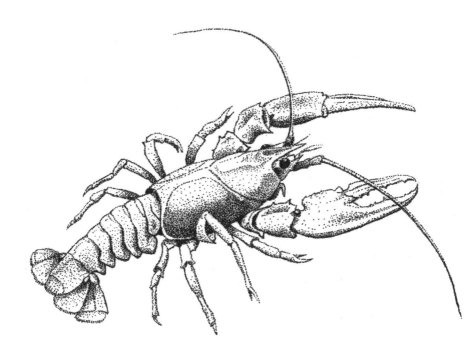

was on and gave directions to a motel where we would meet the night before. The die was cast.

Unlike the month of December, with its promise of Christmas and, for those of us too old to look for old Santa, New Year's Eve, the days flew by to my appointment with Cantrell and his band of merry men in Whitesburg. I used the days to prepare more physically than mentally for the assignment.

Cantrell had told me, somewhat to my relief but not to my surprise, that tickling, noodling, and grabbing required no fancy equipment or, for that matter, any equipment at all. Some "slicks" might use chest waders, he said, but most good ole boys just pull off their shoes, roll up their pants, and jump right in.

An office opinion poll on the "sport" I was about to undertake was useless, resulting only in shy grins, snickers, and offers to help count my fingers for inventory purposes. All this served to confirm my fears that snakes, snapping turtles, muskrats, and other "beasts" lurk in the same recesses that look "perfect" for catfish or suckers.

When the appointed day arrived, I tried to put all this out of my mind as I loaded the car with a couple of changes of clothing (figuring things would get pretty wet when the tickling began), a camera, some film, and, of course, a bottle of snakebite medicine. The breathtaking scenery along what turned out to be *good* mountain roads served to soothe my anxious mind somewhat, and it seemed but a short time until I reached the comfortable motel in Whitesburg.

A few hours later I was joined by Cantrell, with Braswell and Coots in tow, and when Prather came in a little later, we were ready to begin what I assumed was a traditional ritual associated with tickling etc.—card playing. Braswell was apparently the more experienced in this phase of the game, judging by how he almost always held more cards with the same numbers on them than did anybody else (of course, all he relieved us of was a lifetime supply of kitchen matches, right?).

Following the ritual of the cards, morning came all too soon and after a quick breakfast we were off to the creek where I was to be introduced to the world of tickling, noodling, and grabbing. Actually, I was doing pretty well at that point and keeping the assignment in perspective—no sweaty palms or dry mouth—but that was before we got out of the car. When we began to walk toward the stream, apprehension began to build and when I spied a large boulder resting in the swirling waters, I blurted out that opening statement about how insane it all seemed.

With that, Braswell and Coots allowed as how they were the instructors, Prather was the chief demonstrator, I was the chief pupil and it was high time we all got our feet wet. We waded in and Prather approached a moderate-sized rock. Under direct supervision from Coots, he began feeling around underneath the structure and almost immediately began spouting off about feeling something down there.

My heart bled for him, but he kept after his prey, fearlessly bumping it with his hands and channeling it into his grip, all the while guarding against the fish darting away. At that point I wasn't too sure that fish wasn't a snake or something equally frightening (to me, at least) but in a matter of minutes Prather closed his fists and drew out a four-inch sucker—not quite a keeper, but now we knew how it was done.

And that, dear friends, was the only fish our stream stroll produced that morning. Braswell, Coots, and Prather continued to work the submerged rocks—I was too busy with the camera, of course—and they did spook a few fish but none were taken. After a while my picture-taking excuses seemed lame even to me and I realized my time had come—I had to get my hands wet, too.

With great apprehension I approached a rock and began feeling for a depression under the water. Then, against my better judgment, I let my hands stray to a large hole beneath the front of the rock. I surveyed the area completely and, much as I would like to make this a success story and tell you I produced a monstrous catfish, the truth is, I didn't find a thing.

But I was hooked, so to speak, on grabbing (or trying to grab) fish. For excitement, the sport is hard to match, combining quiet stalking in the water with the high drama of never knowing if a fish, or perhaps something else, is lurking beneath a rock, and once I overcame my initial fears, I actually enjoyed the day.

We confined our activities, for the most part, to stream rocks, but there was one bank depression that Coots found too inviting to resist. I didn't have that problem—resisting it was easy for me, since they'd said earlier that fish would be found under stream rocks and anything else under them would probably just move away, but that holes in the bank often serve as lairs for turtles, minks, muskrats, or even snakes. So I held my breath as

Jerry rolled up his sleeves and snaked his arm into the hole, but he came up empty. A good thing, too, apparently, since we later found tracks along the bank that made it pretty evident Jerry had been feeling around a turtle hole.

After about two hours we had worked a quarter of a mile of stream and figured we'd earned lunch, so we retreated to a country store that served the best bologna sandwiches in Letcher County. There began Part III of the tickling, noodling, and grabbing ritual—tall tales. And it was a good thing I heard later rather than sooner (before our foray) about the man who had little skin left on his forearms due to continual "spining" by catfish.

"In fact," Coots said, "most of these pro grabbers will get down flat in the water, sort of like a water spider, on top of the rocks and really search under them. A good team of two to ten men can work a long stretch of stream in an hour and turn a limit [fifteen rough fish per day, but no more than five catfish]."

He pointed out three things that had hampered our success that morning. First, the water was running murky and it was hard to find many of the totally submerged rocks where fish might have been hiding. Second, the really successful "grabbers" are people who have been at it for many years and have mentally marked the rocks and laps where the fish will be. In that way, they can move quickly from rock to rock and turn a fish at virtually every stop. Finally, Coots said, with an "Amen" from Prather, tickling, noodling, and grabbing is a sport which is most successful when catfish are on the nest, in late spring or early summer, rather than in late August.

(The success of those taking fish by hand in certain streams and during certain parts of the season is of special interest to Prather, who is conducting an in-depth study of the sport as a result of recently voiced concern about its possible harm to rough fish populations. The project, which began last summer in the South Fork of the Kentucky River, is scheduled for completion in about three years.)

The season for taking rough fish by hand has passed for this year, but if you're looking for an alternative sport next summer and don't mind risking a finger or two, you may want to try it. Since I'm still typing with all ten digits, I have no regrets, just some good memories.

SIDNEY SAYLOR FARR

Meats: Game and Tame (An Excerpt)

From *More Than Moonshine* (1983)

FATHER AND OTHER MEN in the community went hunting for wild game to supplement food supplies. It always seemed to me it would be more fun to go tramping through the mountains hunting than staying home doing endless chores that faced women and girls every day—although I would never have brought myself to the point where I could have shot at a wild animal or bird. I used to feel such outrage when Father brought home a mother squirrel, a pheasant, or other wild game. And I had a hard time reconciling myself to eating the meals where game was served. But hunger helps one overcome many scruples, and I always managed to get enough objectivity to keep from starving. The women were very ingenious in finding many ways to prepare the wild game. Mother baked groundhog with sweet potatoes, for example, which was a favorite dish of the whole family.

Father would bring the dressed carcass to Mother. She would cut it into serving pieces and parboil them in her black iron kettle. She sent one of the children to the spice bush which grew back of the house to bring in some branches. She broke the branches into lengths to fit the kettle. After putting the meat into the kettle with sufficient water, she added the spice branches and cooked the meat for twenty-five to thirty minutes, or until the meat was just beginning to be tender. Then she poured off the water and rinsed each piece of meat in cold water.

While the meat was cooking in the first water, she would send another child to the smokehouse to get a pan of sweet potatoes. These she peeled and cut into quarters lengthways. She rubbed each piece of meat with salt and pepper and placed it in a baking dish. Around the edges of the meat she arranged the sweet potatoes. Then she put in one and a half tablespoons lard and two cups water and put the pan in the oven. The groundhog and sweet potatoes would bake, sending out savory odors every time the oven door was opened.

People in the hills still eat groundhog, and squirrel, rabbit, and quail, but are adapting cooking methods. A friend of ours, Frank Farr, gave me a recipe for barbecued groundhog.

BARBECUED GROUNDHOG

> 1 groundhog, dressed and cut into bite-sized chunks
> 2 tablespoons lard, approximately
> Barbecue sauce

Brown meat in lard in heavy skillet. Drain off excess lard and drippings. Pour barbecue sauce over meat until each piece is covered. Simmer on stove until meat is tender. Serve with vegetables and bread.

Frank also gave me a modern recipe for fixing venison in a crockpot. Mountain people do adapt their ways of cooking as modern conveniences are brought in. Most homes today have electric skillets, crockpots, and gas or electric stoves.

VENISON POT ROAST

To prepare the roast, soak venison in a solution of salt, vinegar, and water for 3 hours. (For each cup of water, mix in ½ cup vinegar and ¼ cup salt.) Pour off solution and run cold water over meat. Put salt and water (1 cup water to ¼ cup salt) into container and soak venison overnight. Take out of container and rinse in

cold water. Put meat in kettle or crockpot and pour enough water over the meat to cover it. Add carrots, onions, potatoes, celery,
and cook very slowly—8 hours in crockpot or 4 hours in a kettle.
You may sprinkle garlic salt over meat if you like. Venison should
be cooked slowly for it to taste best.

In addition to groundhog, Father brought in rabbits, squirrels, and sometimes, if the season had not been good for wild
game, he brought opossums for the table. He caught possums
which had grown fat from the corn in our fields. I never liked
possum, but for those who did the following recipe was a favorite. Possum meat is strong and gamey, and elaborate methods of
cooking had to be used to make it palatable.

BAKED POSSUM

   1 dressed possum
   1 tablespoon butter
   1 large onion
   1 cup bread crumbs
   ½ teaspoon chopped red pepper
   Dash of steak sauce
   1 hard-boiled egg, chopped
   Salt to taste
   Small amount of water
   1 or 2 sprigs of sassafras root

Dress the possum or have it done for you. For the stuffing: Melt
butter in frying pan and add onion. When onion begins to brown,
add chopped liver of possum and cook until tender and well done.
Add bread crumbs, red pepper, steak sauce, egg, salt, and water to
moisten mixture.

   Stuff the possum with the mixture and sew up the opening. Put
in a roasting pan, add 2 tablespoons water, and roast in moder-

ate oven (300–350 degrees) until meat is very tender and a golden brown. Baste the possum frequently with its own fat. When it is done, take from oven, remove stitches, and put possum on a hot platter. Skim the grease from the drippings and serve gravy in a separate dish.

To add flavor, slip a sprig or two of sassafras root down into the stuffing between the stitches after you have sewed the possum up.

Serve the possum with baked sweet potatoes and green vegetables along with cornbread and coffee or milk.

FRIED RABBIT

Dress rabbit and cut into serving pieces. Put in a kettle with a sufficient amount of water and boil for 5 to 10 minutes. Remove kettle from heat and let stand until meat is cold. Dry each piece and dip into a beaten egg, then roll in flour, seasoned with salt and pepper to taste. Fry in an equal mixture of lard and butter until pieces are nicely browned. Remove pieces of rabbit and keep hot. In the drippings remaining in the skillet, put in flour enough to make a creamy paste, pour in a cup of milk or cream and let the mixture come to a boil. When it is of desired consistency, pour over the rabbit and serve with green vegetables, fried or creamed potatoes, and coffee or milk.

STEWED RABBIT

Dress the rabbit and cut into serving pieces. Put 4 tablespoons butter or lard in a skillet and brown the rabbit. Remove the meat and add 1 pint boiling water to the butter; then stir in 1 tablespoon flour and mix until you have a smooth creamy paste. Season with salt and a little grated onion. Return meat to broth and let it come to a boil; reduce heat and cook slowly until tender. Serve hot.

BAKED SQUIRREL

Clean and dress squirrel. Let stand in salted water for at least an hour. Place pieces of meat in a pan or skillet, sprinkle with pepper and salt, and place in oven. Turn the pieces so all surfaces will brown. Good served with hot biscuits and milk gravy.

BROILED SQUIRREL

Clean and dress squirrel. Cut into serving pieces. Place pieces in salted water and soak for at least an hour. Wipe pieces dry, and broil until tender. When done, place on a platter with melted butter and season with salt and pepper. Serve hot.

COOKED SQUIRREL AND GRAVY

Clean squirrel and cut into serving pieces. Soak the meat at least an hour in salt water. Take out and put in a heavy kettle and pour water over to cover meat. Cook on moderate heat until meat is tender. Put ½ cup flour in cold water and stir until mixture is a smooth paste. Slowly pour into kettle and stir until thickened into gravy. Put pieces of meat into a big bowl and pour gravy over all. Serve with vegetables, cornbread or biscuits, and hot coffee.

Both men and women fished the creeks for trout and other small fish on Stoney Fork, and in Straight Creek, which fed into the Cumberland River, for catfish. In places Straight Creek was so shallow that it barely covered the rocks and gravel, but in other places there would be really deep holes of water. One of these places, so deep the water was green, was called Elm Hole; it was located just in back of my Granny Brock's house. Father and Granny Brock loved to fish, and sometimes Mother would let me join them. I never caught many fish, but it was fun to be with them and listen to them talk. One night they stayed until dark and the moon came over Pine Mountain to light the place up almost as bright as day. Mother was persuaded to let me go and stay with them until they came home. Father had set three fishing poles butt-end into the ground and baited lines in the water and Granny sat patiently holding her line in the water. We sat awhile and they decided the fish had stopped biting for the night. I helped Father bring in his lines and wrap them around the cane poles. When I started to take in the third one I thought, "I'll just give it a quick yank in case there's a fish nearby," and I did. To my surprise I felt a heavy tug on the line and almost dropped the pole. Father came to help and we landed a big catfish. Father figured it must have been just taking the bait into its mouth when I jerked on the line. The hook was buried in its thick lip.

In my usual tenderhearted way, I would have put it back into the water if Father had allowed me to do so. I hated the way he killed catfish. Mother would heat boiling water and Father would pour it over the live fish and literally boil it alive. Mother cleaned the fish and rolled it in cornmeal and fried it. We liked catfish best because there was more meat and fewer bones.

Here is one method for fixing fish, especially if they are not more than ten inches long.

FRIED FISH

Clean and cut the fish into strips for frying. Put ½ to 1 cup (depending on how many fish you are frying) of cornmeal into a paper sack and add salt and pepper to taste. Put a strip or two of fish into the bag at a time and shake until well coated. Do this until all the pieces are coated with cornmeal. It will help if you dip the fish in milk or water first, so the cornmeal will stick. Put a large heavy skillet over medium heat and lay strips of bacon across bottom of pan. Put a layer of fish crosswise over the strips of bacon. Fry until the bottom side is golden brown. Take a flat lid or tin plate and lay it on top of fish. Tilt skillet sideways and pour off all the grease, then turn the fish out onto the lid or plate. Start all over again by placing more strips of bacon on the bottom of the skillet and put the fish into the skillet, browned side up. Fry. When done you will have fried fish held together with the bacon. Serve with hushpuppies and vegetables of your choice.

Sometimes at night the men and boys in the community fixed carbide lights on hard hats (such as miners wore), took long gigging forks (resembling a pitchfork, but smaller, with three tines that were very sharp), and went wading in Straight Creek to hunt for frogs. Father cleaned the frog legs and expected Mother to fry them, which she never wanted to do because of the way the involuntary muscles kept the legs jerking in the skillet.

FRIED FROG LEGS

> Frog legs
> 2 eggs
> 1 cup milk
> Salt and pepper to taste

Boil frog legs in salt water for 3 minutes; drain. Beat eggs in milk, add salt and pepper, and mix well. Dip each frog leg in egg and milk mixture, then in cracker crumbs or flour. Fry in heavy skillet in very hot lard or cooking oil. Fry until rich brown and serve at once.

JOHN FOX JR.

Fox-Hunting in Kentucky (An Excerpt)

From *Blue-grass and Rhododendron* (1901)

IN KENTUCKY, the hunting of the red fox antedates the war but little. The old Kentucky fox-hound was of every color, loose in build, with open feet and a cowhide tail. He had a good nose, and he was slow, but he was fast enough for the gray fox and the deer. Somewhere about 1855 the fox-hunters discovered that their hounds were chasing something they could not catch. A little later a mule-driver came through Cumberland Gap with a young hound that he called Lead. Lead caught the eye of old General Maupin, who lived in Madison County, and whose name is now known to every fox-hunter North and South. Maupin started poor, and made a fortune in a frolic. He would go out hunting with his hounds, and would come back home with a drove of sheep and cattle. He was a keen trader, and would buy anything. He bought Lead, and, in the first chase, Lead slipped away from the old deer-hounds as though he knew what he was after; and it was not long before he captured the strange little beast that had been puzzling man and dog so long. Lead was thus the first hound to catch a red fox in Kentucky; and since every fox-hound in the State worthy of the name goes back to Lead, he is a very important personage. General Maupin never learned Lead's exact origin; perhaps he did not try very hard, for he soon ran across a suspicion that Lead had been stolen. He tried other dogs from the same locality in Tennessee from which he supposed the hound came, but with no good results. Lead was a

85

lusus naturæ, and old fox-hunters say that his like was never before him, and has never been since.

People came for miles to see the red fox that Lead ran down, and the event was naturally an epoch in the history of the chase in Kentucky. Nobody knows why it took the red fox so long to make up his mind to emigrate to Kentucky, not being one of the second families of Virginia, and nobody knows why he came at all. Perhaps the shrewd little beast learned that over the mountains the dogs were slow and old-fashioned, and that he could have great fun with them and die of old age; perhaps the prescience of the war moved him; but certain it is that he did not take the "Wilderness Road" until the fifties, when began the inexplicable movement of his race south and southwest. But he took the trail of the gray fox then, just as the tide-water Virginians took the trail of the pioneers, and the gray fox gave way, and went farther west, as did the pioneer, and let the little red-coated aristocrat stamp his individuality on the Blue-grass as his human brother had done. For a long while he did have fun with

those clumsy old hounds, running a hundred easy lengths ahead, dawdling time and again past his den, disdaining to take refuge, and turning back to run past the hounds when they had given up the chase—great fun, until old Lead came. After that, General Maupin and the Walkers imported Martha and Rifler from England, and, since then, the red fox has been kept to his best pace so steadily that he now shows a proper respect for even a young Kentucky fox-hound. He was a great solace after the war, for Kentucky was less impoverished than other Southern States, horses were plentiful, it was inexpensive to keep hounds, and other game was killed off. But fox-hunting got into disrepute. Hunting in Southern fashion requires a genius for leisure that was taken advantage of by ne'er-do-wells and scapegraces, young and old, who used it as a cloak for idleness, drinking, and general mischief. They broke down the farmer's fences, left his gates open, trampled his grain, and brought a reproach on the fox-hunter that is alive yet. It is dying rapidly, however, and families like the Clays, of Bourbon, the Robinsons and Hamiltons, of Mount Sterling, the Millers and Winns, of Clark, and the Walkers, of Garrard, are lifting the chase into high favor. Hitherto, the hunting has been done individually. Now hunt clubs are being formed. Chief among them are the Bourbon Kennels, the Strodes Valley Hunt Club, and the Iroquois Club, the last having been in existence for ten years. This club does not confine itself to foxes, but is democratic enough to include coons and rabbits.

Except in Maine and Massachusetts, where the fox is shot before the hounds, fox-hunting in the North is modelled after English ways. In Kentucky and elsewhere in the South, it is almost another sport. The Englishman wants his pack uniform in color, size, tongue, and speed—a hound that is too fast must be counted out. The Kentuckian wants his hound to leave the rest behind, if he can. He has no whipper-in, no master of the hounds. Each man cries on his own dog. Nor has he any hunting terms, like "cross-country riding," or "riding to hounds." To hunt for the pleasure of the ride is his last thought. The fun is in the actual chase, in knowing the ways of the plucky little animal, in knowing the hounds individually, and the tongue of each, in the competition of one man's dog with another, or of favorites in the same pack. It is not often that the hounds are followed steadily. The stake-and-ridered fences everywhere, and the barbed wire in the Blue-grass, would make following impossible, even if it were desirable. Instead, the hunters ride from ridge to ridge to wait, to listen, and to see. The Walkers hunt chiefly at night. The fox is then making his circuit for food, and the scent is better. Less stock is moving about to be frightened, or among which the fox can confuse the hounds. The music has a mysterious sweetness, the hounds hunt better, it seems less a waste of time, and it is more picturesque. At night the hounds trot at the horses' heels until a fire is built on some ridge. Then they go out to hunt a trail, while the hunters tie their horses in the brush, and sit around the fire telling stories until some steady old hound gives tongue.

"There's old Rock! Whoop-ee! Go it, old boy!" Only he doesn't say "old boy" exactly. The actual epithet is bad, though it is endearing. It reaches old Rock if he is three miles away, and the crowd listens.

"There's Ranger! Go it, Alice, old girl! Lead's ahead!"

Then they listen to the music. Sometimes the fox takes an un-suspected turn, and they mount and ride for another ridge; and the reckless, daredevil race they make through the woods in the dark is to an outsider pure insanity. Sometimes a man will want to go on one side of the tree when his horse prefers another, and the man is carried home senseless. Sometimes a horse is killed, but no lesson is learned. The idea prevails that the more reckless one is, the better is his chance to get through alive, and it seems to hold good. In their country, the Walkers have both hills and blue-grass in which to hunt. The fox, they say, is leaving the hills, and taking up his home in the plantations, because he can get his living there with more ease. They hunt at least three nights out of the week all the year around, and they say that May is the best month of the year. The fox is rearing her young then. The hunters build a fire near a den, the she-fox barks to attract the attention of the dogs, and the race begins. At that time, the fox will not take a straight line to the mountains and end the chase as at other times of the year, but will circle about the den. It is true, perhaps, that at such times the male fox relieves the mother and takes his turn in keeping the hounds busy. The hunters thus get their pleasure without being obliged to leave their camp-fire. Rarely at this time is the fox caught, and provided he has had the fun of the chase, the Kentucky hunter is secretly glad, I believe, that the little fellow has gone scot-free.

W. D. "BILL" GAITHER

Fishing with the Stewart Brothers

From *The Northern Kentucky Fly Fishers', Ink* (August 2004)

THE FISH WERE skimming along just under the surface of the placid water. Now and then one would rise and suck a tidbit offered up by the drifting current. Seventy-five yards downstream, a riffle gurgled as the stream's course was altered by the resisting limestone, etched and eroded by centuries of flow. The rigid stone rose up from the edge of the riffle, and curved along the waterway path, forcing a gentle bend to the right, and down to the pool beneath the riffle. The stream, the fish, and me, a trilogy perhaps as old as man's appetite for fish and nature, produced one of those peaceful moments that only flowing water anglers can know. Then, "Ouch!" my tranquility was shattered by the sharp bite of a "cow fly" on the back of my neck. (A *Chrysops* spp., known as deer flies throughout much of their range, but they were "cow flies" to young Kentucky lads.)

Slapping at the fly, I must have moved too quickly, spooking the fish. In an instant the school dove for the depths, leaving a dozen swirling eddies on the smooth surface in their wake. Muttering words a sixteen-year-old boy uses only when his mother is not within hearing range, I sat down on a fallen log and waited for the fish to return to their surface browsing. My tackle was simple then, as were my clothing and habits. A new Shakespeare "Wonder" rod lay across my knees; it was rated for a "D" weight line. The rod was fitted with a Pfleuger Medalist reel filled with a Cortland "Bug taper" floating line in the new bright green finish, and a couple of hundred yards of Gladding "Squidding" line as backing. The fly line was tipped with eight feet of eight-pound test leader pulled from one of those little plastic spools. The "leader" had been pulled between a folded square of inner tube rubber to remove the kinks, and tied carefully to one of those little barbed screw-eyed thingies that one stuffed into the end of the fly line.

In my shirt pocket was an old aluminum fly box from the Utica company, as I recall. The box was filled with an assortment of flies that were *de rigueur* at the time: McGinty Bee, Black Gnat, White Ibis, Parmachene Bell, and some of those "new" Irresistibles, along with an assortment of nymphs, bluegill flies, a few streamers, and some well-tied humpies in white with sparse wings and a newfangled parachute hackle wound three sparse turns around the wing feather shafts, beneath the deer hair bodies. A pair of expensive, $12 waders, from the army-surplus store on Madison Avenue in Covington, covered my legs to the crotch. A Ludlow Merchant's baseball cap was curled and cocked on my flat-topped head. An old U.S. Army gas mask case (army surplus—50¢) served as my possibilities bag. The old OD bag was crammed with a sandwich, a canteen full of Kool-Aid, and several candy bars (5¢, anywhere). Spare leaders and sundry tackle and tools filled out the crevices and side pockets of that war-surplus carry-all.

Reaching into the bag, and retrieving a Hershey bar, I sat back to wait for the fish to resume feeding. Halfway through the bar, eaten one little square at a time, the fish returned to their surface prowling. Stuffing the bar into my shirt pocket, I watched the fish cruise into casting range. There was no chance to false cast, since the least sudden motion would certainly send the fish to the bottom once again. Stripping some line from the reel, I fed a rod's length of line out from the rod tip and spooled several more yards into my left hand. Without standing, the fly rod was eased back and with a gentle rolling motion the little humpie was sent out twenty feet to settle onto the surface a few yards ahead of the lead fish. When the fly was just above its snout, the fish rose gently and slurped the fly. Rising to my feet, I set the hook.

The fish turned and raced downstream, making the riffle in less time than it will take the reader to finish this sentence. The hooked prey bored down the riffle like a torpedo racing to its target, sending a bulge of water up and over the streamlined body. Running downstream, I reached the riffle just as the fish turned the bend of the stream and broke my leader across an extending deadfall lying in the water at the inside of the bend. More words my mother would never hear. At lunchtime I met up with my fishing partner, Tom Stewart, the mentor who hooked me on fly fishing more than fifty years ago. Comparing notes while munching sandwiches, we totaled a score of fish nine, Stewart two, and this writer, none—that's zilch, nada, zip for yours truly.

Over the decades since that summer's day, my wildlife art and pursuits have taken me to waters all across the globe. From Appalachian streams to the Odori River in Japan, the Mersey in Australia, the Nigini, Limpopo, Huehuele, Orinoco, Nile, and dozens of other rivers, some whose names I cannot pronounce, and many forgotten. Every game fish in North America, most in South America and Africa and Asia, have fought and lost to my tackle over the years. Landed fish range from the tiny ayu *(Plecoglossus)* in Japan to giant Nile perch *(Lates niloticus)* in Lake Rudolf. I have traveled to Alaska no less than twenty-six times over the years to pursue the finest cold-water fishing on earth. Today, as a resident of the Texas coast, my lines remain taut because of the likes of red-fish, speckled trout, tarpon, king and Spanish mackerel, dolphin, blackfin tuna, and other species. My studio extends out over the waters of Galveston Bay, and when all else fails, there are dozens of speckled trout in my dock lights each night. They are easy prey for most any white or chartreuse streamer, and many evenings are spent casting to them with a little four-weight rod. My girlfriend says that she is not sure if I am a fishing fool, or a fool that fishes.

Getting back to that day long ago, you may have asked yourself, which species of fish was the object of the angling? Which river were the anglers fishing? Without further suspense, let me say simply that those noble fish were carp, *Cyprinus carpio*, the giant members of the minnow family known by many names across the world. The "noble" stream we fished that day was the Little Miami River, just downstream from Batavia in Clermont County, Ohio. Back home in Kentucky, carp were sometimes called "bugle mouth bass" or "golden bass," "sewer bass," and a host of names I dare not recall.

Tom Stewart introduced me to carp on a fly long before my twelfth birthday. Each summer when the cottonwoods bloom, those stately trees carpet streams with downy seeds. Carp feed on those little parachutes, cruising just beneath the surface and slurping them in for hours at a time. Slow-moving pools with a canopy of trees above are best. The foliage blocks out sunlight, creating shade for the photophobic carp.

Tom and his brother, Jess, were consummate fly rodders. Both were railroad men who worked for the Southern System. They lived in Ludlow at the time, since the Southern RR yards were located in that little river town where I grew up. Our home was a block south of Tom Stewart's house on Carneal Street. Tom and his brother were avid bass fishermen. My father and the Stewart brothers often fished together. Dad's favorite method of bass fishing was with casting rod and lures, a method disdained by the brothers. I am not sure if either of the Stewarts owned anything other than a fly rod. Both brothers were mechanically inclined and of the old school, which teaches that equipment made by self is superior to anything one can purchase. To that end, they made their own landing nets, wrapped their own rods, and tied flies without parallel.

If my math is correct, this past year was another year of the cicada in the Cincinnati area. That buzzing pest which emerges from the earth every seventeen years (thirteen in some broods) may be a lot of things to a lot of folks, but it is a rare food for the black bass. The Stewarts knew that and they designed a bass bug to mimic the cicadas. The bug, a popper, was called the "Handlebar Hank." Now I am not sure if either of the Stewart boys actually invented the "Hank" or just borrowed the design from another fly rodder. Whichever the case, it was the Stewarts who made it famous for catching ole *Micropterus*.

The poppers they built were made from stopper corks five-eighths inch in diameter at the large end. The corks were split into halves so that the down side was flat. Wings of polar bear hair, calf tail, and sometimes deer tail were threaded through the cork with a large needle and glued at each side. The tail was tied to a bent-shank "popper" hook and made of similar material. Each wing was from one and a half to two inches long, and the tail extended about one inch behind the body. The bodies were mostly painted with black gloss lacquer, but some versions were brown, green, or white. Two eyes, each with yellow iris and black pupil, were applied to the front, above the hook's eye, with a matchstick or nail head, and a series of "vees" were painted on the flat bottom—one would assume to represent the legs of the cicada.

The "Hank" was designed to float high on the water and was retrieved with a series of very short, gentle pulls. The idea was to allow the forward motion to cock the long wings, which would rebound, causing the popper to reverse directions a bit at the end of each forward tug. Sometimes it was "skittered" along the surface, dangled from the end of an outstretched fly rod. Old Tom liked to dangle the "Handlebar" just a few feet beneath the tip of his fly rod as he sculled (this was long before the electric trolling motor) a boat along deep rock shorelines with an abundance of overhanging trees. He knew that bass like to suspend in the shade along those shorelines in midday and can't resist an unfortunate insect that drops from the limbs above. Now, don't get me wrong, Tom was a big fellow who could cast well into his backing when conditions called for that, but he was a past master at feeding that fly rod in and out of overhanging brush to place his fly where most anglers fear to tread. When a bass pounded the popper, Tom would set the hook and then scull back, away from the shoreline. He knew that the fish would dive for the deep water along the ledge, allowing him time to position the boat so that the angle of the line was down and away from the tree limbs and deadfalls. I have seen the man land many six- to eight-pound bass in that manner, during the heat of midday in July when other fishermen were playing cards or taking power naps. I still use the method to this day when fishing deep-water lakes, and it is just as valid now as it was fifty years ago.

The Stewarts were just two of a number of northern Kentuckians devoted to fly fishing. Other anglers of mention include Jimmy Singleton and Preston Graham of Crescent Springs, Jack Mader from Fort Thomas, Frank "Spider" Godsey, Walley Muhlenchamp and Fred Wergus, Mort Eisman, Don Wolf, "Big Hamp" Hampton, and perhaps the most dedicated angler of them all, "Chippy" Thompson. Now Chippy was not just a man who fished; he was a man whose entire life was dedicated to fishing. Chippy was my father's main fishing partner. Actually, I suppose, he was any man's fishing partner on the right day, since my father, unlike his friend, worked most weeks.

During the spring of 1949, Chippy's wife, Ivy, finally laid down the law. She told him in no uncertain words that it was "Either those danged fish or me!" I remember well the night that Ivy called my mother and said her husband was "gone." That was a time when telephones were communication devices and not weapons of mass marketing. When the phone rang, it was important, else why would someone call? Any time the phone rang after nine o'clock at night, someone had died, suffered an accident, or was stricken with something much more insidious than routine disease. Ivy had phoned at nearly midnight. That was cause for the entire family to rush to the phone. In those days, there was but one phone in a home. (Owning more than one was considered foolish extravagance.) Ivy came over soon after that, sobbing her eyes out. She related the ultimatum she had given her husband the past Friday. My father muttered something that sounded like a word my mother wouldn't like to hear, gathered my brother and me, and we headed upstairs to bed, leaving the women to sort things out.

Chippy surfaced four years later. He had moved to Sarasota, Florida, and opened a fishing camp and guide service in the land of big Dunellon bass. He pulled up in front of our house one day, driving a surplus U.S. Army jeep with a trailer attached to the rear. Inside the trailer was a tub full of alligators, a box of rattlesnakes, and albums full of trophy largemouth bass photos. I remember trying to devise a scheme then and there that would result in my returning to Florida with the man. Of course, my mother vetoed that, and to my surprise, her motion was seconded by my father. Like I said, Chippy was a fishing fanatic, and for years, my hero.

Northern Kentuckians were not blessed with a trout stream whose very name symbolizes the sport of fly fishing. We don't have many streams with fancy names either. Only Kinniconick Creek has a name that is old and mysterious. Instead of the Au Sable or Rappahannock or Oconaluftee, we have streams with names like Licking, Tradewater, Salt, Green, Kentucky, Rough, Dix, and Barren. To the east there are the Big and Little Sandy Rivers, to the west, the terminus of the Cumberland and Tennessee, the Little and the Pond Rivers. Of course, Elkhorn and Gunpowder and Big Bone Creeks each have names that would lend well to trout lore, if there were trout living in those waters. Most trout waters, sadly, are a long weekend trip or a hard-earned vacation away from Boone, Kenton, and Campbell Counties. Trout fishing was mostly a dream for most of us living on either side of the Licking River Valley.

Actually, aside from the fluff and pomp stories in *Field & Stream*, *Outdoor Life*, and *Sports Afield*, most northern Kentuckians knew little about trout and cared less. Maybe our streams didn't have fancy names, but they were complete with a wide variety of fish. The Stewart brothers often traveled far and wide to catch trout, but I honestly believe they did that simply out of boredom, and not because they preferred fishing for those cold-water species. Those of us who couldn't afford the luxury of travel were content to fish for native species. Actually, after a lifetime of fishing, this old man can state honestly that a saucer-sized bluegill rising slowly to a drifted fly stirs just as much excitement as an approaching permit cruising a tidal flat. There are few words that describe the thrill felt when a two-foot-long largemouth bass rises up to a floating Messenger Frog and sits there nose to deer hair making up its mind if it will engulf the offering or not. Those are the eye-to-eye moments that are seldom offered up on even the best freestone streams.

My mentors, the Stewarts and their kin, didn't seem to differentiate between carp and brown trout. One was an exotic, the other locally abundant. Ask yourself, which offers up the most sport? Having caught plenty of both, I can say that the contest would be a tie. Perhaps the carp would have a slugger's edge over all but the meanest, big-headed, hook-nosed browns. A Baptist minister from Chattanooga taught me to catch carp on nymphs around 1956. We vacationed each year at Eagle Lodge on Watts Bar Lake in Tennessee. The preacher, named Werk, vacationed there at the same time each year. He was a fly fisherman. So was I. He was knowledgeable, I was eager. We often fished together, the teacher and the novice. Several miles from Eagle Lodge there is an island. The island is shaped like a crescent and is named, aptly, Half-Moon. On the west side of Half-Moon there extends a large flat that is around one-quarter mile square.

The water covering that flat is from one to four feet deep. During the day, hundreds of large carp and buffalo fish *(Ictiobus)* cruise those flats slowly as they probe the bottom for Ephemerid and Odonata nymphs and other macro-invertebrates. The cruising carp are as wary as any bonefish I have ever seen. They must be stalked, cast to gently and with accuracy and timing that only practice can teach. A fly must be presented well ahead of and in line with the feeding fish. The cast must be timed so that the fly settles to the bottom very near the fish and then inched slowly to the front of that vacuum cleaner mouth. A line slap, or a sudden motion, sends the carp racing for the safety of deep water.

When an angler is fortunate enough to hook up with the tailing carp, the fish immediately makes a dash for deep water that has to be experienced to be believed. Perhaps the carp is a tad slower than the bonefish, but it makes up for the lack of speed with brute strength. The carp on that flat average ten pounds, and some are three times that heavy. Since the deep-water shelf may be up to 500 yards away, one spends a lot of time watching backing race off the reel.

No matter where I have fished, or with whom I have fished, no matter where I may fish tomorrow or beyond the limits of this earth, I will never forget my first Elkhorn smallmouth or the big Kinniconick muskie and the bluegill and crappie I caught as a boy in Kentucky. It is hard to compare a spotted bass from Grassy Creek to a British Columbia steelhead, but all things are comparable. Like my friend Mark Sosin said to me one day a while back, "These big fish are beginning to be more work than pleasure." I am sure that the little streams I fished with my father or the Stewarts as a boy are much different today than they once were. Many of the farm ponds have no doubt gone to progress or eutrophication, the gravel bars are dredged from the Ohio River, and too many streams sag under the weight of pollution, but I miss fishing the little waters that adorn the Bluegrass State.

Those of you who still ply those old limestone bed creeks and streams are far more fortunate than many other anglers around the planet. The next time you string up that flea flicker and wade out into a fork of the upper Licking, thank God for Kentucky and for folks like the Stewarts, who not only followed the kinder and gentler methods but passed the lore on to a freckle-faced kid so long ago.

GARY GARTH

When the Cork Goes Under (2005)

FOR ONCE, bureaucracy took a backseat to common sense. Some farsighted folks who worked for the Jefferson County Parks Department approached state game and fish officials with a simple idea: Stock one of the Louisville Metro Park lakes with an extra helping of catfish; solicit local businesspeople to chip in for the needed bait and tackle and throw in a few bucks for hot dogs and soft drinks; round up some volunteers to help bait hooks, untangle lines, and release fish; and then let some city kids fish for a few hours. No license. No charge. No hassle. The game and fish people thought it was a grand idea. A date was set. The lake was stocked. Bus transportation was arranged.

The day arrived—a splendid Saturday without the smoldering humidity that turns so much of the summer into a soggy mess. The response was astounding. Fishers outnumbered volunteers fifty to one. From kindergartners to teenagers, the youngsters (mostly inner-city kids) lined the bank three deep and patiently waited their turn to cast, crank, catch, laugh, and squeal. The project director, a bighearted man who would like to put a fishing pole into the hands of every kid in America, eyed the swelling crowd and announced that everyone who wanted to fish would have the opportunity to do so. Organizers had planned to fish until noon. They stayed until dark.

I watched and wondered how the kids would remember this day and what they would recall about it. Many were fishing for the first time; some maybe for the only time. There was no way to tell. But they would all leave with a story.

Fishing generates memories that last a lifetime and then live on. Recall your own experiences: The glow of your father's cigarette while he sculled a plywood boat in the predawn light—the only sound the rhythmic *slurp-drip-drip, slurp-drip-drip* of water streaming from the ash paddle. A beaver pond the color of leaden silver under a May moon. Backwater carp tailing in the muddy fringes of the Ohio. A steely-eyed fisherman gripping a wooden-handled gig, the pose reflecting a half-mad, modern-day Poseidon stripped to the waist and wearing cutoff jeans. Mayflies fogging an overhanging willow in a fold of Sugar Bay, the bedding bream slurping them like popcorn. Rough River Lake frothing from white bass in the jumps, a half acre of fish here and gone and back again. Noodling—fishing's version of hand-to-hand combat—where the human participant knows that the mouth lurking along the mud bank is almost certainly a flathead cat but could be a snapping turtle or worse. A thick, low summer fog blanketing the Cumberland tailwater, an anomaly that turns a July sunrise boat ride into a bone-numbing experience. Bass. Bluegill. Bonefish. Carp. Catfish. Crappies. Muskellunge. Pike. Salmon. Sauger. Tarpon. Trout. A line stretched as tight as the pounding of your heart that vanishes into the blue water then emerges 100 yards distant connected to 300 pounds of marlin. The brown trout that materializes at dusk and quietly inhales a No. 16 Green Wing Olive, then twists the 5-weight into a square knot before leaving the line slack and the fisherman gasping for breath. A five-year-old's first perch. Your grandfather's last trip to his favorite farm pond where he (and you) learned to fish.

But for all its simple charms, fishing sometimes seems to be overdosing on itself. Tackle boxes are the size of suitcases. Five dollars won't buy a bass plug. A boat costs as much as a small house. Show up at the ramp with your battered flat-bottom aluminum and feel the stares from the guys waiting to launch their gleaming 20-foot neon-flaked beauties.

It is the era of tournament mania. Bass, crappie, trout, marlin, carp—nothing seems immune from the lure of competition. Fishermen are media stars who double as pitchmen touting lures, boats, electronics, rods, reels, line, shirts, sunglasses, batteries, and more. We're becoming programmed to believe that we cannot fish without a sack of gadgets that seem more suited for the space shuttle than a tackle bag. To walk into a tackle shop is to experience sensory overload. And for some, fishing has even become a spectator sport. But there's hope.

A famous bass pro was shaking hands and signing autographs at the Louisville boat show. Surrounded by all the trappings of the modern-day bass warrior, this former guide had caught the tournament wave early and ridden it to fame and fortune. He was stationed at a sponsor's booth under a poster touting his Saturday morning TV show, all smiles and goodwill. The line waiting to shake his hand curled out of sight. It was a life that appeared to be the fulfillment of every bass-man's dream—the endless travel and heartrending divorce notwithstanding. The line eventually dissolved, and during a coffee break I asked if he still had the time or inclination to fish for fun.

"Oh sure," he said between doughnut bites. "But you know what I really like?"

The man's shirt was a billboard. I expected a product lecture. "What?"

He glanced at his watch, then at the crowd gathering around the sponsor's booth. He wasn't paid to be late. He licked the sugar from the corner of his mouth and drained his coffee cup, then used his hand as a napkin. Underneath all the sponsor polish and product gleam was a guy you could fish with.

"There's a little lake a couple of miles from my house. Just a pond, really," he said, the deep-set crow's-feet around his eyes crinkling at the memory. "When my kids were little, we'd go down there with worms or minnows—whatever we had. We'd usually dig our own worms. But anyway, we'd go down there and catch bluegills under an old cork bobber. We'd fish from the bank or paddle around in an old boat I had. We'd catch them by the dozens. We did the same thing when I was a kid." A crooked-toothed smile split his face, a face burnt a permanent brown from more than thirty summers of chasing tournament bass under a sizzling sun.

"I still like to do that. I really do," he said. "I absolutely love it when the cork goes under."

The writer of Proverbs is very clear: "Train a child in the way he should go, and when he is old he will not turn from it." I doubt the author had fishing in mind, but you never know.

JANICE HOLT GILES

An Excerpt from *40 Acres and No Mule* (1967)

ALL SUMMER we had sneaked time from the tobacco and the
canning and the improvements on the house to fish and to study
birds, and Green River was perfect for both. Green River! Ah,
everyone should have Green River flowing at the foot of the
ridge as we do. Beautiful, emerald, winding stream, chattering
over the rapids, purling around the shoals, stilling over the deep
places. "Lonely river, weary water." Henry sings a song that begins with those words, and I never go to the river without thinking of them. Lonely river, weary water.

Only when the tide comes is the water ever muddy, and then
quickly it clears to its lovely, cool green emerald again. Someday I'm going to find out why the hill people, a hundred and
fifty years removed from their residence by the sea, still speak
of a rise in water on the creeks and rivers as the tide coming, but
as yet I have found no clue other than the one that applies to so
many of their sayings: That's the way their fathers spoke of it,
and their fathers before them, and their fathers. "It's allus been
that way!"

Green River flows shallow under the bridge where the pike
crosses, noisy over the pebbled shoals. Then it tunnels under
the willows and deepens, slowing and flowing genteelly, like a
lady who has been slightly hurried, but who now preens herself
and straightens her skirts. Green, green water, jeweled in the
sun. Deep and cool and still. Here it bends around a bank, high-
cut and steep. The water is roiled at the edge, disturbed. Then

come the rapids, noisy and rushing, water-whitened and restless. And then, the travail past, comes a long, clean stretch of water, slow-moving and sweet. Here the canes grow down to the water's edge, and it is here that we come to fish.

I do not hunt with Henry very often. Not that I mind the hunting, or even the killing of game. I like to eat it too well to be sentimental about its death. It would not be very consistent of me to enjoy the rewards of hunting and object to its methods. I don't enjoy hunting because I am a physically lazy person and Henry goes much too far and too fast for my comfort. When he is hunting, he forgets all about me, as he should, and I am left to fend for myself. We go uphill and downhill, through brush and timber, and my legs are weary and my tongue is hanging out long before Henry has begun to think of turning toward home. I am just a millstone around his neck when I go along. And it may be sheer rationalization, but I think he should be allowed to keep one thing entirely for his own. He seems glad to have me go, on those rare occasions when I want to go. But I know he never has as good a time as when he goes alone, or with another man.

But fishing—now, that is an entirely different story. I am ready to go fishing almost any time Henry says the word. But we drive down to the river and then all I have to do is sit on the bank and hold a pole. That's the kind of thing I do best. Oh, I like to fly-fish too, and I'll work hard at it without even noticing the passing of time. But we don't have much fly-fishing in Kentucky, and I have never got the knack of casting. I can get my line snarled up with a backlash quicker than you can say Jack Robinson. Consistently too. Not many people can do it as completely and as frequently as I. A double-action reel is just beyond me. I never could do two things at once, and casting and thumbing the line are like rubbing your head and patting your stomach, as far as I'm concerned.

Henry was patient with me for a while. "If you can handle a fly rod, you can certainly learn to cast," he said. He just didn't know.

But the day I lost two Hawaiian Wigglers for him within thirty minutes he learned, and his patience was surprisingly and suddenly exhausted. I don't know why he can cast millions of times and never lose a lure. And then let me get hold of the thing and if I ever get my line unsnarled long enough to cast at all, the dratted lure snaps off. The first time it happened he didn't say a word. Didn't even look crossly at me. He just fastened another Wiggler on and told me to try again. And it's the truth, so help me, on the very first cast *that* Wiggler snapped off. He didn't say anything then, either. He merely reached out and took the rod.

With a single-action reel I know where I am all the time. I can whip my line out and never once get it snarled—nor in the top of a tree, either. And the feel of it threaded through my left hand gives me a sense of control. The rod is long and sensitive, and I react automatically when I get a strike. The only time I ever caught a fish casting, I didn't even know I had it. I just reeled the dratted thing in. Of course it *was* minuscule in size, but I'd have felt it with a fly rod.

So, fishing being what it is in Kentucky, and I being the kind of fisherman I am, I usually put a worm on a hook, drop it in a still, shadowed pool near the root of a tree, and catch a nice little string of bream, rock bass, bluegill, and sunfish. Henry turns his nose up at that kind of fishing, but he never fails to eat what I catch. Game fish are scarce in the fresh-water streams around here, and while occasionally Henry nets a nice bass, more often than not he comes home empty-handed. I have yet to fail to bring home enough fish for a nice meal.

We keep a boat in a small inlet on the river. It is only an old, leaky rowboat, but it's handy to have when you want to get out in the stream and cast into the rooty, reedy places near the bank. At such times I become the oarsman of the boat, and, if I do say so myself, I am very proficient at the job. I have to be. One splash of the oars, one thoughtless creak, too fast or too slow, and I should promptly be put ashore. I don't know how other people row for a fisherman, but I don't. I paddle. I can use the paddle for a rudder, and an occasional dip, about every five minutes, is enough to keep the boat moving at the snail's pace Henry requires.

We spend long hours that way many summer afternoons, perhaps not speaking the entire time. I don't believe if it were left up to Henry he would ever quit fishing. Always that next cast is going to hook the big fellow. Just around that bend, just there by that gnarled root, just here near the reeds. Now, once more. . . . Darkness is the enemy that puts him to rout. We rarely come home from the river before night.

One day he had the moment for which he had been waiting and patiently casting times without end. The water was slow and the day was still and windless. It was about four o'clock. We had rowed up to the rapids and were slowly drifting back to the inlet. The river shoals on the far side along there, and, almost idly, Henry cast toward the shoal. I saw his arm jerk, and then *z-z-zing*, the reel sang, and Henry was on his feet in that split second. We both saw the big fellow plainly when he arched clean out of the water. He looked as big as a whale! A flash of his sides and the churning water—that was all—but it was enough for us to know that *this* was the fish. My heart ballooned into my throat and I chunked it back down with a gulp, praying and praying that the hook was firmly set, that the leader would hold, and that I should have sense enough to know what to do with the boat when Henry needed me.

But my very excitement almost fouled up the whole works. I dropped the oar! And of course I did what anyone would do under the circumstances. I grabbed for it frantically. That rocked the boat, naturally, and Henry came very near pitching out into the water. He clutched at me to recover balance and got me by the hair, nearly pulling me bald-headed. But it was enough of a hold to steady him, and at the same time I managed to recover the oar. "In a crisis," he said bitterly, "you can always be depended on to be detrimental to the cause."

I could have batted him down with the oar. Did he think I had purposely dropped the thing? And my head still hurt where he'd yanked my hair. "You," I snapped at him, "can get out and walk!"

The line sang again then and we both forgot everything but the whopper. "Thank God he's headed for deep water," Henry muttered.

Oh, it was beautiful to watch that battle—a battle between strength and skill! The big fellow was such a gallant fighter, turning, twisting, swimming deep down trying to dislodge the hook, flashing clear of the water occasionally, angry, frustrated, and strong. But Henry's skill was patient, and in the end the big fellow tired, and when we netted him, he had accepted the inevitable. At such times you feel like giving the tired old warrior back to the water. After all, you've had the hook on your side. We looked at him as he lay in the bottom of the boat, and then we looked at each other. "I'd throw him back," Henry said, "if I thought he wouldn't end up in someone's net or trap."

For all the men who fish Green River are not sportsmen. All too many will use any method at all to catch fish. There are fish traps, nets, baskets, all up and down the river. And men even shoot them on occasion. That this big fellow had escaped a net or trap so long was just pure luck. When we measured him, he was just under eighteen inches, and he tipped the scales at two pounds, fourteen ounces. Not a giant of a fish, certainly, but he was far and away the largest smallmouth bass we had ever seen caught here.

We called it a day, then, for any further fishing would have been an anticlimax. When you've had the best, there's no use asking for anything more. The big fellow made several meals of succulent fillets, and he made fireside talk for many months. "When Henry caught the whopper . . ." and the story is told over and over again. Of course it wasn't long until the fish had grown in size. Two full feet long and a good four pounds. But if a fisherman can't lie about the fish he catches, the world has indeed come to a sad state of affairs.

JAMES A. HENSHALL, MD

The Philosophy of Angling

From *More about the Black Bass* (1889)

THE ART OF ANGLING, with the improvements and appliances thereunto pertaining, will not suffer by a comparison with the progress of any other out-door recreation. The love of angling increases with the lapse of years, for its love grows by what it feeds on.

Wiser and more healthful and more humane sentiments now prevail among the guild than formerly, so that its practice more nearly approaches and deserves its appellation of the "gentle art."

Fishing for count, and the slaughter of the innocents, and the torturing of the fish, when caught, by a lingering death, now meet with the opprobrium of all true disciples of the craft, and have become abhorrent and despicable practices.

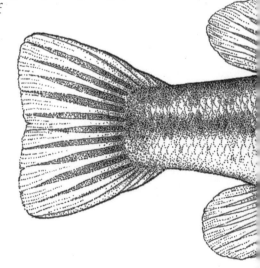

The genuine angler "loves" *angling* for its own sake; the pot-fisher "likes" *fishing* for the spoils it brings, whether captured by the hook, spear or seine.

The angler wending his way by the silvery stream,

or resting upon its grassy banks, has an innate love for all his surroundings—the trees, the birds, the flowers—which become part and parcel of his pursuit; become true and tried friends and allies without whom he could no more love his art, nor practice it, than the astronomer could view the heavens with pleasure on a cloudy, starless night.

It is the love of the stream in its turnings and windings, its depths and its shallows, its overhanging branches and grassy slopes, that gives to the art of angling its chiefest charm, and presents the bass or the trout to the angler in its true and proper setting of leaves and flowers and sparkling water. If it were otherwise he would find as much pleasure in fishing in the flume of the fish-culturist, or in viewing the fish in the fish-monger's stall.

Truly, the stream and its surroundings are all in all to the angler. I am not much given to preaching, though I come of a race of preachers; but I can not refrain from presenting to the reader the following eloquent similitude and beautiful comparison be-

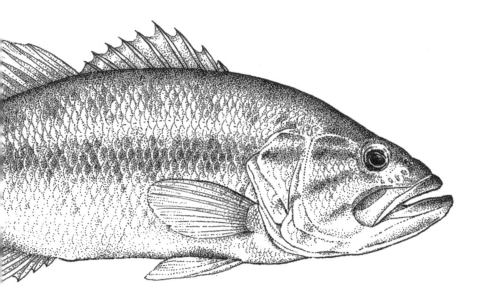

tween the angler's stream and the stream of Life; showing the easy and natural transition from the love of angling to the love of nature and nature's God. I feel more like presenting it because it is an extract from a sermon of one (Rev. Dr. H.) who has both the love of God and the love of angling deeply engrafted in his heart:

Act, therefore, while the day calls. Live its life as if life were complete in it. Not that it contains all varieties of experience, but so joins the days before and after as to make them one stream, which your spirit should wade cheerily as the trout fisher wades his brook.

His brook is wild, because the trout love waters where boats can not follow them, nor even lumber logs roll free; waters that twist and plunge, and shoot and eddy, with many a snag in the midst and fallen tree across.

And there the fisher seeks them by an instinct like their own—loving the bends that lock the pools, the shoals that embank the deep, the concealment of trackless woods, with their twilight noons and mystic noises, and every difficulty that teases him to more eager quest of his water-sprites.

When no upward flash meets his fly he reels his line in expectation to give a merrier hum to the next throw, and again to the next, until all expectations are fulfilled at once when his wrist tingles to the trout's jerk and swirl and jump.

And still that wrist tingles through casts that take no prize, until another capture renews its thrill. Broken leaders, snarled lines, torn garments, bruised limbs, do not spoil his hilarity, which feels the whole day's sport in every minute, the whole brook's beauty at every step.

And so with life. It is to be lived as a whole. Happiness comes from an energetic sense of its entire significance in every passing phase of it—in mystery, as giving value to knowledge—in failure, as the gauge of success—in evil, as the condition of good, which indeed is but evil overcome, and without the evil could not be—and in all alike as strides and casts of the confident soul, whose trout-stream from end to end is God.

And if by these the soul gains nought else, it gains immortal health; fills its creel with secrets of infinite love and wisdom—wisdom too loving to wish less than man's perfection—love too wise to spare any pain necessary to attain Godlike end. Luck enough for time or eternity. Nay, eternal sport in time.

JAMES A. HENSHALL, MD

Bass, Pike, and Perch (An Excerpt)

From *Bass, Pike, Perch and Others* (1903)

THE DIFFERENCES of opinion among anglers, of all men, pertaining to the practice of their art, has become axiomatic. Some will differ even to the estimation of a hair in the legs of an artificial fly, while it is averred others will go so far as to "divide a hair 'twixt south and southwest side," as Butler has it. But, seriously, there are several moot points which I have endeavored to discuss in the following piscatorial polemic.

Two friends went fishing. Both were famous black-bass anglers, with the enthusiasm born of a genuine love and an inherent appreciation of the gentle art so common among Kentucky gentlemen. One was a fly-fisher, the other a bait-fisher. Each was a devotee to his especial mode of angling, though generously tolerant of the other's method. They had fished together for years when the dogwood and redbud blossomed in the spring, and when the autumnal tints clothed the hillsides with scarlet and gold.

They differed in their methods of fishing from choice, or from some peculiar, personal idiosyncrasy, for each was an adept with both bait and fly. But this difference in their piscatorial practices, like the diversity of nature, produced perfect harmony instead of discord. Each extolled the advantages and sportsmanship of his own method, but always in a brotherly and kindly manner; never dictatorial or opinionated in argument, or vainglorious and boastful as to his skill, for both were possessed of the generous impulses of gentlemen and the kindly influences of the gentle art. Moreover, they were innately conscious of a common aim, and differed only as to the ways and means of best attaining that end, which, while dissimilar, were not inharmonious.

And so the Silver Doctor and the Golden Shiner, as they dubbed each other, went trudging along the bank of the merry stream together. The Doctor, lightly equipped with only rod, flybook, and creel, sometimes relieved the Shiner by toting his minnow bucket or minnow net. They were fishing a rocky, gently flowing river, characteristic of the Blue Grass section.

They stopped at a broad, lakelike expansion of the stream, caused by a mill-dam, and, in a quiet cove at the entrance of a clear brook, Golden Shiner proceeded to fill his minnow bucket with lively minnows, using for the purpose an umbrella-like folding net. This he attached to a long, stout pole, and, after baiting it with crushed biscuit, lowered it into the water. In a short time he had all the bait necessary—chubs, shiners, and steelbacks.

"The golden shiner is the best of all," said he, "especially for roily or milky water; but the chub and steelback are stronger and livelier on the hook, and for very clear water are good enough."

They then proceeded below the mill-dam, where there was a strong riffle, with likely-looking pools and eddies.

"The proper way to hook a minnow is through the lips," continued Golden Shiner, "especially for casting. One can give a more natural motion to the minnow on drawing it through the water. For still-fishing, hooking through the tail or under the back fin will answer; but even then I prefer my method, unless the minnow is less than two inches in length." And he made a long cast toward the eddy of a large boulder.

"For the same reason," acquiesced Silver Doctor, "artificial flies are tied with the head next the snell"—industriously casting to right and left over the riffle.

"But some flies are tied with the tail next to the snell," ventured Shiner.

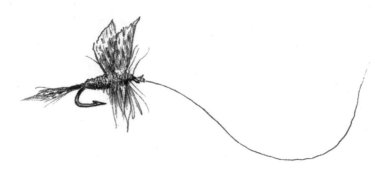

"That is true, but it is unnatural. I never saw an insect swim tail first up-stream. Nature is the best teacher, and one should endeavor to follow her lead." Just then the Doctor snapped off his point fly. Upon examination he found that the snell was dry and brittle next to the head of the fly, though he had previously soaked it well in a glass of water. He discovered that a drop of shellac varnish had encroached beyond the head of the fly for perhaps the sixteenth of an inch on the snell. This portion, being waterproof, remained dry and brittle—a very common fault with cheap flies.

"This fly," said the Doctor, "was given to me for trial by Judge Hackle. He tied it himself. The broken end of the snell still shows a portion of shellac coating."

"I never thought of that before," remarked Shiner. "No doubt many flies are cracked off from the same cause."

"Without a doubt, as you say. I know a lady," continued the Doctor, "who, as Walton says, 'has a fine hand,' and who superintends an extensive artificial fly establishment—and who has written the best book ever published on the subject of artificial flies—who personally inspects every fly turned out by her tyers. And, moreover, she varnishes the head of every fly herself, in order that not the least particle of shellac may touch the snell. Such careful supervision and honest work, to quote Walton again, 'like virtue, bring their own reward,'" and the Doctor resumed his casting with another fly.

"Well, Doctor, I sympathize with you; but my snells are clear-quill and no varnish. I may throw off a minnow once in a while by a very long cast, but it is soon replaced, and costs nothing. And, speaking of casting, I observed that you made half a dozen casts to reach yonder rock but sixty feet away, while I placed my minnow, by a single cast, a hundred feet in the other direction. Moreover, I reel my line toward me through undisturbed water, while you whipped the entire distance by several preliminary casts."

"That is necessarily true," answered the Doctor; "but while you must recover all of your line for a new cast, I can cast repeatedly with the extreme length of my line in any direction; so I think honors are easy on the question of casting."

"But," persisted Shiner, "with my quadruple multiplying reel, it is only a matter of a few seconds to prepare for a new cast. Then again, I have better control of a hooked fish, and can give and take line much faster than you with your single-action click reel."

"While I grant your reel has a great advantage in speed, I hold that a single-action click reel is all-sufficient to play and land a hooked fish. Your reel is intended particularly to make long initial casts, and it is admirably adapted for that especial purpose; but in playing a bass it has no advantage over a click reel; in fact, I prefer the latter for that purpose. Really, the engine of destruction to the hooked fish is the rod. Its constant strain and yielding resistance, even without a reel of any kind, will soon place him *hors de combat*."

Golden Shiner was not slow to perceive the force of the Doctor's arguments and held his peace. In the meantime both anglers had succeeded in killing some half-dozen bass, the largest ones falling to the rod of the bait-fisher, as is usually the case. The sun was now climbing toward the zenith, and the Doctor's flies seemed to have lost their attractiveness for the wary bass, while the Shiner, seeking deeper water, was still successful in his efforts. The day, however, was becoming uncomfortably warm.

"You will admit, Doctor, that you must cast your flies early in the day or late in the afternoon to insure much success, while I can fish during the middle of the day in deeper water and still have a measure of reward, which I consider quite an advantage of bait over fly."

"Granted. Fish rise to the fly only in comparatively shallow water, and are found in such situations in bright weather only early and late in the day. But I prefer to fish at just those times. I do not care to fish during the middle portion of the day in summer." And the Doctor proceeded to reel in his final cast.

Just then his friend hooked the largest fish of the morning's outing. It was an unusually gamy bass, and leaped several times in rapid succession from the water, shaking itself violently each time. But the Shiner was equal to "his tricks and his manners," and soon had him in the landing-net.

"Doctor, why does a hooked bass break water and shake his head? Is it through fear or rage?"

"It is to rid his jaws of the hook. He can neither pick his teeth with a fin, nor remove a foreign substance from his mouth with his tail. His mouth is his prehensile organ. A horse, cow, dog, or fowl will shake the head violently to rid its mouth of an offending object. But a fish, having no neck to speak of, can only shake his head by shaking his body, and that only in a lateral direction. As a bass cannot shake himself energetically enough beneath the water to dislodge the hook, owing to the resistance of the denser medium, he naturally leaps into the air for that purpose; and he always does so with widely extended jaws, as you have seen time and again this morning. He probably also fortifies himself at the same time by taking in oxygen from the air. He does so, at all events, willy-nilly."

"How high can a black-bass leap from the water, do you think?"

"A foot or two at most, as you well know," replied the Doctor. "In rocky streams like this, one has a good gauge for measuring the leap. I never saw a bass leap as high as yonder boulder, which is about three feet above the water; and as you have taken several fish in its eddy, you might have proved it by your own observation, as I did myself."

"I distinctly remember, now," affirmed Shiner, "that my last catch—the big fellow—leaped several times very near that same rock, and he did not go half as high."

The two friends then repaired to a cool spring beneath a spreading beech, to enjoy a luncheon and a quiet pipe—well satisfied with their morning's sport—and to continue the *argumentum ad hominem* anent fly and bait, with the usual result that, "A man convinced against his will, is of the same opinion still."

SILAS HOUSE

A Place of Noble Trees (2005)

FOR THE PAST forty-five years, my family has been spending at least one week out of the year on Dale Hollow Lake, straddling the Kentucky-Tennessee border. Mine was a family that, in the 1950s, had just begun to crawl up out of poverty and was still decidedly lower middle class. They were coal miners, factory workers, lunch ladies, and waitresses. They were farmers and milkmen, gas station attendants and truck-stop cashiers. They were people who had known the deepest poverty but had never been mired down by that. Instead, they had kept their eyes focused on going forward, on bettering themselves.

So, when my family first took a vacation, in 1960, it seemed only natural that it would be a camping trip. My Uncle Dave was a great adventurer and had made his first fishing trip to Dale Hollow in the early 1950s with some of his coworkers from the coal mine. For years, the family heard Dave talk about the crystal-clear water ("You can see all the way to the bottom in fifty feet of water"), the fish ("So many they practically jump in the boat. You catch them before your hook is even wet"), the miles and miles of shoreline and the tall cedars that shaded the campsites, and the bobbing marinas with beautiful names: Wisdom Dock, Cedar Hill, Wolf River Marina. For ten years or so, Dave tried to talk the family into going to the lake with him. He dreamed of everyone going together, pitching tents on an island, and staying an entire week. Many of the others found this laughable. If they had a week off from work, they couldn't just run off to laze about on the water. A week off from work would more likely be devoted to working around the house or yard. But Dave was a determined man who exaggerated and bragged about Dale Hollow Lake as if it were some kind of promised land. He never stopped trying to convince them. In 1955, when the world-record smallmouth bass (11 pounds, 15 ounces) was caught on Dale Hollow, he carried this news to them. He spoke of the clean air, the 30,000 acres of water, the 620 miles of shoreline. Finally, they were all convinced. They loaded up practically everything they could fit into their trucks and lit out.

That first trip there were about fifteen family members. Only two of them owned johnboats. No matter, though. They'd get everyone across the water. They traveled about 130 miles on winding mountain roads, through Hyden and Manchester, London and Somerset, Monticello and Albany, and finally came to Wisdom Dock, where they piled their tents and stoves and Coleman lanterns into the little yellow boats. Two at a time, they crossed the water until everyone—and everything—had been safely deposited on a small, cactus-covered island that stood in the water on the Kentucky side of the lake. It was important that they camp in Kentucky—a matter of state pride.

I first went to Dale Hollow in utero. My mother was seven months' pregnant in June of 1971, and by that time, the lake vacation had become a family tradition. Both my parents worked—my father was a celebrated mechanic at the Shell station in London (his talent with engines and compassionate service to customers got him written up in the *Louisville Courier-Journal*), and my mother worked in a refrigerator factory. They didn't have the money or the desire to go to Myrtle Beach or even the Great Smoky Mountains, but a vacation at the lake was doable. I picture my mother there on the shale banks of the lake, lounging in a recently purchased lawn chair, one hand on her belly as she lay in the sun, the waves washing up to nip at her toes. Some parents sing to pregnant bellies. Some play Mozart to their waiting babies or read to them through the layers of skin and muscle. But my parents gave me something even better. While I was in my mother's belly, I was soaking up the spirit and beauty of Dale Hollow Lake. Maybe that's why I love it so much.

When I look back on my childhood, I feel as if I practically grew up on the lake. By that time, my family was spending two weeks at Dale Hollow each year (one week in June and one in September), as the individual members became more prosperous and gained more vacation time. All of them had purchased boats by now—sleek little runabouts with walk-through windshields and black Mercury motors that glistened in the sun. Everyone owned their own Zebco 33 fishing reels. Receiving mine on my fifth birthday filled me with the same overwhelming joy that other boys feel when they get their first hunting rifles.

As soon as the children were big enough, they were required to work at the lake like everyone else. It took a full day to pack all our stuff across the water and then up the hill to our campsite. My family took everything: huge fabric tents, tarps, stoves, lanterns, kettles and cookers, metal tables. In those days, soft drinks were available only in bottles, so we would carry carton after carton of 16-ounce Pepsi and Dr. Pepper up to the camp (and then ferry the empties back home, for the bottle deposits). We had to bring so much because there were no sandwiches or hot dogs on our camping trips. We had full-fledged meals there on the lake. Aunt Sis went to the lake for two things: to fish and to cook. She would spend the whole day cooking green beans, preparing chicken and dumplings, making cornbread in the little hinged pan that could bake things on a Coleman stove, cutting up cantaloupe, making lemon pies. We had two huge meals a day. Breakfast was never simply doughnuts purchased at the dock. No, every day we had bacon, eggs, fried potatoes, gravy, biscuits (made in the hinged baker), pancakes, and whatever else they could think of. Lunch was a hastily grabbed can of Vienna sausages or Beenie Weenies (mostly because we didn't want to take time out during the hot part of the day to cook or eat). Then, in the evenings, we had suppers that were more extravagant than most people's Thanksgiving dinners.

It is important to point out that we didn't stay in a regulated camping area. We didn't even know that such a thing existed. We simply picked an island in the middle of the lake, docked our boats there, and went about clearing a space to meet the needs of our camp. We cleared brush and grass, raked the ground of pinecones and rocks and branches, made paths up into the woods, nailed together lumber to build cooking stations against the trees. The forest was our bathroom, the lake our bathtub. At first we stayed on narrow little Cactus Island, where we had first camped, but we soon outgrew it. Besides the whole family, our friends began to join us, too. At one point in the late 1970s, more than forty of us camped together on Dale Hollow Lake. We found a heavily shaded place tucked into a nice fishing bay and called it Spider Island, because of the abundance of granddaddies that managed to find their way into our tents no matter how tightly zipped. Then we moved to Carp Island, so named because of the fish that constantly fed at the edge of the water throughout the night. Carp was one of my favorite places because it had an old root cellar, left behind by the Corps of Engineers when the people of the valley had been run out so the lake could be built. Although the adults repeatedly warned us not to approach the cellar, of course, we did. We managed to get the door open and found that it was still stocked with Mason jars full of beans and kraut, tomato juice and blackberry jam.

I was probably only about ten when this happened, but even then, I realized that we were invading that place. I thought about the people who had lived there before, and I felt sad for them, but only momentarily. Quickly, my childish selfishness overtook me, and I was thankful that those natives had had to leave the valley to make way for the lake, which had become so important to me.

However, the haunted nature of the lake loomed larger once my family started camping on what we called Ghost Island. We found a large cemetery there, in the woods some ten yards behind the camping area we had cleared. Ghost Island was the best campsite we had had so far. It was incredibly flat, and shaded with the most noble cedars and maples I have ever seen. It was also roomy. During one trip, we stretched twenty tents on that island. There was a creek that trickled down one side, where we could catch crawdads and minnows. A deep ditch that ran down the other side of the island was perfect for seeking refuge during windstorms or the occasional tornado threat. The shoreline was less sloped than on other islands, so the women could comfortably sunbathe in their outstretched folding chairs. There was also a sycamore tree that stood out in the water just far enough (in June, at least) for us to nail planks to it and build a diving platform in the intersection of its strong limbs. I must have jumped from that sycamore a thousand times. But best of all, there was the graveyard.

That graveyard looms large in my childhood. Every night at the edge of dark, all the children would prepare for the trek to the cemetery. We located our flashlights, found ourselves good walking sticks (which, in truth, we carried for protection more than anything else), consulted the crude maps we had made of the island (even though we knew its geography better than that of our own town), appointed a leader, and walked up the path through the fragrant pines. This took a long time, as we were constantly stopping because someone would say, "I heard something" or "What was that?" Halfway to the graveyard, someone always turned back, the beam of the flashlight bouncing haphazardly against the treetops as he or she ran back to camp in terror. But we braver ones would make our way to the graveyard and have séances or tell ghost stories, always with our flashlights turned to our faces for a more frightening effect. Eventually, someone would claim to have seen a ghost, or someone would hear a branch snap when none of us were moving, and we would run back through the woods screaming maniacally until we reached camp, where our family was gathered around the campfire listening to the crickets and frogs.

Often I went to the graveyard alone, but only in the daylight. It was creepy at night, but in the day there was a holiness about it. So silent, so still. It wasn't a cemetery by any practical means, but it was obvious that it once had been. The graves had been dug up by the Corps of Engineers. This, somehow, was eerier than anything else. There were sinkholes where the caskets had lain. I imagine that the graves had been hastily refilled by Corps workers, then left to settle and sink until it became apparent again that this had been a graveyard. The sinkholes were too purposely laid out for it to be anything else. The gravestones had been removed too. But there was a crumbling fence around the sinkholes and an obvious cleared space where a road had led to the cemetery during its heyday. Occasionally we found a plastic funeral flower or metal grave marker if we pushed enough leaves away. Some of the graves were small, and we knew that these had held babies. This was too sad to bear, so we kept clear of those.

I went there because it was where I could best imagine the people who had lived in this valley before the lake had been formed in the 1940s. I could see them coming down that old road in various states of grief. Six men carrying a casket. Women in netted hats and long wool coats. A preacher in a collarless

shirt and a booming voice. People had died here, had been buried here. What bigger reminder that people had once lived here?
And their histories lay beneath the clear waters. When I thought
too much about this, I would run back to camp, but never in fear;
I felt only a strange kind of shared grief with the people who had
called this magical place home.

I thought about that when we went fishing in the evenings,
too. I would cast my line and wonder if there was a house down
there, many feet below the water. Were there tricycles and toys
rusting on the bottom of the lake? What mysteries would never
be recovered? Although most of the time we were just enjoying
Dale Hollow Lake, my family always paid homage to this remarkable past in some way, even if it was only to acknowledge
it by saying, "What a pretty place they had to leave." We loved
the place so much that we had to overlook what had been taken
from its original residents; otherwise, we couldn't have enjoyed
it anymore.

And enjoy it we did. Our day went like this: We arose early
and stoked the simmering fire that had been left the night before, standing around it sleepy-eyed as we stretched. We children were allowed to drink coffee while at the lake, and it has
never tasted better than it did on those cool mornings when
the sharp sounds of tents unzipping were the only thing inter-
rupting the green sounds of morning. Beyond us we could see
the mist moving down into the cleavage where two mountains
came together, or hovering just above the surface of the water.
There was so much birdcall in the mornings—the drill of woodpeckers in the deepest parts of the forest, ringing out across the
water, swallows singing in the day, redbirds calling *birdie birdie
birdie*. We had our big breakfast—like all our meals, accompanied by much laughter and joking. Then a quick change into our
swimsuits so we could run down to the shore and dive into the
lake. No matter how cold the mornings were, we would jump in,
not wanting to waste one minute of the day. Many of the adults

stayed within the shade of the camp throughout the day. They worked on their rods and reels, swept out the tents, restructured the campfire, polished the water skis, cooked. But many other adults came down to lie on the rocky bank or swim or simply look out at the water, breathing in its cleanness. After the adults had tended to everything, they would come down and take us water-skiing or inner-tubing. We rode the boats—by this time, many of us owned stylish bass boats with metal-flake paint jobs that flashed in the sun—to the docks for ice cream or candy bars or ice, which was always in great demand. We spent the day playing —riding the waves, floating on air mattresses, swimming, diving from our beloved sycamore tree, building dams in the little creek, fashioning miniature villages out of moss and brush and rocks. Not once did I ever hear a child complain about being bored on that island. When it had cooled down enough, everyone pitched in and cooked supper. Sis had usually already prepared the main course—fried chicken or a turkey breast or salmon patties—but there were always the potatoes to fry, the bread to bake, and the macaroni and tomatoes to boil. My mother and aunts were in charge of all this, and they greatly enjoyed complaining about it as the sweat ran down into their eyes. Everyone ate together, talking and telling stories the whole time. Great waves of laughter rolled out of our camp and out onto the water, perhaps finding their way to other campers along the banks who heard our joy and smiled at it.

Then everyone outfitted themselves properly and headed down to the boats to go fishing. Often there were a few children, myself included, who wanted to stay behind and squeeze a little more time out of the day to swim or play, so an older cousin was usually elected to stay behind and watch over them. Most of the time, this task fell to my sister Eleshia, who would get in and swim with us or take us on long journeys to explore the island or spend hours helping us gather the tiny seashells and chips of quartz that lined the bottom of the lake near the shoreline.

When I didn't stay behind to join in on these activities, I often went fishing.

My favorite picture is of me catching my first bluegill all by myself, when I was about five. I am wearing one of those awful orange life jackets that simply slide down over your head and always ride too high on your chest. I am holding up my little Zebco with one hand and clutching onto the fishing line with the other, my eyes fixed on the bluegill that dangles there. That rush of joy and exhilaration and surprise at catching a fish is evident in my face, in my huge smile. My mother and Sis are laughing in the cramped yellow johnboat. My father is reaching out to help me take the fish off the hook. Behind us the lake stretches out like a painting. Sandbar willows as green as new limes sit half submerged in the water. The sky is peach with the nearing twilight, and our faces are lit with this wonder of the gloaming. The picture doesn't capture that I refused to let any of them help me, that I took the bluegill off myself, just as I had baited the hook myself. It doesn't contain the moment that my father said, "Do you want to let it go?" and I said, "Naw, I want to eat it!" And later I did eat it, delicious in cornmeal batter, and felt simultaneously thankful to and grief-stricken for the little fish.

Those evenings on the lake—fishing with all our boats sitting close together in cliff-lined coves or weedy bays where the bluegill fed best when they were "on the nest"—were golden. We would talk softly to one another, never too loud for fear of scaring away the fish. The adults told us their own fishing stories, stories we had heard a million times but never tired of. Often we had brought along cans of peaches or packs of Nabs and would nibble on them as we watched the sky move, watched the water change with the sky, watched our lines for any sign of movement.

When we returned from fishing, the children and babysitter who had stayed behind would run down to the bank with flashlights or Coleman lantern in hand to guide us into the shore. They were always laughing and hollering ("What'd you catch?"

"We saw a ghost while you were gone!" "Who caught the biggest one?") and happy that we had returned. Then a lantern—issuing that hollow whistle that is so comforting and warm—was hung in the branch of a tree and everyone cleaned their catch. Ziploc bags were filled with the most beautiful white meat, which we saved for the last day of our vacation, when we had a fish fry so large that we often had to drive over to the dock and give the leftovers to the men who had pumped our gas or handed us ice throughout the week. The water always seemed twice as warm at night (just as it did after a good rain) when we washed the blood and scales from our hands.

If the fishing proved too messy, we were sometimes allowed to take a quick bath under the cover of darkness. We threw the cake of soap back and forth to one another (always Ivory, since it floated and was therefore harder to lose) and put too much shampoo into our hair and dove in to wash it out. Often I would submerge and stay completely still, listening to the underwater sounds of the lake at night. The water felt like warm milk.

One of the best parts of the day was when we all gathered around the campfire at night. Someone always built a great fire of tall, licking flames (and then various members of the family tended to it throughout the night, poking at the logs to stoke them, telling a child to get another piece of wood to throw on). Everyone brought down their chairs and formed a circle around the fire, and people told stories—stories oft repeated and stories we had never heard before. The children caught lightning bugs or frogs, played hide-and-seek, terrorized each other in the woods. But eventually we made our way to the fire, where we climbed up into our parents' laps, exhausted from the joy of our day.

There was nothing, in those hours, except human voices and the crack of the fire and the night sounds: crickets, katydids, cicadas, frogs. Best of all, there was always a whip-poor-will that settled in a tree close enough for us to hear its song throughout the night. Each time it called we would grow silent for a moment. My father would usually say something like, "There's no prettier sound than a whip-poor-will," and then Sis would say, "But that's the lonesomest old song." And then someone else would launch into an old or new story and I would refuse to go to sleep, even though my eyes were unbearably heavy as I lay stretched out on my mother's or father's or aunt's or uncle's or cousin's lap. But eventually I was carried off to my good, comfortable bed in the tent, and the songs of the woods whispered me to sleep. And in the morning, it all started over again.

When I grew up and married, I began to take my own family there. Now my children know the wise old woods, the noble trees that have seen families who lived there and buried their dead there, as well as those who camped there and came running up the bank to show off how many fish they had caught. My children learned how to swim in that same water, heard those same sounds, caught their first fish there.

Shortly after my second child was born, a lot changed, though. The Corps of Engineers stopped letting people camp on the place we had named Ghost Island. Pine beetles ravaged the area and caused many campsites to be uninhabitable. Pretty soon, the Corps made people take out permits if they wanted to camp on the islands. Usually, the limited number of permits are taken up far in advance by people who are not even from Kentucky or Tennessee. In addition, several members of my family are now elderly, and it became too hard for them to pack all the tents and tarps and cases of pop up to the campsites anyway. So slowly, they all began to buy RVs, and we relocated to a managed campsite on the lake called Lillydale. Once crowded with trees, it too was nearly devastated by the pine beetles. Now it bears only a few old hardwoods that stand next to many, many saplings that have been planted to provide shade sometime far in the future. The whole family still goes to Dale Hollow. We line our campers up side by side for the whole week, and in the evenings we line up our boats when we go fishing. But now we have a shower house and a bathroom and electricity and running water. It's not the same as the campsite of my childhood. The new campground is quiet and sweet with the scent of water and leaves, but it's not wild, and it's not a place of wild things. The lake itself hasn't changed, though. That mist still moves on the water in the mornings. Those whip-poor-will songs still find their way to us. And Sis and my mother still cook huge meals. Stories are still told. Respect is still paid to the people who lived there before we ever visited, before we were even born. And it's still more than a lake to all of us. It's a thread in our family history.

HARLAN HUBBARD

An Excerpt from *Shantyboat* (1953)

I AM NOT a true fisherman. Many are drawn to the river by a desire to fish, but this was not even a minor reason for my becoming a shantyboater. Perhaps it could be said, since I am not a thorough fisherman, that I am not a genuine river rat. I have become a consistent fisherman, but only because fish are so valuable to us. I enjoy it, too, but all the pleasure of fishing does not come from catching fish.

To make a beginning, our hopes lay in Andy. He was a real fisherman, and it was fishing that first attracted him to the river. This was in his early days when he was working in the coal mines, soon after his arrival in this country from Germany. At Brent he still used his bank cap and miner's carbide lamp for night fishing.

We were pleased when Andy promised to help us, and we bought the specified hooks and two sizes of cotton twine. After a long delay, waiting for the June rise to be over, and, I think, because Andy was somewhat reluctant, after all, to give away his secrets, we put out a trotline.

First there had been some preparatory work. Andy "stagin'd" about fifty hooks, showing us the clever way in which he tied each hook to a short piece of light twine he called a staging. Then we selected two heavy anchor stones of the right weight and shape, for Andy was particular about details, cutting shallow notches in them so the line would not slip off. For a buoy, a square gallon can was preferred, though a jug or block of wood could be used just as well. A few small weights were the last requirement.

One evening Andy and I went out in our johnboat with this equipment and a bucket of live minnows for bait. One end of the heavy line was tied to a stone, which was dropped overboard some distance off shore. As I rowed out into the river, holding against the current, Andy payed out the line. He soon tied on another piece of heavy twine to which the buoy can was fastened. This was tossed overboard. When the other end of the main line was reached, it was tied to the second stone, and that was heaved overboard far out into the river. Thus the line lay on the river bottom, stretched between the two stones, at right angles to the current.

We now rowed over to the buoy can, and raising the line to the surface, tied on the "stagin'd" hooks, about three feet apart. A live minnow was strung on each hook in a peculiar way that was Andy's secret. Weights were attached at intervals to hold the line on the bottom. When all the hooks were tied on, the line was let go, and we rowed back to shore.

Next morning when we traced our line I was surprised to find several nice catfish on it. Andy took it as a matter of course. When we got back to shore, Andy began catching minnows, and putting them in a floating box, ready for use in the evening. We let our line rest during the day, for Andy's experience had been that not enough fish could be caught then to make it worthwhile to bait up in the daytime. The minnows were caught in a glass trap, a jug-shaped affair with a glass funnel built into the large end. The trap was placed in shallow water near shore where the slow current fed out the bread crumbs which had been put in it for bait. It was quite effective if you set it out where and when the minnows were running.

This kind of fishing, with a trotline, is generally practiced around Brent. As we went down the river we found many variations of it, and also new methods of which we had never heard.

We were delighted to have some fish, and put into service a live box I had found in the drift, tying it to our boat in true shantyboat style. Fishing now became a daily chore for all of us, and a satisfactory division of labor worked itself out. Andy, or Sadie, caught the minnows, using their precious glass trap. They could not have been more careful of the Ark, removing all nearby stones, and sitting by in a shady place ready to snatch it up if threatened by waves from a passing boat. Occasionally the minnows must be emptied out and fresh bait put in. As this was often done by little Jerry, his grandson, Andy's contemplation of the river would be undisturbed for hours.

Our part was to supply all equipment and do all the heavy work—rowing, tracing the line mornings, for the fogs bothered Andy, and baiting the line in cool or wet weather.

The fish we caught were mostly catfish. There were channel cats, mud cats, and some light blue ones which Andy called, correctly, Mississippi blue cats. None of these were large, the average being a pound, perhaps. The largest we caught that summer weighed four pounds.

Fish became a main part of our diet. They still are. When they are available, which means a large part of the year, we eat them day after day, always with relish. The dogs eat fish, too, and the heads and trimmings cooked with vegetables and cereal. We soon experimented with smoking fish, making a smokehouse out of an oil drum. Smoked catfish turned out to be a delicacy, but perhaps smoked eel is best of all. We canned fish for winter use, dried, and salted them. Anna has learned and invented many ways of cooking fish, and can even make a tasty dish out of gar.

From our observation, river people seldom eat fish.

We never became acquainted with a boat which consumed as much fish as ours does. Farmers and Negroes seem to be the most fish-hungry. Our partners at Brent were no exception to the rule, and only now and then did Sadie cook a few perch for Andy.

Soon there was a surplus of fish in our box. We gave some to our friends, and Sadie, who was an old hand at the business, said we must sell some. When the word got around in the neighborhood, we soon had all the customers we could take care of. It was a nuisance at times, but we enjoyed our fish buyers, and made some good friends among the farmers, railroaders, and retired boatmen who came down to the boat. Sadie's salesmanship was worth listening to, over and over. If the fish were large, she praised their size. Of the small ones she would say, "Them's the kind we eat, sweetest of all. Hold him tight, Harlan, or he'll fin you."

At the end of the summer our share of the take was $67. We figured that by giving most of our time to the work, having four or five lines out instead of one or two, we could have earned, clear, more than $400. This would be a small income, but our overhead was small, and after all, $400 would last a long time on the river.

I enjoyed the fishing that summer. It was sweet to head out into the river in the summer dawn, through the rising mist, or perhaps a fog so thick that one must steer by the sound of roost-

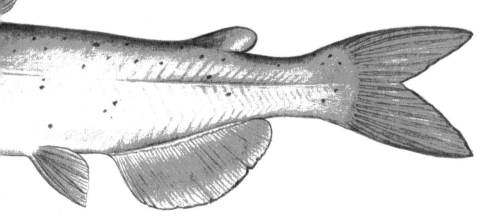

ers' crowing, or a Carolina wren, or a passing train. As we sat out there in the twilight, baiting up, shore sounds came to us over the water—children playing, their mother calling them in, the mooing of a cow, or barking of a dog. A steamboat comes up in the distance, columns of smoke rising from her stacks. You raise your eyes now and then, trying to judge whether you will be finished baiting before she reaches you. Or you see another fisherman tracing his line—a tall figure standing in the end of a johnboat, a boy with a steering oar in the stern. As the sunset fades, you smell the night coming on; the roar of water over the dam becomes louder, and the last evening song of the thrush comes from the hillside.

Life flowed back into Andy when he was out fishing. As he deftly baited hooks, he told many yarns about the river—about fishermen, steamboats, steamboat whistles, and some of his own experiences. He had traveled up and down the river, far up tributaries which were known to us only by name. He towed his houseboat with a little gasoline stern-wheeler, one of many he had built. One room of his boat was fitted up as a store, a sort of condensed dime store, with tin cups, dishes, notions, and such. He would trade with the natives for junk which he carried in a small flat alongside and sold in the first large city he came to. Andy had done much drifting and had a special little flat for his "beadle" hounds. One of these dogs, when he felt the urge, would swim ashore to hunt, and Andy would hear him as he coursed the hills. Later the dog would swim out to the boat when far below. We have often wished that our dogs would learn to do this.

Andy said that bigger fish could be caught by baiting up a second time after dark, and talked me into going out on the line during the night. All the rest of the summer I crawled out of bed at whatever time I happened to wake up, and rowed out into the dark. I picked up the buoy can by nocturnal landmarks, and took off what fish there were, then baited up in the light of a miner's lamp worn on my cap, for I had acquired one like Andy's. When finished, I put out the light, and rowing slowly back, watched Cassiopeia rising in the eastern sky. She seemed to draw up her fish line, which was Perseus, with the misty Pleiades as bait, and bright Venus caught. All was growing dim in the faint beginning of dawn. Then I felt I was fishing with the One who made the river and set it flowing. I felt its length and sinuous curving, fed by swift streams in the wooded mountains, and somewhere, after a long course through country unknown to me except by hearsay, past the mouths of new rivers and strange towns, it would at last enter an ocean and lose its identity, as I would, too, at the end of my devious drifting.

BARBARA KINGSOLVER

The Memory Place (An Excerpt)

From *High Tide in Tucson* (1995)

THIS IS THE KIND of April morning no other month can touch:
a world tinted in watercolor pastels of redbud, dogtooth violet,
and gentle rain. The trees are beginning to shrug off winter; the
dark, leggy maple woods are shot through with gleaming con-
stellations of white dogwood blossoms. The road winds through
deep forest near Cumberland Falls, Kentucky, carrying us across
the Cumberland Plateau toward Horse Lick Creek. Camille is
quiet beside me in the front seat, until at last she sighs and says,
with a child's poetic logic, "This reminds me of the place I always like to think about."

Me too, I tell her. It's the exact truth. I grew up roaming
wooded hollows like these, though they were more hemmed-in,
keeping their secrets between the wide-open cattle pastures and
tobacco fields of Nicholas County, Kentucky. My brother and
sister and I would hoist cane fishing poles over our shoulders, as
if we intended to make ourselves useful, and head out to spend a
Saturday doing nothing of the kind. We haunted places we called
the Crawdad Creek, the Downy Woods (for downy woodpeckers
and also for milkweed fluff), and—thrillingly, because we'd once
found big bones there—Dead Horse Draw. We caught crawfish
with nothing but patience and our hands, boiled them with wild
onions over a campfire, and ate them and declared them the best
food on earth. We collected banana-scented pawpaw fruits, and
were tempted by fleshy, fawn-colored mushrooms but left those

138

alone. We watched birds whose names we didn't know build nests in trees whose names we generally did. We witnessed the unfurling of hickory and oak and maple leaves in the springtime, so tender as to appear nearly edible; we collected them and pressed them with a hot iron under waxed paper when they blushed and dropped in the fall. Then we waited again for spring, even more impatiently than we waited for Christmas, because its gifts were more abundant, needed no batteries, and somehow seemed more exclusively ours. I can't imagine that any discovery I ever make, in the rest of my life, will give me the same electric thrill I felt when I first found little righteous Jack in his crimson-curtained pulpit poking up from the base of a rotted log.

These were the adventures of my childhood: tame, I guess, by the standards established by Mowgli the Jungle Boy or even Laura Ingalls Wilder. Nevertheless, it was the experience of nature, with its powerful lessons in static change and predictable surprise. Much of what I know about life, and almost everything I believe about the way I want to live, was formed in those woods. In times of acute worry or insomnia or physical pain, when I close my eyes and bring to mind the place I always like to think about, it looks like the woods in Kentucky.

ART LANDER JR.

Partners in the Web of Life (2004)

WE ARE HUNTERS by instinct. Something in our genes tells us to go into the forest and emulate wild creatures. We admire the animal stealth, cunning, and will to survive that so many humans have lost touch with or altogether ignore. Petroglyphs on the walls of caves tell of the exploits of ancient hunters who lived by the chase and celebrated their kill. Without fresh meat, their families perished. Without hunting, primitive man would have passed into oblivion.

The accomplished hunter has always been looked at in awe. Praised in life and immortalized in literature. A ghost who moves through the forest in silence, with his nose to the wind and the sun at his back. A creature of shadows who thinks and acts like the wild game he pursues. If only we could glide through the dark timber like a Cooper's hawk.

Hunters share a bond with their prey. For eons, predator and prey have been on a journey through an ever-changing pathway. There are glimpses of this passage in the rush of water that alters the course of rivers and in the process of plant succession, which turns fields into forests.

In pioneer Kentucky, the hunter was the provider for camp— the chosen one who killed so that many could live. He was the leatherstocking who ventured into the wilderness with little more than a knife, a tomahawk, and a longrifle.

Hunting white-tailed deer with a flintlock longrifle is our heritage, our roots, as old as these ancestral hunting grounds that were once the property of the Shawnee. The deer moves through the forest like an afternoon shadow, slowly and quietly on damp leaves. A flicker of an ear, then legs and shoulders appear, until the whole animal materializes among the branches and leaves. Finally, the deer is in my sights. The dark gray English flint sparks and sets off the main charge in my rifle with a *woooosh*. The big doe stumbles and then goes down.

We have eaten squash, corn, and green beans from the garden all summer. Now we will have fresh meat.

Charlie Wallingford's hand-forged blade makes quick work of field-dressing. The carcass is carried from the woods, hung, and rinsed clean. The loins are carefully removed, to be cooked with garlic and olive oil in our old iron skillet. Tomorrow morning I will skin the deer, cut away the thick backstraps from both sides of the backbone, and debone the hams. The shoulders will be kept whole for cooking over hickory coals.

The air has grown cold, and the moon is a bright yellow crescent above the horizon when we get to the house. I clean my rifle in front of the fire. The embers are glowing red like the sun setting in a winter sky.

The day has ended like so many in the life of a hunter, generations of hunters. This primal act of gathering food has brought us closer to the natural world. Life sustains life, and death is never an end but a new beginning. Native Americans believe that when an animal gives itself to a hunter, the animal invites the hunter into its spiritual journey through the sacred circle of creation.

We welcome that journey, for we are hunters, partners in the web of life.

ART LANDER JR.

King of the Spring Woodlands

From the *Lexington Herald-Leader* (April 26, 1992)

THE CLOUDS ON the horizon were backlit with crimson and yellow light when the turkey started gobbling. It was a lusty, rattling call that echoed through the woods, shattering the predawn calm. From a ridgetop down the creek, it was impossible to pinpoint the exact location of his roost tree. So I walked, almost ran, as fast as I dared down the hill and through the valley.

Doves fluttered from cedars. In the half light, unseen branches grabbed at my arms and poked my face. The wet underbrush pulled at my legs and soaked my boots. The gobbles became more frantic, one after another. I remember thinking, "If he sees a hen, it will be over before I can get there." To be safe, I opened the action of my pump shotgun as I scrambled from rock to rock crossing the creek. After I stepped over a sagging barbed-wire fence, I re-chambered the round.

A deer trail led up through the woods to a flat, open clearing. Farther back I could see the tops of big oak trees.

I remember this place. There's the old log house with its roof caved in. The rock chimney is standing as straight and true as the day it was built. The apple trees have long been swallowed up by the forest. The little flat by the creek, where once there was a garden plot, is covered with grass and trees. Tall, slender walnuts have taken root in the dark, rich soil. The old homestead has been abandoned for more than 50 years, but on this crisp, spring morning, it pulses with life, with wildness.

The king of the spring woodlands has ascended his throne.

I am crawling in the leaves to get where I can see into the clearing, at the base of the big oaks. My heart is pounding. Beads of sweat are rolling down my neck. Seated with my shotgun up on my knees, I slip in the thin reed of latex and push it up against the roof of my mouth. I utter a sharp cluck on the mouth diaphragm. He gobbles. I yelp softly. He cuts me off with a thundering double gobble.

Wing beats. The leaves rustle. He is on the ground and coming fast. I click off my shotgun's safety.

It is a moment, and a hunt, I will never forget as long as I live. How many generations has it been since a gobbler called this woods home? It may have been more than 100 years since a hunter took a bird here.

The big tom bursts into view and gobbles so loud it's startling. His head is up when I block it out with the front bead on my shotgun barrel.

BOOM. Then there is stillness. For the first time all morning I notice how loud the songbirds are singing.

My gobbler is down for keeps. It is 25 steps to where he lays outstretched on a carpet of leaves, iridescent feathers shining. The forest floor is covered with patches of beautiful wildflowers —larkspur, Virginia bluebells, bloodroot, trilliums, and violets. I pull off my headnet and sit back down against the base of the tree. The sound of the creek is like a gentle song. There's a cool breeze stirring.

The return of the wild turkey to Kentucky's woodlands is a story about recapturing a part of our natural heritage. Restoration has taken 15 years, at a cost of about $2 million, with 4,000 wild turkeys stocked in 280 sites across the commonwealth. Sportsmen gladly forked over the money to make restoration happen, but they didn't do it just so they could hunt these noble birds. They did it to bring back what has been lost to generations of Kentuckians, hunters and nonhunters alike—a piece in the ecological puzzle.

From the Big Sandy to the Mississippi, Kentucky was once a vast forest, interspersed with open savanna. A spring morning in 1780 must have been one long crescendo of gobbling. The wild turkey was abundant, a staple on every settler's dinner table. But the big bird was also an inspiration, a symbol of freedom and America's rich natural resources.

It's a wonderful feeling to know that a long-lost native species has returned.

Our Creek Is Full of Memories

From *The Best of Crawfish and Minnows* (2000)

WHAT IS THE DIFFERENCE between a creek and a river? Myth has it that to be a river, the stream must be at least 100 miles long. And according to this same myth, Elkhorn Creek falls one mile short of this magical distance, and therefore does not qualify as a river.

All of this, however, is just a myth. The real difference between a creek and a river is memories. A creek has memories. A river has large boats and barges and pollution, but never memories.

Elkhorn Creek is a treasury of memories for me. It was my family's park for our annual Fourth of July picnic. The cool spring below Degaris Mill dam provided the fresh drinking water and the spot to cool the watermelon we had lugged from across town with each child taking turns carrying it.

The deep hole at Big Bend was the swimming pool for those skilled swimmers who could dive from the 10-foot platform attached between branches of that old sycamore tree that is now just a stump.

The beginners, like myself, waded and learned to swim in Toad's Hole. It was not too deep, and best of all, the bullies usually were never there.

The fondest memories of Elkhorn Creek, though, are the many, many hours my dad and I waded and fished together in this grand old stream.

We caught fish by the hundreds. There were redeyes and bass, catfish and carp. There were days when we got skunked. But there was never a day we didn't have a great time. For a young boy, this was what living was all about.

There have been a lot of changes in Scott County since my boyhood days, but this creek and its memories seem to be the same.

You don't catch nearly as many fish as you did years ago, and there is a lot more development along its banks. The boat ramps and fiberglass boats with high-powered motors have replaced our old leaky wooden boats and their back-breaking oars.

But after all, Elkhorn Creek is a creek, and a creek is a place of memories, and memories never change and they never die.

I still go back to these same secret holes that I fished nearly a half century ago. It is then that I am once again the little young-ster fishing alongside my dad. We sometimes got caught in a storm or slipped and fell down and got soaking wet. We still joke about the heart attack he had while fishing—he wouldn't leave because the fish were hitting so good. Yes, there is still that 50-cent bet on who would catch the biggest fish.

Today we celebrate Father's Day. I think I'll eat supper a lit-tle early and head for a certain spot below Robinson Dam. I'll go alone, but I know for sure my old fishing buddy will be wait-ing there at the Cathole wondering what took me so long to get there.

BOBBIE ANN MASON

An Excerpt from *Clear Springs* (1999)

IT HAD BEEN an unusually hot summer, and my mother had gotten out of the habit of stirring about, although she still drove to her garden at the farm each morning. When she lived at the farm, she had kept active all summer, but at the new house, she felt inhibited from going outside. There were so many houses around, with people to see her and make her feel self-conscious. She was stiffening up with arthritis, and her muscles were still weak from her stroke a year ago. The doctor told her she had severe osteoporosis, but he didn't seem to think that was unusual for someone her age—seventy-seven. Her daughters nagged at her about exercise. They went on and went on about muscle tone and skeletal support. It made her tired to listen to them.

Now that it was autumn, the weather was a little cooler, and she longed to go fishing. Her daughters had given her a new rod and reel for her birthday over a year ago, but she had hardly made use of it. She knew the fish were growing big. When Wilburn restocked the pond, just before he died, he had included two five-pound catfish.

One sunny day in early October, after her dinner at noon, she impulsively went fishing. Leaving the dirty dishes on the table and the pots and pans on the counter, she stowed her tackle box and her rod and reel in the car and drove to the farm. She parked the car in the shade by the stable, near her garden, and headed across the soybean field toward the pond. She knew the fish would be biting. She was quicker in her step than she had been lately, but she picked her way carefully through the stubbly field. The soybeans had been recently harvested, but she did not know if the men who leased the land had gathered the popcorn they had planted in the back fields. It had been several years since she had been across the creeks to the back acreage.

She was walking through the field behind Granny's house. Only one car was in the driveway, and she did not see any of the renters. The trampoline in the yard reminded her of a misshapen hospital cot. The black dog chained to the wash-house regarded her skeptically, pawed at the ground, and sat down lazily. With his chain, he had worn away her grapevine and turned the grass into a crescent of dirt. The old place had so much time and heart invested in it, too much to comprehend. Now it seemed derelict and unloved.

She was out of breath when she reached the pond, but she recovered quickly in the warm air. The leaves on the trees along the creek were beginning to turn yellow and brown. The pond was full and still. The pondweed had diminished somewhat this year because Don had released two grass-eating carp into the water. They were supposed to eat their weight in pondweed daily. She had told Don to make sure they were the same sex. She didn't want the pond overrun with carp, which could be a worse calamity than pondweed.

She felt good, eager to fish. She baited her hook with a piece of a chicken gizzard she had bought the week before. It was ripe, a piece of stink bait to lure a catfish. After wiping her hands on the grass, she cast out and reeled in slowly. It was pleasant to stand on the bank and watch the arc of her line fly out. She was standing at the deep bend of the pond, near the old lane. The water was exceptionally high, nearly reaching the rim of the pond. The wind was blowing from the east, and her floater drifted to the left. She reeled it toward her.

Lately she had been reviewing her life, reflecting on the hardships she had endured. She bridled at the way the women always had to serve the men. The men always sat down in the evening, but the women kept going. Why had the women agreed to that arrangement? How had they stood it? What if she had had an opportunity for something different? Wilburn, amazed by her paintings, once said, "Why, if you'd had a chance, there's no telling what you could have accomplished." She didn't know. The thought weighed her down, taunting her with something lost she could never retrieve, like a stillborn child.

After a while, she got a bite. Her cork plunged down and then took off. A fish was carrying the bait across the pond, against the wind, rippling the water, flying across. She reeled in and felt the fish pull steady. It was a big one, but she didn't allow her hopes to rise yet. It seemed heavy, though. She worked it back and forth, feeling the deep pleasure of hooking a fish. It grew lively then. It was a fighter. As it resisted, she gradually realized its strength. She was afraid her line wasn't strong enough to bring it in. She would have to play it delicately.

She had never felt such a huge fish pulling at her. With growing anticipation, she worked the fish for an hour or more. But time seemed to drift like a cloud. She thought of LaNelle's Lark at the bottom of the pond. Wilburn had sunk the dilapidated car at the high end of the pond to reinforce the levee. Its hulk would be like a cow's skeleton, she thought. She did not allow the fish to take her line near that area.

She thought she knew exactly which fish she had hooked. She had had her eye on it for years. It was the prize fish of the whole pond. She had seen this great fish now and then, a monster that would occasionally surface and roll. It would wallow around like a whale. Since the first time she'd seen it, she had been out to get the "old big one." Her quest had become legendary in the family. "Mama's going to get that old big fish," they'd say. But she hadn't imagined this would be the day. It was as though the fish had been waiting for her, growing formidably, until this day. It had caught *her* by surprise.

Slowly, the fish lost its strength. She could see its mouth as she drew it nearer, as it relaxed and let her float it in. The fish was gigantic, more immense than any fish she had ever caught. From the feel of it and now the glimpse of it in the murky water, she thought it might weigh thirty pounds. If only she could see Wilburn's face when she brought this fish in.

She had never landed a fish larger than eleven pounds. She had caught a ten-pound catfish at a pay-pond once, and she had hooked the eleven-pounder in this pond. She knew that landing this one would be a challenge. She would have to drag it out, instead of raising it and flipping it out of the water.

Finally, the fish was at the bank, its mouth shut on the line like a clamp-top canning jar, its whiskers working like knitting needles. It was enormous. She was astonished. It touched the bank, but without the smooth glide of the water to support it, the fish was dead weight. She couldn't pull it all the way up the bank. She couldn't lift it with her rod, nor could she drag it through the weeds of the bank. She was more worn out than the fish was, she thought. She held the line taut, so that the fish couldn't slip back in the water, and she tugged, but it didn't give. The mud was sucking it, holding it fast. Its head was out of the water, and with those whiskers and its wide wraparound mouth, it seemed to be smiling at her. She stepped carefully through scrubby dried weeds and clumps of grass, making her way down the shallow bank toward the fish. Knots of pondweed bordered the water. Gingerly, she placed her left foot on a patch of dried vegetation and reached toward the fish.

The patch appeared solid. For a fraction of a second, the surprise of its give was like the strangeness of the taste of Coca-Cola when the tongue had expected iced tea. The ground gave way under her foot and she slid straight into the pond. It wasn't a hard fall, for her weight slid right into the water, almost gracefully. On the way, she grabbed at a willow bush but missed it. She still had hold of the line, even though her rod and reel slipped

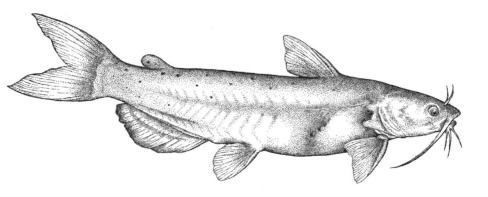

into the water. She clutched at dried weeds as she slid, and the brittle leaves crumpled in her hands. Then the fish was slipping back into the water, dragging the rod. She snatched the rod and felt the fish still weighting the end of the line. Quickly, she heaved the rod to the bank. She caught hold of the fish and held it tight, her fingernails studding its skin.

She was gasping at the chill of the water. She could not touch bottom. She was clutching the edge of the bank, and the water was up to her neck.

She hadn't imagined the pond was so deep next to the bank. The fish in her hands, she hugged the bank, propping herself against it with her elbows. She tried to get a toehold against the side of the pond, but as she shifted her weight, the solid matter fell away and her foot seemed to float free. She kept a tight hold on the fish, pointing its head away from her so it would not grab her fingers. Sometimes a channel catfish would grip bait and not let go, even after the fish was dead. It could bite a person's finger off.

She still couldn't touch the bottom, but she balanced herself against the side of the pond and held the fish's head out of the water. The water helped buoy the weight of the fish. The fish gaped, and the baited hook floated for a moment. The hook was not even sunk into its flesh. Then the fish clamped onto the hook again.

The fish was a fine one, she thought. It would make good eating. She was pleased, even amazed that she had caught it. It had lost much of its strength. She would have to wait for it to die. When the mouth stayed open, it would be dead, even if it still seemed to be breathing.

She managed to scoot it up onto the bank, inching it in front of her. She laid it in the ooze, placing it by the gills. Its gills were still working, its mouth loosened now. She held it down hard against the mud. The fish gaped, and she lessened her pressure. She floundered in the water, repositioning herself against the muck. She realized the water no longer seemed chilly.

The water was high, submerging the lower branches of the willow bushes. The willows were only a few feet away, but she did not want to get near those bushes. She was sure there were snakes around the roots of the willows. The snaky tendrils of the pond-weed brushed her legs. She kicked and stirred the water while holding on to a tuft of grass.

To make her way to the shallow end, she would have to maneuver around the willows. But she would have to launch too far out into the pond to do that. She wasn't sure she could swim, yet her clothes did not feel heavy. She was wearing her old tan stretch-knit pants and a thin blouse and a cotton shirt and tennis shoes.

She noticed it was shady in the direction of the shallow end, so she decided to stay where she was, where she could feel the sunshine. She expected that someone would see her presently and come to help her out. With difficulty, she twisted her body toward the road, where cars were passing. She let out a holler. More cars passed. She hollered again. The cars were driven by the blind and the deaf. Their windows were rolled up tight.

"Hey!" She let out a yodeling sound, and then a pig call. "Soo-eeee!" She tried all the calls she knew, calls she used when she had to reach the men working in the fields, sounds that could carry across creeks and hollers. "Sook, cow!" she called, as if summoning a herd of milk cows.

There was no one at the house now, but she thought the renters would be there soon. The car she had seen was gone. Her car gleamed fire-red at the stable. In the smooth surface of the pond before her, stretching toward the soybean field and then the road, she saw the upside-down reflection of the chicken-feed mill. The sky was bright autumn blue, and the reflection of the tower was like a picturesque postcard, still and important-looking.

Balancing against the bank in the water up to her neck, she gazed across the field toward the houses and the road. In that panorama, her whole life lay before her—a rug at the foot of the feed-mill tower. She saw her own small house in the clump of trees. The bulldozer still had not come to demolish it. She was sure the house could be fixed up, if she could only tend to it. Leaving it vacant had caused it to deteriorate. The loss of her house probably hurt her more than anything about the farm. But she couldn't keep everything up. It was too much for her. She'd had the stable repainted—a clear red—but it needed more work. Her thoughts weighed her down with the heaviness of the farm's history. Her memories mixed together in a mosaic of hard bits, like chicken grit. She saw the calves, the horses, the corncrib, the gardens, the henhouses, and other buildings no longer there. She saw the onions and potatoes she stored in one of the stalls. She saw mules and tractors and bonfires of leaves. What she saw before her eyes now was the consequence and basis of her labor. Years of toil were finished now; sometimes she wondered what it had all been for.

She seized a clump of grass but could not nudge her weight onto the bank. It was like trying to chin herself on a high bar. She did not have the energy. Then the grass pulled loose. The fish gaped again, and she managed to push it farther up the bank. She avoided its mouth.

Time passed. For a while, she lay horizontal in the water, clutching grass; then she rested vertically against the sludge of the bank. When occasionally her grip loosened, she had to dog-paddle to keep afloat.

She was panting. She held herself steady until she gathered her strength, then she tried again to pull herself up. She could not. The water seemed quite warm now. She thrashed, to scare off snakes. If she could grab a willow branch, she was sure she could pull herself out, but the thought of snakes underwater around the willow roots made her tremble. Snapping turtles were there too, she felt sure.

THE SHADE COVERING the shallow end had grown deeper and longer now. She needed to stay here in the sun.

A pack of coyotes could eat a person. Wilburn had said that was not true, but she believed it was. Last year, one of the neighbor women carried dinner to the farmhands at work in one of her back fields. She parked her car on a lane beside the field, and as she started toward the gate with the dinner she saw some coyotes running at her, a whole caboodle of them. She raced back to the car and slammed the door just in time. The coyotes clambered all over the car, sniffing.

Sometimes the siren of a passing ambulance started the coyotes howling. All along the creek, a long ribbon of eerie sound followed the siren. If the coyotes found her in the pond, she could not escape. They might smell the fish, she thought. That would draw them like bait. Her dread hardened into a knot. She thought she ought to pray. She hadn't been to church much lately. She had trouble hearing, now that they had a microphone. Its squealing hurt her ears.

Cars passed. She thought she saw her son's van under the trees. She thought he might be sawing wood. She hollered to the air. After a while, she could tell that what she had thought was the van was only some scrap metal glinting in the sun.

The soybeans had been harvested only a week before, and the combine had missed multitudes of beans. She could see clumps of them dotting the field. There was so much waste. It bothered her. The land itself was washing into the creek. She pictured herself in the pond, washing over the levee in a hard rain and then sweeping on down through the creek.

If Wilburn came along and saw her here, he would grin at her and say, "What are you fooling around in the pond for? Got time on your hands?" She wondered what it would be like to while away the hours in a country club swimming pool. She had never had time to idle like that. She did not know how people could piddle their lives away and not go crazy. She had stopped going on the senior-citizen bus tours because they wasted so much time at shopping malls. She told them she'd rather eat a worm.

She recalled falling into water before—it was familiar. She was a little thing, fishing in Panther Creek with her grandmother and aunt. Suddenly she slid off a log, down the bank, and into the water. Mammy Hicks and Aunt Hattie laughed at her. "You got wet, didn't you?" Hattie said, bobbing her pole. A whole life passed between those two splashings.

Her hands were raw. She thought she could see snakes swirling and swimming along the bank some yards away. She had never seen a cottonmouth at this pond, but a snake was a snake, poisonous or not. She shuddered and tightened her grasp on the grass. She kicked her feet behind her. Her shoes were sodden.

A pain jerked through her leg—a charley horse. She waited for it to subside. She did not know how much time had passed, but the sun was low. She was starting to feel cooler. Her legs were numb. She realized she could be having another stroke. For the first time, it occurred to her that she might really be stranded here and no one would know. No one knew she had come fishing.

She scrambled clumsily at the bank. Now she knew she had to

get out. No one was going to come for her. She knew she should have tried earlier, when she had more strength, but she had believed someone would spot her and come to help her. She worked more industriously now, not in panic but with single-minded purpose. She paused to take some deep breaths. Then she began to pull, gripping the mud, holding herself against it. She was panting hard. Little by little, she pulled herself up the mud bank. She crawled out of the water an inch at a time, stopping to rest after each small gain. She did not know if she felt desperation. She was so heavy. Her teeth were chattering from the cold, and she was too weak to rise. Finally she was on the bank, lying on her belly, but her legs remained in the water. She twisted around, trying to raise herself up. She saw a car turn into the driveway. She hollered as loud as she could. Her teeth rattled. After a moment, the car backed up and drove away.

The western sun was still beating down. She lay still and let it dry her. As her clothes dried, she felt warmer. But her legs remained in the water, her shoes like laden satchels. She pulled and pulled and crawled until her legs emerged from the water. She felt the sun drawing the water from her clammy legs. But as the sun sank, she felt cooler. She crawled with the sun—moving with it, grabbing grass.

When she finally uprighted herself, the sun was going down. She stood still, letting her strength gather. Then she placed one foot in front of her, then the other.

She had to get the fish. Stooping, she pulled it onto the grass, but she could not lift it, and she knew she could not pack it to the car. It was dead, though its gills still worked like a bellows, slowly expanding and collapsing. It had let go of the hook. Leaving the fish, she struck out across the soybean field toward the car. No one was at the house. She reached the car. Luckily, the key had not washed out of her pocket while she was in the pond. In the dim light, she couldn't see how to get it in the ignition. For an interminable time, she fumbled with the key. Then it turned.

Instead of following the path around the edge of the field, she steered the car straight across the beanfield. She stopped before the rise to the pond and got out. As she climbed toward the pond, her feet became tangled in some greenbrier vines and she fell backwards into a clump of high grass. Her head was lower than her feet. She managed to twist herself around so that she was headed up the bank, but she was too weak to stand.

She lay there in the grass for some time, probably half an hour. She dozed, then jarred awake, remembering the fish. Slowly, she eased up the bank and eventually stood. When she reached the fish, it appeared as a silhouette, the day had grown so dark. She dragged the fish to the car and heaved it up through the door, then scooted it onto the floorboard behind the driver's seat. She paused to catch her breath.

The sun was down now. In the car, she made her way out of the field to the road. Cars were whizzing by. She was not sure her lights were working. They seemed to burn only dimly. She hugged the edge of the narrow road, which had no shoulders, just deep ditches. Cars with blazing headlights roared past. She slowed down. By the time she got into town, the streetlights were on. She could not see where to turn into her street. A car behind her honked. Flustered, she made her turn.

When she got home, the kitchen clock said 7:25. She had been at the pond for seven hours. She opened the back door, and Chester the cat darted in, then skidded to a stop and stared at her, his eyes bugged out. She laughed.

"Chester, you don't know me! Do I smell like the pond?"

Chester retreated under the kitchen table, where he kept a wary lookout.

"Come here, baby," she said softly. "Come on." He backed away from her.

She got into the shower, where she let hot water beat on her. Memories of the afternoon's ordeal mingled in her mind like dreams, the sensations running together and contorting out of shape. She thought that later she would be angry with herself for not pulling herself out of the pond sooner—she could have ventured into those willow bushes—but now she felt nothing but relief.

After she was clean and warm, she went to the kitchen. Chester reappeared. He rubbed against her legs.

"Chester," she crooned. "You didn't know me." She laughed at him again.

She fed Chester and warmed up some leftovers for her supper. She hadn't been hungry all those hours, and she was too tired to eat now, but she ate anyway. She ate quickly. Then she went out to the garage and dragged the fish out of the car.

She wrestled it into the kitchen. She couldn't find her hatchet. But she thought she was too weak to hack its head off now. Using the step stool, she managed, in stages, to get the fish up onto the counter. She located her camera. The flash didn't work, but she took a picture of the fish anyway, knowing it probably wouldn't turn out. She didn't know where her kitchen scales were—lost in the move somewhere. She was too tired to look for them. She found her tape measure in a tool drawer.

The fish was thirty-eight and a half inches long. It was the largest fish she had ever caught.

"Look at that fish, Chester," she said.

With her butcher knife, she gutted the fish into a bucket. The fish was full—intestines and pondweed and debris and un-identifiable black masses squished out.

She could feel herself grinning. She had not let go of the fish when she was working it, and she had gotten back home with the old big one. She imagined telling Wilburn about the fish. He would be sitting in front of the TV, and she would call him from the kitchen. "Just wait till you see what I reeled in at the pond," she would say. "Come in here and see. Hurry!" He would know immediately what she had caught. She had a habit of giving away a secret prematurely. Her grinning face—and her laughing voice—gave her away. When she had a surprise for the children, she couldn't wait to tell them. She wanted to see their faces, the delight over something she had bought them for Christmas or some surprise she had planned. "Wake up, get out of bed. Guess what! Hurry!"

CHAD MASON

Inheritance (An Excerpt)

From *Voices on the Wind* (2002)

IT WAS A balmy day in July 1994 when my wife and I went to my parents' home for a weekend visit. My father called me aside after supper.

"There are some things in the downstairs bedroom that I want you to look at," he said. "We brought back all of Papaw's hunting gear. It's too small for your brother and me, but Papaw was about your size." Papaw had died on Christmas Eve 1993.

Like wine that is sweet on my tongue and bitter in my throat, the downstairs bedroom confronted me with conflicting emotions. Here was a shrine to an obscure man who had loved misty mornings, fox squirrels, bobwhite whistling, and the anxious whimper of pointers itching to run. Hats, vests, pants, jackets, and boots covered the bed. I put on the old canvas hunting coat, with its bloodstained game bag and missing button, then slipped into the brush pants that were loose and frayed from countless battles with green briars and multiflora rose. Finally, I picked up the Remington Model 1100 Light-20 autoloader. It was not the sort of gun I would choose for myself; it would not break open to rest in the fold of my arm. It was a piece of ordnance, not a piece of ornamentation. However, some guns are beautiful for no intrinsic merit of their mechanics, but for the hands that once held them. So I picked up the gun and reflected on the memory of those hands.

"MORNIN', SON. You ready to shoot some quail?"

Papaw always called me "son," the same term of endearment he used for my father. It was 6 A.M., too early for a college boy accustomed to late nights and late awakenings. It was Christmas vacation, 1988, and I was home for the holidays.

"Yeah, let's go get 'em," I replied.

"How 'bout you, Joe?" Papaw asked.

My brother wasn't in much better shape than I was, but he mustered all the enthusiasm he could, which amounted to no more than a "Yup." The three of us piled into Papaw's tan '78 Chevy pickup with tobacco stains on the driver's side and headed out from Greenville toward Rockport, near the Green River. We drove to an area Papaw called the spoil banks, an old reclaimed strip-mining area of about a square mile. Looking at it, I expected to see a band of pronghorns. It was rolling, treeless, rocky ground covered with dry, brown grasses. It looked oddly out of place among the native woodlands of Kentucky, but supported a thriving quail population.

We reached the spoil banks before sunrise and rolled down the windows to listen for bobs. It was a calm, clear morning, perfect for hearing the sharp *bob . . . WHITE* wakeup calls of quail. Papaw whistled twice to elicit a response. Soon quail were whistling all over the surrounding hills, and the dogs were beginning to whine.

Chief, a lemon-and-white pointer, seemed especially anxious. His bracemate for the day was Maggie, a white setter pup. Chief wore an electronic collar, or, as Papaw called it, a "steering wheel." Papaw bought the collar when Chief refused to leave Maggie alone, taking every hunting trip as an opportunity for sweet congress with his nubile hunting partner. Papaw reasoned that a shock collar would make Chief more chivalrous with the ladies, though his plan could well have backfired. After all, politically correct trainers refer to such correction as stimulation. It

is true of all species that their reason is at lowest ebb during the copulative act. A stout shock administered during mid-mount might only heighten the ecstasy and be received by Chief as the best he'd ever had. Fortunately, the plan worked as hoped, and Papaw once again had himself two dogs that could concentrate on quail.

Chief's tail thumped the side of the truck bed in rapid cadence, but he would just have to wait. We sipped much-needed coffee, letting the sun get above the trees to allow the quail time to move around and spread their scent.

At last the wait was over. We released the dogs and headed toward a swale where we had heard considerable whistling. The dogs got birdy immediately. But after a few brief, false points from Chief, it became apparent that the birds had vacated the premises. We stomped and circled and stomped some more, but to no avail.

The hunt became one of those mysterious, exasperating days when the best-laid plans come to naught and weary hunters are left scratching their heads, wondering where the quail have gone. The area had to be full of birds. We saw sign everywhere, and the dogs acted birdy throughout the morning, but we still were not moving any quail. Maybe the scenting conditions were tough, with the ground, as some old-timers say, "soaking up scent." Whatever the reason, we were striking out.

Finally, Chief and Maggie struck a real point—nostrils pulsating, tails motionless, muscles taut and quivering. God, what a sight! I have owned nine breeds of sporting dogs and watched several others in field trials or hunting tests. I have taken eight species of upland birds and nine species of ducks while hunting in five states. I have killed whitetails and pronghorns, climbed vertical rock faces in the Rockies, cast dry flies to feeding browns in the amber light of evening, hooked trophy rainbows feeding behind spawning salmon, and stalked to within forty feet of a bull elk. I have watched a tom turkey come to a call and seen ten thousand geese descend on a prairie marsh. But none of these experiences stirs me like the sight of a white dog turned to stone.

Why all this fervor at the sight of a dog standing still? A solid point compresses the anticipation of all my hours afield into a single moment of silence. I find an intense, predatory excitement in knowing the quarry is present before the quarry is visible, since a visible bird does not make my temples pound quite like a potential bird does. A dog on point is potential, a sight pregnant with possibility. In that sight, I see all that I love about hunting but cannot quite articulate when people ask me why I do it. If only they could see a white pointer with quail in his nose they would understand. Or maybe they wouldn't.

Chief and Maggie were well outside shotgun range, just like proper pointing dogs should be. Not wanting to leave anything to chance, Joel and I hustled to reach the dogs. I don't know why I looked back, but I glanced over my shoulder at Papaw and noticed that he could not keep up with us. Today, with the mental clarity afforded by time, I realize that an inevitable turning of tables had occurred. Years earlier, he paused frequently to wait for his grandsons to catch up. Now the grandsons slowed to accommodate his gradual progress on legs made weary from thirty-two years of toil in underground mines.

I looked toward the dogs just in time to see the flush, as the covey decided not to wait for a proper gentleman's walk-up. They exploded like shrapnel, and one rocketed high in front of me, right to left. I could see he was a cock, and my eyes locked on his white throat patch as I fired a quick shot. The shot felt so good, I was too surprised to fire a second one when the bird didn't fall. My brother didn't fare any better, missing twice. I thought, "Man, could we start this day over?" We hunted a little longer without success, until we'd finally had enough punishment for one day.

I returned to college the following week, then moved to Colorado a few months later. Papaw and I would not hunt together again. Sometimes I wish we could have shot a limit of quail on our last hunt together, but in a way it is fitting that we had a *hunt* and not a *shoot*.

"YOU CAN TAKE that little 20-gauge home with you, if you want it," Dad said. I hadn't noticed he was watching me, and wondered how long he had been standing in the doorway.

"It's too short for me and your brother," he continued. "Take good care of it, though, and keep it always. It's an heirloom." Dad retired to the den, leaving me alone.

Suddenly an imaginary covey of quail erupted from under the nose of an imaginary pointer. The gun came up quickly, the part of my body that had been missing all these years. Two imaginary blasts, whispered "POW!" on my lips, brought the instant demise of two bobs, and the pointer became a lemon-and-white blur. He retrieved the birds, both cocks, to hand. I patted him on the head and slipped the imaginary quail into the game pocket on the old canvas coat.

"Good boy, Chief," I whispered.

Many writers have attempted to explain why they hunt. They wax eloquent about predatory instincts, primal desires, and ancient connections with the land. They expound on the profound paradox of loving game, yet reducing it to possession. They cast a wary glance at the general populace, who condemn hunters while exchanging money for packaged flesh at the supermarket. Sometimes I too am prone to such raving apologetics. But hunting was not that complicated for Lee Roy Mason. He did not hunt for abstractions. He approached hunting like he approached all of life, with that embodied knowledge typical of peasants. I have come to adopt the wisdom of his simplicity, seeing that there is no meaning behind a quail covey. That is not to say a quail covey has no meaning. The meaning, whatever it is, resides within the covey itself, and is not a thing separate from the quail. At the moment I begin to look for meanings and justifications behind the act of hunting, I hinder myself from receiving the gift within the game. We are born, we live, we hunt, we die, we hope to live again, Lord willing. Maybe that is all that needs to be said.

Last week while driving to the feed store to buy dog food I passed a woman walking by the side of the road. She was an arresting sight. Tall, slender, and tan, she moved with confident, effortless rhythm. Strands of her wavy, coal-black hair blew across her face, and she smoothed them aside with her long fingers. Her sleeveless blue dress billowed in the wind like waves on a fertile sea. She was an evocative portrait of youth and vigor. A real head-turner.

About a half mile down the road I passed another woman. Gray, shriveled, and stooped, she moved in geriatric staccato, aided by a walking cane with four rubber feet. She strained, through thick glasses, to see the road before her. Her brown shirt quivered in the wind like sun-baked leaves on a dying tree. She was a haunting portrait of age and barrenness. A real head-shaker.

Then I realized that over the past half mile I had traveled on a journey through time, a journey framed by two glimpses of the selfsame woman. Even the sultriest beauty will return to the dust. I did not want to face that reality when Papaw was dying, but I can no longer ignore it. I am, after all, a hunter like my peasant grandfather before me. I hold this reality in my hand every time my dog brings me a quail I have killed. As Charles Fergus has written, "I kill quickly, eat what I slay, and keep the knowledge of my own death close at hand." In retrospect, that is a lesson I learned from Lee Roy Mason, both in his life and in his death.

In the summer of his days he was an agile sportsman. In the autumn of his days he passed that heritage on to me. Autumn gave way to winter, and he was gone. Now he awaits the glorious spring of resurrection.

Some men and women bequeath little of monetary value but leave legacies that remain unweathered by the relentless wind of time. We who follow them receive a joyous inheritance immune from taxation.

FRANK F. MATHIAS

They Called Him Lucky (An Excerpt)

From *The GI Generation* (2000)

MOM CALLED HIM Charlie, his sisters called him Charles, his sons called him Dad, but everyone else in his world called him Lucky. He signed Lucky to his checks and letters. Mail to him from acquaintances was always addressed to Lucky Mathias. Few people in town knew his real name. He liked it that way; I never once heard him complain.

He did not remember how he picked up his nickname but assumed with everyone else that fishing had something to do with it. Few would argue that he was not the best fisherman in the county. Some held that A. R. "Tickie" Fisher, or Hicel Asbury, or Stan Hutchings, or even Superintendent Pfanstiel— all of them fast friends of his—could hold their own with him. That was probably true on a given day, but week in and week out Lucky had no peers. He fished in every season of every year in every body of water available in Nicholas and surrounding counties. And unlike most others he had plenty of time to fish, for he was completely divorced from any temptation to allow his sales job to take on time-clock dimensions.

Lucky was known everywhere and warmly welcomed to ponds and lakes the owners stoutly denied to most fishermen. He was known as a sportsman who had no intention of "fishing the place out." A few "keepers," usually bass, newlight (crappie), or bream, satisfied him; he carefully dehooked and threw back smaller fish. His disgust with "fish hogs" carrying a string of forty or fifty tiny fish was total. He despised even more the illegal methods some used to get fish. "Dynamiting" was one method, the stunned fish scooped up by the poacher. Another was to get down in the water and "feel them off the nest." This got the fish but kept next year's crop from hatching. Yet another was called "telegraphing." This required a car battery with two pokers, one wired to the positive and the other to the negative pole. When stuck into the water, the electricity stunned nearby fish, and they could be scooped up as they floated to the surface.

Lucky was seldom a sit-down fisherman. He usually walked as he fished, especially if he was after bass. He had a good casting rod with a well-oiled Pflueger reel. He called his casts like a pool hustler calling his pockets: "There's a big bass under that root over there just waiting for me," and with a flick of his wrist the plug invariably lit softly within inches of his target. He seldom lost plug or bait since he nearly always hit where he aimed. Lucky made it look so easy.

Following Lucky as he walked and casted along Licking, Hinkston, Stoner, and other streams was a chore for Speck and me. He was as much at home in this element as a bullfrog or shykpoke (heron). Lucky confidently attacked all obstacles head-on, whether briars, fallen trees with grapevine tangles, overgrown water gaps, collapsed banks, swamps, snakes, farmers' dogs, and the unexpected stuff that came up each trip. His one object was the stream and its fish; all else was secondary, and this sometimes included Speck and me!

We struggled along after him, catching up

when he stopped to cast to "a likely spot over by that stump." We had been with him many times on rough-and-tumble hikes. We knew what to expect. He always headed to his favorite stretches of a stream where he stopped and spent several leisurely hours strolling and casting. But he often got there the hard way, fishing his way through thickets so as not to "miss that big bass I nearly hooked here the last time." Once at his favorite spot, however, he settled down. If it was noontime we had a picnic of sardines, Vienna sausage, and crackers. Speck and I did not think it got much better than that!

Dad's favorite spots were cherished swimming holes for Speck and me, not that we swam near him. On South Licking, for example, an old brick gristmill had tumbled into the river near the village of Berry. Dad fished on the downstream side and we swam above it. The clear water revealed the brick-clad bottom through our fifty-cent water goggles, our early version of snorkeling. When on Fleming Creek, the "blue hole" held our atten-

tion on hot summer afternoons. Hinkston and Fox Creek had exciting stretches of smooth water dappled with sun and shade, and both offered lovely covered bridges to play in and initial and date with our pen knives.

Then there was the johnboat at Millersburg dam. A grocer owned this long, lean, homemade rowboat and let Dad use it whenever he wanted. It took us ten minutes to row upstream to Dad's favorite spot. For some reason he nearly always rinsed off his false teeth on this trip, pulling them out, swishing them in the river, snapping them at us, then putting them back in his mouth. We always tied the johnboat to the same easy-to-get-to tree. The river here was deep, with steep banks and no shallow spots for swimmers to rest. The place always bored my brother and me after fifteen minutes of paddling around.

One afternoon, when Lucky was pole fishing for newlights, I eased from the boat with my goggles, swam underwater twenty feet, tugged his bait hard, then swam underwater back to the boat. He was a study in concentration, mumbling something about either a big turtle or water dog grabbing his line. The next time I did it I had to come up for air before reaching the boat. "I knew it was a water dog," he laughed, throwing a handful of clods splashing about me.

Water dogs deserve mention. They are tailed amphibians with toothy dog-shaped heads and four small legs. They can reach a foot and a half in length and weigh around two pounds. Trot-line fishermen hate them because they bite chunks out of hooked fish. But they often hook themselves when they do this. Every fisherman of my generation knew what had to be done with a caught water dog. Tradition held that the only way one of these baleful looking creatures could be killed was to pound a wooden stake through its heart, pinning it helplessly to the bank. We who did this sensed that we were taking part in a mystery rather than acting foolish. Then came the night several pals and I shuddered through a movie at the Lyric titled *Dracula*. We used much longer and sharper stakes on water dogs after that, often looking over our shoulders as we did so.

Lucky knew the denizens of Kentucky's lakes and streams as well as Ed Metcalfe knew his cattle when he was a Montana cowboy. He was at home there and wanted his sons to be the same. We were, up to a point, but that point was reached when it came to "feeling for turtles." He had done this often, he said, when he was a boy, and he was determined to show us how it was done.

Turtles hang around half-submerged brush piles and overgrown water gaps. They sun themselves on protruding brush or branches. Dad decided to show us how to catch them one afternoon. He peeled down to his BVDS and started feeling his way along a brush-burdened water gap. Water gaps are gatelike affairs of fencing and boards hung across small streams to keep livestock in their assigned fields. Lucky talked as he slowly moved, keeping his hands underwater to feel for a turtle among the morass of sticks and brush.

"You will always know when you touch something alive," he advised. "Always feel your way around the top edge of the turtle's shell until you get to his tail; a snapper can give you a bad bite if you grab his head instead of his tail."

As he talked he felt the tail of something alive. In one quick splashy motion he sent a big water snake flipping through the air, just missing Speck and me. We ducked but saw no room for comment; we had swum with plenty of water snakes. They were a nasty-tempered lot, compared with field snakes, but we knew that the only dangerous ones, cottonmouth water moccasins, did not live in the Bluegrass.

We thanked Dad for showing us how to feel out turtles—he found none at this gap—but we secretly drew the line at water gaps and soggy brush piles. Down in that sunless morass there was bound to be a grabbing, grasping, biting something or other we would be better off to leave strictly alone!

JOHN E. MURPHY

Fly-Fishing Time

From the *Kentucky Post* (September 6, 1963)

SEPTEMBER DRAWS the first delicate blushes from the country-side. Streams gurgle with their most fervent seasonal serenity. The fish and wildlife have reared the young, who are less handsome but more confident by this time than their tired parents.

If there is a specific season of fly-fishing, it is now. For this is the calm interim of nature, a likely matching of man, mind, and the quiet dimension of angling.

FLY-FISHING is a heritage. Pioneer Kentuckians, if they were not feather-flickers, were long rod bait fishermen, and the single-action spool preceded the now-famous "Kentucky multiplying reel," which was lashed to the cane reed rod and stood alongside the Kentucky rifle in the cabin corner.

This oldest form of sport fishing is geared to peace. The disciple of the fly rod will invariably let his pipe grow cold frequently, will countenance a thorough bird dog, and will be in no rush to reach the next pool. Thus fly-fishing is well-bred through leisure. Its very character and rhythm are flowing and cannot be hurried, which is its blessing. Time in centuries has changed it but little.

FLY-FISHING, like walking alone, needs no additional goal.

Swallowed flies are a bonus, often the awakening from the

abstract that envelops the methodical fly-fisherman. The encounter is more stimulating than combative. And the harvest is much like the destructive cracking of a shiny nut that has been smooth and pleasant to the touch.

FLY-FISHING is exact and limitless. It is the world of the inchworm, searching in a graceful arc of sensitivity.

The deception is in the hands of the angler through the light divining rod, and the bulk of the terminal enticement is but a minor factor.

All fish love flies, and it is their innate longing rather than their lust and savagery that causes them to engage the fly rod angler.

MOST STABLE is the fly-fisherman's tackle, as steady as the art's emotion.

The ancient aura is constant, but the progressive individual rays are perhaps more opaque in the light of improved equipment accompanying the dream. This banishes the nightmares!

There is no small, cussed corner in the household of the contented modern fly-fisher, user of synthetics.

DWELL, THEN, on September, and the reverie of fly-fishing. Linger.

THOMAS D. SCHIFFER

The Kentucky Longrifle (2004)

> But Jackson he was wide awake
> He wasn't scar'd at trifles
> for well he knew what aim we take
> With our Kentucky Rifles.

THE KENTUCKY LONGRIFLE occupies an integral part in the legend, song, and story of American history. It dates from the time pioneers attempted to cross the mountains and break away from the eastern seaboard. In the hands of legendary men such as Daniel Boone, Ebenezer Zane, Benjamin Logan, Simon Kenton, and many others, it was, and is, a symbol of pioneering and of confronting the unknown—a symbol not far removed, if at all, from the minutemen of Revolutionary War fame.

The lines quoted above are from a popular ballad by Samuel Woodworth called "The Hunters of Kentucky." It was written in celebration of the Kentuckian's role, under Andrew Jackson, in winning the Battle of New Orleans in 1815. As will be seen, the Kentucky longrifle was the primary tool of both the hunter and the militiaman, who were, for the most part, one and the same. I would not be surprised to learn that Woodworth's ballad is responsible for etching the name "Kentucky rifle" permanently into our present-day lexicon.

The Kentucky longrifle holds a fascination for me for several reasons, not the least of which is the graceful way the makers combined the basic elements of lock, stock, and barrel. Having caught my eye, it soon became apparent that a lot of interesting and important history was made with the Kentucky rifle in the hands of people both ordinary and extraordinary. A closer look showed me that it was a thoroughly practical and efficient tool as pioneers ranged farther into hostile territory. These venues were often far from any source of supply, and any vestiges of civilization had to be carried long distances by manpower or by canoe or pack horse. Often the best roads were game trails and rivers.

The Kentucky longrifle was developed to fit into this picture. It gradually evolved from a form of rifle used in Europe, where a strict guild system held sway. It is my opinion that the new-found freedom of thought and action in the New World hastened the evolution of a somewhat moribund design. The needs of the frontier called for lighter (smaller) calibers to conserve ammunition. Calibers were not reckoned in inches back then, but rather in gauge—how many lead balls (that is, bullets) to the pound. To give you a frame of reference, a .36-caliber would take 98 balls to the pound; a .45-caliber would take about 52, a .50-caliber about 39, a .54-caliber about 32, and a .58-caliber about 26. A .73-caliber rifle would take a bullet weighing in at 12 balls to the pound, or a 12-gauge shotgun, if you will. (Remember that the weight goes up with the cube of the diameter.) For people setting off into the unknown, that would be something to consider. In the Kentucky longrifle, a caliber somewhere around 50 to the pound was reckoned to be optimum, considering power, range, and weight.

I don't know what amount of powder was used in rifles on the frontier, but if a charge weighing 70 grains was used, the velocity would be close to 2,000 feet per second (fps); with 100 grains, over 2,300 fps. With the former, a frontiersman could get 100 loads out of a pound of powder; 70 loads with the latter. "Loaded for bear" might mean an even bigger charge with two balls in place—not a load one would want to get in front of, and no joy to be behind, either, considering the effects of re-coil. Even the 70-grain load far exceeds the muzzle energy of the famous .44-40 cartridge fired from a rifle. And some experts have rated the .44-40 as the greatest deer harvester in history.

Though it tended to have a smaller caliber, the barrel on the Kentucky longrifle grew longer than that of the parent Jaeger (hunting) rifles of the old country. The commonly held belief is that the longer barrel provided more velocity with a given pow-der charge. While this is certainly true, I think the longer bar-rel design had more practical reasons. For one thing, eyeglasses were rare in those days, and with the sight placed farther from the eye, targets were easier to acquire and line up. (Those of you who are past the blush of youth are likely all too familiar with this phenomenon; you youngsters will just have to wonder what we are talking about for a while yet.) Also, the barrel of the Ken-tucky longrifle approached four feet (versus the two and a half feet common in Europe). This put the overall length just shy of five feet. With the butt on the ground and the barrel vertical, this would bring the muzzle to just below chin height in an av-erage man. For a muzzleloader, this was an important factor in terms of safety and efficiency in loading—it put the muzzle right where you could see it and control it.

Despite the differences in caliber and barrel length, the in-spiration of the Jaeger rifle is obvious; the Kentucky longrifle clearly sprang from this Germanic source. But since the iron-clad rules of the old guild system were nonexistent in this coun-try, there was a certain relaxation of workmanship—keeping in mind that functionality was still considered paramount. The

Kentucky longrifle featured changes in dimension and style to suit newfound needs, and it embodied the ideas of the individual craftsmen who fashioned it. The source of ignition was the time-tested flintlock, the barrel continued to be made of iron, the bore contained rifling of about one turn in five or six feet, and the stock simply accommodated the new dimensions. The stock was traditionally made of curly maple stained dark with aqua fortis. The old patchbox in the off-side butt of the stock was retained, and the triggers, either plain or set, were nothing new. The ramrod, still used to load and clean the rifle, was carried under the barrel in pipe keepers. The sights were finely made and set into the top of the barrel, carefully regulated to the point of impact of the bullet. The rifle was often engraved with symbols reflecting religious ideals in a primitive, folk-art style. All these features harked back to the Jaeger rifle. There are those who hold that the system of patching the ball with cloth was a New World innovation, but there is evidence to belie this notion.

Stylistic features (along with length) are what visually set the Kentucky longrifle apart from the Jaeger. This styling is distinctive and has been arranged into "schools" by scholars on the subject, both past and present. Thus, a rifle made in Virginia has stylistic features that set it apart from those made in Pennsylvania or North Carolina; there are even subdivisions of these concepts. Suffice it to say that, for the most part, each individual Kentucky longrifle is unique. Some are mounted with brass fittings, others with iron. Some have a simple grease hole bored in the stock in the place of a patchbox. Despite these differences, the longrifles of all these schools retain a common functionality.

The Kentucky longrifle, along with the axe, became a staple

of pioneer households. It was used to defend the hearth and to harvest some of the frontier bounty for the table. It was the right tool for the job.

Kentucky longrifles were carefully cleaned, dried, and reloaded before venturing into hostile territory or big-game country. With a sharp flint and dry priming, they were very sure of fire, accurate, and sufficiently powerful for the usual game taken, primarily deer, elk, bear, and the occasional bison. For smaller game, such as a squirrel, the "loaded for bear" rifle would tend to render the animal unfit for the table. Because these muzzle-loaders were not easily unloaded and reloaded with a smaller charge, some woodsmen adopted the method of "barking" a squirrel with a full-charge load. This consisted of shooting at the branch under the squirrel; with luck, the flying bark and wood would stun or kill the animal, leaving it intact. Friends of mine who have tried it have had mixed success, but I am convinced that it can be a viable method.

No less a naturalist than John James Audubon told of the Kentucky longrifle's use by frontiersmen competing in shooting matches. One took place in the dead of night, the flame of a candle being the target.

Men were not the only users of the Kentucky longrifle. My former history professor, Dr. Charles Talbert, relates in his biography *Benjamin Logan, Kentucky Frontiersman* (University of Kentucky Press, 1976), that in one shooting match, the prize was simply the lead from the spent bullets in the target, which illustrates just how precious lead was on the frontier. Talbert quotes the Draper Manuscript as saying that William Whitley, upon seeing this rifle match, handed his rifle to his wife, Esther, and urged her to take a turn. "Her first shot beat the best that had been made and the men continued until dark without being able to equal her record."

But it was the Battle of New Orleans in 1815 that launched the Kentucky longrifle into the legendary place it still occupies.

Poems were written in praise of it, and the stories likely lost little in the telling. We often hear in later times (I never heard of such a claim dating from its heyday) that it was not a Kentucky longrifle at all but a Pennsylvania longrifle or a Pennsylvania-Kentucky rifle. What they call one made in Virginia, Maryland, Tennessee, or the Carolinas is not on record. My opinion is that an elephant rifle is still an elephant rifle, regardless of where it was made.

In 1963, some fellows from Pennsylvania rode on horseback down the old warrior's trail to Frankfort, Kentucky, where they literally threw down the gauntlet on Governor Bert T. Combs's desk. They challenged Kentucky to a rifle match to determine, once and for all, the proper name of the rifle. The governor accepted the challenge and turned to Colonel George Chinn (who wrote the definitive work on the machine gun) to ensure that the Kentucky team was recruited by Colonel James Malcom VanDevier. The Kentucky team prevailed in that and subsequent matches held in both Kentucky and Pennsylvania. A prize longrifle, mounted on a suitable plaque, hung in the governor's office for many years. That team and its spirit still exist, and it was my honor to captain the team during much of the 1970s. Competitions are held at Boonesborough every October, and many other states now compete on the same field. It is spectacular to see them standing shoulder to shoulder in period dress and using recently made, originally styled, Kentucky longrifles.

In the late 1920s, Kentucky longrifles had been out of the limelight for many years when a group of fellows around Portsmouth, Ohio, decided to see how the old smoke poles would compare with small-bore rifles. Back then, percussion ignition held full sway among those who decided to go the muzzleloading route. Depending on who was lurking behind the butt plate, the muzzleloader gave a good account of itself. So much fun was had that Oscar Seth, Red Farriss, and others organized the National Muzzle Loading Rifle Association (NMLRA) in 1933 to perpetuate the sport. From humble beginnings, it burgeoned into a multidisciplinary organization that currently owns and operates several shoots per year on 500-plus acres of land in southeastern Indiana. It must be said that a small group of diehards in the hills of eastern Tennessee and Kentucky continues to make and use the old rifles. Another group in Canal Fulton, Ohio, claims to be the oldest continuing muzzleloading club in the country.

As the NMLRA grew in numbers and strength, members initiated a newsletter that evolved into a magazine called *Muzzle Blasts*. For a number of years, percussion ignition was most popular on the firing lines, and flint ignition was only occasionally used by those considered to be on the fringes of sanity. As time went on, flintlock ignition Kentucky longrifles started to edge their way into the percussion matches, where they were tolerated because they were considered disadvantaged. But once a good number of first-place prizes in percussion matches were carried off by the flint boys and girls, they were given matches of their own. Many of us would then shoot the Percussion Offhand Aggregate with our "flinters" as a warmup for the Flintlock Offhand Aggregate. I never felt disadvantaged to enter percussion matches with my flint rifle. Nearly all this flint shooting was done with newly made rifles—the originals were now too valuable to campaign.

The NMLRA embraces far more than just Kentucky longrifles. Programs are put on for rifle, pistol, and shotgun. Rifle matches at ranges from a few yards to over 500 yards are held at the national shoots. Pistol matches for caplocks, flintlocks, and revolvers are offered. Shotgun shooters have a choice of trap, skeet, quail walk, and sporting clays. Some require primitive attire as well as firearms.

I can remember a time when the first five places in the Flintlock Offhand Aggregate were taken by members of the Corps of Kentucky Longriflemen with their Kentucky longrifles, with Jerry Pilyer taking first prize that year. It was my honor to serve the NMLRA as director, vice president, and then president from 1989 to 1992.

The making of new Kentucky longrifles, as well as other reproductions of vintage pieces, became a cottage industry. The first ones were primitive indeed. Workmanship was often quite acceptable, but it was obvious that most of the makers didn't know what the rifles should look like. It is difficult to produce accurate three-dimensional firearms from two-dimensional photographs in books. Eventually, the NMLRA, in conjunction with Western Kentucky University, started a gunsmithing school, offering classes in the arts and crafts necessary to produce such work. Wallace Gusler, master gunsmith of Colonial Williamsburg, John Bivins of the Museum of Early Southern Decorative Arts, master engraver Lynton McKenzie, and Kentuckian Hershel House were a few of the early presenters at these weeklong seminars in the art of rifle making. The school was held for a couple of years at Northern Kentucky University, before returning to Western. The fruit of these labors is breathtaking. In fact, the Minneapolis Institute of Arts mounted a large exhibit of this work entitled "Three Centuries of Tradition: The Renaissance of Custom Sporting Arms in America." The catalog accompanying the exhibit features 192 pages of beautifully photographed currently made firearms, along with some selected original pieces. Not all of these are Kentucky longrifles, but many of them are.

Many years ago, the NMLRA championed the creation of special hunting seasons for primitive weapons. With the cooperation of the Departments of Natural Resources in several states, certain times of the year are now reserved for such activity. Kentucky has such a season. The Kentucky longrifle is well suited to take advantage of such seasons. A rifle of sufficient caliber can be used to take any game in North America by tailoring the load to the game sought. Instead of indulging in the "barking" of squirrels, the rifle is simply loaded down to the level required. Muzzleloading rifles of many descriptions have been used to harvest game all over the world, including Africa. Many hunters use their flint Kentucky longrifles in the regular gun season for big game and get excellent results.

So, you can readily see that a good Kentucky longrifle, with the proper loads and loading, can, even in this day and time, provide endless hours of fun and sport. If you will but listen to its story, it will give you a real appreciation for the many blessings you have inherited. I wish you good shooting. With a Kentucky longrifle, you can do it!

DAVE "MUDCAT" SHUFFETT

The Scolding (2004)

Dedicated to my dad, Judge Billy Shuffett

LITTLE BOYS will always need an occasional "talking to," no matter how old they are. That was the lesson I learned not long ago when, at the age of 46, I got one more scolding from my 81-year-old dad. First he gave me that same old facial expression I'd seen all my life—it's a cross between contemplative and pained. I knew I had done something of which he didn't approve. Trying to be firm in his aging voice, he said, "You're letting little Willie watch too many of those video games. It'll ruin him, if you don't get him away from that stuff. I don't want to tell you what to do, but I am anyway."

With that advice fresh in my mind, I began to ponder just how much my little boy was playing video games. For the most part, Dad was right. We didn't need to get Willie "away from that stuff" totally, but there was no denying he had become addicted to one contraption called the Game Cube.

For those who are as technologically inept as I am, the Game Cube is a little box that can turn your TV screen into a state-of-the-art video game. Since we got the Game Cube, Willie had become increasingly disinterested in the outdoors and all the other things little fellows have done for countless generations to occupy their time, and his parents were willing accomplices. When he played that thing, he was completely enamored, allowing mom and dad to get other things done. Sound familiar?

Back in 1961, Dad took me on my first fishing trip. The Green

River was the backdrop of my introduction to the great outdoors. I was only three, but I swear I can still remember that trip. For sure I can recall the dozens of float trips in the years afterward.

Dad loved to fish for smallmouth bass and goggle-eye, and always, in the back of his mind, were grand thoughts of a monstrous muskie taking his Heddon "River Runt." It was all a rush for me. I can vividly recall looking up at bright puffy clouds against a turquoise-blue sky, gazing at upside down reflections of trees and boulders. There was the unforgettable feeling of a fighting smallmouth bass—with a one-two punch that sets him apart from other fish—and the sound of our old wooden johnboat raking against rocks as it stopped against a gravel bar when it was time for dinner, which in those days meant the noontime meal.

The river runs right through the heart of my little hometown of Greensburg. Residents have had a close kinship with the river since the town was settled in the late 1700s. Before them, the Native Americans hunted along her banks and fished her waters with bone fishhooks.

I look at the Green as if she were an old woman who's always been there—a provider to the children who have borrowed from her waters for more than 10,000 years. That kind of love is deep-rooted and passed down from great-great-grandfathers, whom I wish I could have known. Also, I believe that some kind of genetic memory comes into play when something is such an integral part of one's heritage. Had I been raised a thousand miles from the Green, I believe that somehow, I still would have known her. If, on some fateful day, I had the good fortune to encounter her while drifting and casting for smallmouths, I believe a sense of déjà vu would have come over me as a hundred ancestors whispered "welcome home."

But river passions can turn to rage, as happened back in 1965, when a controversy over the state-record muskie packed the courtrooms. Public documents state that Green River fisherman Quentin Vance set out two bank poles baited with live suckers and proceeded to leave the scene. Then Otha Durrett entered the picture. According to Durrett's testimony, he tested Vance's lines and found a baitless hook. He claimed  that he rebaited the hook with another sucker and soon got a strike. Allegedly, a giant muskie leaped 10 feet out of the water and broke the line. The fish flopped into shallow water, where Durrett jumped in and caught the fish by hand. The muskie weighed 51 pounds, handily beating the previous state record.

The story ran in the *Greensburg Record-Herald* and, as you would expect in a small town, was read by Quentin Vance, who filed suit claiming the muskie as his own. A jury awarded Vance $750 in damages and the state-record title; however, Durrett and his team of lawyers appealed the case, which floundered in packed courtrooms for years before Vance gave up his pursuit.

And there are the little stories that survive because you can see it happening so easily in your imagination. According to Dad, he and his brother-in-law, Sam Moore, were floating the Green one spring day in about 1939 when they pulled up to a weed bed next to a gravel bar. Spooked by the boat and trapped by the weeds, a largemouth bass jumped into the boat and right into Sam's open tackle box. The fish flopped around and then jumped back in the water adorned with five or six of Sam's favorite handmade lures.

And there are the countless memories of my own—of Dad paddling with one arm and fishing with the other, and when I caught one, he would yell (I can still hear him, plain as day), "That-a-boy! Bring him in here!"

Dad knew he was building character by spending unforgettable, precious moments with his children. Unknown to me at the time, those hours together in the outdoors were laying a foundation I could fall back on, after the wildness of my late teens and early twenties. Eventually, I rediscovered those old rushes of adrenaline—the kind when a smallmouth violently bursts from the water trying to shake off a Rapala.

These days, my dear old dad, now a widower, is slowing down. The deep wrinkles in his face are time lines from a life of magnificent experiences—from the young, courageous soldier in the Second World War to the great father he came home to be. That one last scolding he provided was perhaps the most important one I've had. I recently took little Willie to his first Cub Scout meeting. We've got a lake fishing trip planned for the spring, and a half dozen Green River float-fishing trips are on the calendar, too. Day hikes, camping, and long talks around the campfire await us, all thanks to the man who never gave up his role as father, grandfather, and lover of the Green.

STEPHEN M. VEST

Chapter Added to Rich History

From *Kentucky Monthly* (June 2000)

LONG BEFORE written histories documented the fact, Kentucky was a hunting ground for the Iroquois, the Shawnee, and the Algonquin.

In 1763 Elisha Walden led a dozen Long Hunters through the Cumberland Gap into Kentucky. They described it as a virgin wilderness teeming with "game waiting to be killed . . . clear streams filled with delectable fish eager to be caught." Kentucky was a paradise populated by "countless turkeys and other fowls [that] longed to be eaten."

Within three years Virginian and Carolinian Long Hunters had made it west to the Mississippi. They would hunt all they could carry. In June 1769, according to hunter Abraham Bledsoe, 20 Long Hunters netted 2,300 deer in one trip.

The Long Hunters, nicknamed for the distance and time they would spend away from home, hunted mostly for the pelts, which angered the Indians they came in contact with and caused much tension between them.

Many of the commonwealth's early settlers—Daniel Boone, Simon Kenton, and James Knox—were Long Hunters. Charlie Kramer, Shelby County's tourism director, could be called a Long Hunter, and he would like to see Kentucky build on its hunting heritage and use hunting and fishing to draw tourism to some of the state's less-populated areas.

"Who wouldn't want to come to Kentucky with all we have to offer in terms of the outdoors?" Kramer asked. "We just need a way to get the word out."

Kramer loves hunting and he loves telling others how much he loves hunting and how much they would love it if they would just explore the opportunities.

It was this hunting passion that led him to call me with an invitation to join him for a western Kentucky turkey hunt. "When you see that turkey for the first time, your heart will race and the hairs will stand up on the back of your neck," he said.

You must understand that my own hunting heritage is scant at best. My maternal grandfather owned a wooden duck call, and my uncle Gus in Florida once killed a bear—evidenced by my aunt Mabel's bearskin rug. My dad once owned a .410 shotgun he used for hunting rabbits near Verona, but he traded the gun for a wristwatch upon his return from World War II.

As shocking as it may sound, I had never been hunting before. I had never before worn camouflage nor fired a shotgun.

My non-Baptist relations supposedly went Wild Turkey hunting every Thanksgiving, but I think that was for the liquid variety that is bottled near Lawrenceburg. I can't remember them ever bringing home a bird, but they always seemed happy after the hunt.

I explained my naivete to Kramer, which I figured would dissuade him from inviting me, but I was wrong. My claims, "Uh, I don't own a gun . . . I don't own a vest (yes, I'm named Vest, but I don't own one) . . . I don't have any boots . . . don't have a hunting license," were answered one by one. If I would just get a license and drive as far as the Morgantown Dairy Queen, Kramer would take care of the rest.

It was a little after 9 P.M. when I made my rendezvous with Kramer and Loyd Forbes, upon whose family farm my indoctrination into the world of tick repellent would take place. Forbes lives on 240 acres in Butler County, southwest of Morgantown.

The house where we spent the night is one of several on the farm that goes back six generations.

Climbing out of bed a little before 5 A.M., I layered two camouflage shirts over a vest and then strapped on another camouflage vest complete with a seat cushion to make sitting in the woods a little less aggravating. The amount of camouflage needed amazed me. My boots, my gloves, even my 12-gauge shotgun, on loan from Kramer, were camouflage.

Slipping off the paved road near an old family cemetery, we proceeded down a hill, across a stream, and into a clearing cut for utility towers. "The birds often come into this clearing in the morning to sun themselves and feed," Forbes explained. "They've been coming here for weeks unbothered, so they should be back this morning."

My instructors, whispering, showed me how to remain unseen and what to look for. I snuggled my back up against a tree, and they moved into positions to my right. It was almost 5:30 and time to wait. Six A.M. came and went, then 6:30, 7, and 7:30. At about 7:45, Forbes was certain we were wasting our time.

We had heard a few clucks and gobbles but had seen nothing. I had fallen asleep twice. "I don't understand it," he said. "Someone must have been hunting here yesterday, that's all I can guess."

We were now on the move. We scouted each of the rain-soaked lower fields of the Forbes farm. With my boots filling with water, Forbes directed us to our second location of the morning. He placed two inflatable decoys in a path that circled the field where he had scored the 12-point buck that graced the wall above the bed where I had spent the night.

"Right over there is where I shot my first bird," he whispered. "Over there is where I got my first deer."

Nestled in against another tree, I awaited my prey. Forbes stretched out on his belly to my right. Kramer, who had an assortment of birdcalls, was positioned up the hill to my left.

The wait began again. Nine A.M. came and went, then 9:30, 10. I remembered the time the Boy Scouts had taken my Webelos troop snipe hunting.

Scanning left and right without turning my head, I continued to look. Forbes clicked his tongue against the roof of his mouth. Out of the corner of my left eye, I could see the turkey, which was later described to me as a 20-pound, 2-year-old Jake, strolling down the path toward the decoys. I raised the gun, found him in the sights, and tracked him left to right. He passed behind a tree. The barrel then caught on a small twig and he crossed behind yet another tree and then into clear view.

I didn't know if I could do it, but surprising even myself, I pulled the trigger. After more than five hours of peaceful silence, broken only by hushed whispers, the blast startled me nearly as much as it did the bird.

Through the scope, I could see the black-and-red turkey turn, as if startled. He then spun back, making eye contact before rising above the field intended for soybeans. The glorious bird rose to about 30 feet, turned to its left, and slowly climbed over the trees and into the valley below the main house and out of view.

"I guess I missed," I said, drawing muffled chuckles from my partners.

"Well, but you got off a shot," Kramer said. "Some people go weeks without even taking a shot."

"But," I said. "I thought I got him."

"I think you let him get too close," Forbes said. "That gun is designed for 30 yards. When you fired he couldn't have been more than 15 yards away."

We hiked back to the farmhouse in silence.

Charlie and Loyd weren't sure if I had fully enjoyed the experience without tagging a turkey. "You looked like you were sleeping a couple of times," said Loyd.

"I was," I said.

"Did you find it that boring?"

"No, I found it *that* relaxing," I said. "I loved being out in the woods away from the telephone and the fax machine. Just being on the hunt was good enough for me."

After one of the grandest breakfasts I have ever eaten, I loaded up the Grand Am and headed home. Back in Frankfort, I was greeted with the rest of the story.

"Charlie Kramer called," I was told. "He tried to reach you on your cell phone, but you must have had it turned off. They found your turkey and wanted you to come back and get your picture taken with it."

"They found my turkey? Where'd they find my turkey?"

"Kramer said it was the strangest thing. They were going back out and there he was in the valley below the house, just sitting in the road. At first they thought he was sunning himself, but he didn't move. There wasn't a scratch on him. Best they could figure, you'd scared him so bad, he'd had a heart attack."

JOHN WILSON

Old Reels

From *Happy Hunting Ground* (July 1973)

IN 1810, GEORGE SNYDER, a silversmith in Paris, Kentucky, had an idea. Let's assume that it came to him in March, just when the first buds began to appear and only the faintest hint of green colored the fields, came to him during those first few warm days of spring when Snyder, in anticipation of fishing trips to come, was walking along Stoner Creek.

Then, for the next few weeks, while winter returned to play out the last seemingly interminable act of its seasonal drama, Snyder stayed indoors at his lathe while under his hands his idea took shape, and when he once again appeared on Stoner Creek he carried his invention with him.

George Snyder had made the first bait-casting reel with multiplying gears—that is, one turn of the handle causes the spool to revolve several times. It isn't known if he realized that his reel was the first of its kind, but what happened on that historic first cast is almost certain. He baited his hook with a big minnow (or maybe a nightcrawler or two), leaned back and tried to throw his bait all the way across the river, then watched in amazement as all his line tried to jump off the spool at the same time, tangling itself into the most incredible series of knots and snarls imaginable.

History mercifully does not record what Snyder called this first backlash, but variations, all equally unprintable, have been used by fishermen ever since. In any event, Snyder soon learned to use his thumb to control the spool and began making a few more reels to sell to his friends and neighbors. This was in the days before mass manufacturing and merchandising, so he remained content to keep his reel making as a small sideline to his jewelry and silversmithing business.

Snyder never knew the impact his invention would have on fishing throughout the world, never foresaw the hundreds and thousands of anglers who would use the direct descendants of his reel to catch everything from bluegill to sailfish, never guessed that tournament casting would develop into an international sport. In fact, Snyder's role in developing the casting reel was virtually forgotten until the 1930s, when he was rediscovered by Mrs. Wade H. Whitley, a Bourbon County historian.

It's only about 40 miles from Paris to Frankfort, but in the early 1800s, that was at least a five-hour trip. News, like everything else then, traveled slowly, and it was over 20 years after Snyder made his first reel that Jonathan Meek, a Frankfort jeweler, was commissioned to produce a similar article. Here again the historical record is scant, and we'll probably never know the exact date or circumstances of the first Frankfort reel.

Different versions of the story place it as early as 1832 to as late as 1839 when Judge Mason Brown learned about the Snyder reel and asked Meek to make him one. Some sources say that Brown had invited some friends from Paris to Frankfort for a fishing trip and they brought a couple of Snyder's reels with them. Brown liked them, and took one to Meek for him to copy. Another version has it that Brown owned a Snyder reel and hired Meek to make a replacement when he lost the original. Yet a third story completely discounts Snyder's role and maintains that Brown independently asked Meek to develop a reel for him.

But the important point is that Meek accepted the job and in so doing started an industry in Frankfort that was to last until after World War II. It is probable that Meek turned some, if not all, of the job over to his younger brother Benjamin, who although still a teenager, was purported to be a better craftsman than many men twice his age. It is also very likely that there was a young apprentice, Benjamin Milam, in the Meeks' shop when the first reel was made.

This reel was probably made of brass and had a 4:1 gear ratio —the first "quadruple multiplying" reel. This gearing became and still is standard on most reels. Brown liked his reel, and soon the Meeks started receiving orders for others. Since the reels were entirely handmade, production was slow, seldom exceeding at its peak seven reels a month. Until 1853, all reels made were stamped "J. F. and B. F. Meek," although Ben Meek and Ben Milam accounted for the total output. Between 1853 and 1880, the reels were stamped "Meek & Milam," but all were made by Milam, Meek having gotten completely out of the reel business for the time being in 1855. A "Milam" reel is one made between 1880 and 1927, with the later ones built by Ben Milam's son John after his father's death in 1904.

Ben Meek moved to Louisville, where in 1882 he again started making reels, continuing with his two sons until his death in 1898. He is generally credited with developing most of the refinements in the Kentucky reel, including pivotal gearing and jeweled bearings. According to one source, he was also instrumental in perfecting an early level-wind mechanism. He was sent a prototype level-wind device in which, in use, according to its inventor, "a noise was produced resembling the onward movement of an ice wagon." Meek improved the device, charging $75 for his services. But his client was so impressed with the workmanship that he sent Meek an extra $10 in appreciation.

Another well-known Frankfort reel maker was the firm of George W. Gayle & Son, a company that is still in business in Frankfort, although no longer making reels. Gayle was a worker in the Meeks' shop, and in 1882 he, along with his son Clarence (then 16), began making reels. Clarence Gayle continued to build

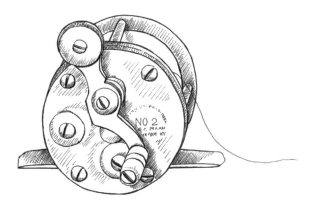

reels through the 1940s, making him the last representative of the traditional Kentucky reel craftsmen.

There's an interesting story connected with the Gayle reels. Just before World War II, the company was mass-producing a stamped metal reel that sold for a quarter. The Japanese, however, copied the reel, and the imported version was being sold in the dime stores for 10 cents. Then, during the war, the Gayle Company contracted with the government to make some small precision parts for the military. Clarence Gayle, who was then in his late seventies, worked himself relentlessly, even having a barber chair brought into his shop so he could obey his doctor's orders to lie down and yet, by swiveling his chair, supervise all phases of the work. When asked why he was working so hard, he replied that in addition to the war efforts he had a personal grudge against the Japanese because they had stolen his reel. It was only after the war was over that he learned just how effective his labors had been: the parts he had made were used in the atomic bomb.

Anyone examining these early Kentucky reels for the first time will be surprised by their beauty, precision, and elegance. The men who made them were jewelers and silversmiths as well as skilled machinists and proud craftsmen, and in both their materials and their attitudes they blended an aesthetic quality with sound functional design, producing an end product that no modern assembly line can hope to match.

The majority of these reels were made of German silver (although some early ones were brass), and each part was painstakingly measured and matched by hand to the others. Each reel was unique, and parts were not interchangeable. In fact, in some models even the screws and screw holes were correspondingly numbered so that each screw could be replaced in its proper slot.

These old masters took no patents on their reels, knowing that their own skill was better protection against imitation than the whole legal system, and in fact they issued a challenge welcoming anyone who thought he could make a better product, or even one as good, to try his hand. This quality they built into their reels is best shown by their longevity—reels that have been used for 60, 70, or even 100 years show no appreciable signs of wear and still operate as smoothly and flawlessly as when they left the hands of their creators.

When B. F. Meek or Ben Milam or Clarence Gayle stamped their names on a reel, it was with a sense of accomplishment and achievement similar to what an artist experiences when, with a flourish, he signs his painting. And like other works of art, their handmade reels could and did command prices reflecting the care and skill that went into them. In 1850, the J. F. & B. F. Meek reel sold for $75, and Clarence Gayle in the 1930s advertised models ranging from $100 to $200. If these reels were sold today at prices with the same proportion to the average wage, they would cost anywhere from $750 to $1,500.

It is obvious then that only the wealthy could afford a genuine Frankfort reel, but needless to say, the majority of fishermen then, as now, weren't rich. So before mass production methods made inexpensive reels available, poor but resourceful fishermen came up with quite satisfactory substitutes.

One homemade reel, now owned by Fred Gordon of Frankfort, consists of a spool approximately 5 inches in diameter and one-half inch wide which is grooved about a half-inch deep so it resembles a pulley wheel. This spool is attached by a spindle (a blunted nail) at right angles to another trough-shaped piece of wood which is attached to the rod. The spool can turn freely on the nail, but what makes casting possible is the addition of pork rind washers on either side of the spool where the nail passes through. The grease from the rind produces a constant supply of lubrication and permits quite long casts. One of these reels had not been used for years, but when it was taken out in the sun for photographs, the rinds began oozing grease again and soon the spool was spinning freely.

These reels, both the homemade and the expensive, were used with limber rods sometimes up to 10 feet long. Baits were cast side-armed with a wide sweeping motion. Both to counterbalance the weight of the rod and to serve as a support, the handles of these rods were quite long—18 to 24 inches—and the rod was held so that the section behind the reel rested against the underside of the forearm. Holding the rod in this manner worked well with the side-arm cast and was quite comfortable. Rods were made of cane, hickory, or other suitable native woods, and the reel was sometimes taped or tied to the rod, although the ones generally used with the more expensive reels usually had a metal reel seat and either a polished wooden handle or one wrapped with rope.

The side-arm cast with this type of equipment was popular until after the turn of the century, when the overhead cast with shorter rods came into vogue. It was also around this time that artificial lures started being used and bait-casting tackle began rapidly growing in popularity. Ironically, this popularity marked the virtual end of the handcrafted Kentucky reel—the greatly increased demand made mass production methods necessary, and reel making moved out of the small shop and onto the factory assembly lines.

In one way this was fortunate for the fisherman of average means, because it greatly lowered prices. Today a first-quality casting reel costs between $30 and $50, around $25 less than the handmade ones of 100 years ago, although modern reels, despite the addition of a few later developments such as star drags and anti-backlash devices, have changed very little. Even a popular modern reel made in Sweden clearly shows the direct descent from its ancestors of Paris and Frankfort, not just in its general shape and design but also in its craftsmanship and precision of operation. The Meeks, Milams, and Gayles of Kentucky not only showed the way, they also set standards of excellence that few have been able to equal and probably none surpass.

STEPHEN M. WRINN

A Connecticut Yankee in
a Kentucky Trout Stream

From the *Kentucky Fishing Journal* (August 2002)

AMONG THE MANY MYTHS that outsiders have come to believe about Kentucky is that it has no outstanding trout fishing. Despite 13,000 miles of rivers and streams, and more navigable waterways than any other state except Alaska, it is still widely believed that only bass, catfish, panfish, and the occasional muskie lurk in the commonwealth's depths. Until very recently, I too shared this fiction.

This is the story of my enlightenment, and of the knowledge I gained after one trip to the Cumberland River. I now believe that Kentucky is home to a river that ranks as one of the best trout fisheries on the continent, period. Not just in the South, or in the Midwest, or west of the Appalachians, or east of the Mississippi. Period. Below the Wolf Creek Dam, the Cumberland is a river that, in both natural beauty and trout population, rivals any I've encountered. And I've encountered more than my fair share.

IN MY BRIEFCASE, tucked behind a thick file of paperwork labeled "To Do," I carry a cheap plastic photo album of some of my most memorable fishing trips. I've learned that it comes in handy to keep these photos nearby, especially after one of those long, hard, frustrating days at work. You know, the kind of day we try to forget when we're fishing.

Looking at the album, I'll see some of the gorgeous brown trout I caught in Scotland, the huge steelheads I landed in New York, and the many rainbows from my home state of Connecticut. There are the beautiful little native brookies from New Hampshire, the smallmouth bass in Maine, the northern pike in Vermont, and, of course, the six-pound golden trout I caught in Pennsylvania as my envious father-in-law looked on, which is now mounted on the wall of my office.

There are a lot of pictures and even more memories. When some unfortunate soul with a casual interest in fishing mentions the topic, I reach for the album and narrate the stories of the many gigantic striped bass I've caught off the Rhode Island coast, the countless bluefish in Massachusetts, the flounder in Delaware, the incredible false albacores off the outer banks of North Carolina. I've stalked trout in some of the nation's finest rivers, and, outside of New England, I've caught them in Wyoming, Montana, Idaho, Colorado, West Virginia, Maryland, Virginia, and Washington State. Before my son, Eli, was born 18 months ago, I had caught trout in 18 consecutive months.

While I consider trout my favorite quarry, I'm not one to discriminate against a good tug at the end of my line. Freshwater, saltwater, spinning rods, fly rods, lures, live bait—I'll do whatever it takes (I wish I was exaggerating) to catch fish, wherever, whenever, however. Have I mentioned the redfish I netted in South Carolina, the tarpon in Florida, or the bonefish in Mexico? Occasionally, on business trips, I've been so desperate for a fight that I've fished the Hudson River from the shores of Manhattan, and I even caught shad and catfish in the Potomac River in the heart of our nation's capital. The bumper sticker "Fish tremble when they hear my name" has always held a special resonance for me.

I believe, with the same conviction with which Fox Mulder

pursued the "truth," that the fish are out there, and my philosophy is that any species of fish I haven't yet caught is one I'd like to feel tugging at the end of my line. I don't even eat fish and will release any that my wife doesn't care to consume. At last count, I had caught fish in 22 states and 4 countries—and man, those red snappers in St. Lucia fought like tigers!

Kentucky was definitely not on the list of places where I'd caught fish. In fact, the commonwealth never even ranked as a fishing destination for me.

When word arrived that I was a finalist for a job in Lexington, I did what any devoted fisherman would do. I immediately went online, accessed Google, and typed, "fishing . . . Kentucky." It came as no surprise that the majority of hits discussed the Bluegrass State's many lakes and the bass and panfish opportunities they offered. I wasn't disappointed by what I learned, because some of my best fishing memories come from the four years I lived a few hours north of the Bluegrass. I enjoyed some tremendous farm pond and lake fishing in central Ohio, and, trout or no trout, slamming a hungry largemouth bass on a surface lure is always a great thrill. Within two weeks of moving to Kentucky, I went bass fishing early one morning in a pretty Sadieville farm pond. It was a positively gorgeous setting, and I caught some nice bass, but I assumed that my trout fishing days were over. To my delight, I was approached to write this article, and my education in Kentucky trout fishing was about to begin.

MY GUIDE, Brandon Wade, met me at my apartment at 4:30 A.M. sharp. Even without the benefit of caffeine, he was clearly as excited as I was to get on the water and catch some fish. We briefly discussed the large amount of trout we would undoubtedly slam that day. I always evaluate guides not only by their skill, knowledge, and safety but also by their enthusiasm for their profession. I knew instantly that Brandon shared my passion for fishing in equal measure.

Our photographer for the trip, Drew Sturgill, arrived. He looked groggy but was alert and already outfitted with a mug of coffee. We made our introductions and drove approximately 85 miles south to Russell County. As the sun rose over the hills, I imagined Civil War soldiers encamped on the mist-shrouded fields. The countryside was as inspiring and lovely as any I had encountered, but my mind was focused on catching that first Kentucky trout.

To whip myself up into an even greater frenzy, I blasted an energetic live version of "Cumberland Blues" by the Grateful Dead, though I was confident that I would be far from blue when the day was over. After a quick McDonald's breakfast in Russell Springs, we drove through the historic ghost town of Creelsboro (I thought the name of the town was a good harbinger) and dropped our boat in the water approximately six miles below Wolf Creek Dam. Brandon, Drew, and I would spend the day on a 15-foot drift boat constructed by Brandon himself, and simply put, the boat is a work of art.

I had no excuses. The conditions were ideal for fishing. There was no wind, and it was warm and sunny with occasional cloud cover. My guide grew up fishing on the banks of the Cumberland and knew the river intimately. I also had Brandon's assurance that a 70-fish day wasn't out of the question. Even before setting foot on the boat, I observed several trout rising to a caddis hatch and watched longingly as a nearby angler landed a sizable rainbow. At 50 degrees, where it remains nearly year-round, the temperature was definitely in the trout zone. Most importantly, the height of the river, which is controlled by the dam, was at an optimal level. Brandon tied on a prince nymph trailed by a caddis pupa, and we set off.

The night before our trip, I had read *Tailwater Trout in the South* by Jimmy Jacobs, which described the many state-record trout caught in the Cumberland. At first, the river wasn't at all what I had envisioned, and it certainly didn't resemble most of the blue-ribbon trout rivers I'd fished in the past. The section where we entered was slow and wide, more of a pond than a river, with dead logs and other structure on both banks. The current was almost imperceptible. I remember thinking that it might yield more smallmouth than trout. Of course, it was at precisely this moment that I missed my first hit. Before an hour had passed, the river's complexion had changed to resemble a textbook trout stream complete with riffles, rapids, and deep pools. By the end of the day I concluded that the Cumberland is diverse enough to satisfy the tastes of any trout angler.

A word of caution to those anglers unaccustomed, as I was, to drift boats. Although they offer fly fishermen distinct advantages over wading, such as covering more water with less casting, fishing from a drift boat nonetheless requires adaptation. One must overcome the instinct to continually cast, false cast, and cast again as if working a specific, well-defined section of the stream. Remember, it's not called a *cast* boat. In addition to my unfamiliarity with the drift boat (I know what you're thinking, and you're right, it is a lame excuse), it took me a while to understand that Cumberland trout took our nymphs with extreme delicacy (yes, that's even more lame). The slightest twitch of the yarn strike indicator signaled a hungry trout, and I'm ashamed to say how many I missed before I finally hooked up.

After nearly a dozen misses, I began to worry that Brandon would classify me as a Yankee mutant who couldn't catch a fish in an aquarium. At one point I suggested that we throw Drew overboard because the presence of a photographer was definitely messing with my fishing mojo. I should mention here that patience is another of my favorite characteristics in a guide. Every time I missed a strike, sometimes with unintended comical choreography, Brandon would just smile, tell a funny joke, and put me on top of more fish. His confidence in the Cumberland's potential was reassuring.

Though we enjoyed perfect weather conditions, I was surprised by the dearth of fishermen on either boats or the banks. During our nearly 10 hours on the water, we saw just a dozen other boats and even fewer anglers on the shore—an average crowd on this section of the river, according to Brandon. In my defense, others we talked to complained of it being a slow day. I was just beginning to smell a skunk when I watched a large trout dart from the shadows under a tree to inhale my beadhead copper john. This time I managed to set the hook, and believe me, it was a particularly satisfying fight. After a few minutes of solid resistance and some acrobatics, Brandon netted a 17-inch brown trout. It was one of the loveliest brown trout I had ever observed, its coloration spectacular, resembling a bar of gold. I wondered if it had been introduced to the river as a fingerling, as are thousands of other browns annually. I posed for a photograph, gave the fish a kiss, thanked him for his company, and returned him to the Cumberland.

The extreme beauty and serenity of the river were almost distracting (this is my last excuse, I swear), and it was worth the trip just to see the numerous birds, trees, limestone cliffs, caves, and arches. We shared a lot of laughs and stories in our pursuit of trout that day, not to mention a gourmet lunch on a secluded bank. As it often does, our perseverance paid off. Shortly after landing the brown, I hooked into a spunky rainbow at the tail end of a long pool. These areas where the current begins to accelerate before entering a shallow riffle section had been most productive for us and the other anglers I had watched. My fly was a sowbug imitation, which is abundant in the Cumberland and a favorite food source for trout. This 15-inch rainbow fought with the determination of a much larger fish and made five impressive runs. I posed with him and released him. As we approached our takeout point, I began fishing with streamers and managed to land another rainbow. Though it was not my fortune to catch one that day, I could easily understand why the Cumberland has produced so many of Kentucky's trout records. It's just that good.

EXHAUSTED, JUBILANT, and satisfied, I spent the evening at the Cumberland Lodge in Russell Springs reveling in the trout I had caught and the new friends I had made. To those fishermen who, like me, particularly enjoy a cold beer or seven after a hard day of fishing, be warned that Russell County is dry. But as the friendly manager at the inn said, "If Abe Lincoln didn't need it, why should you?" I slept extremely well that night knowing that Lexington is in such close proximity to a world-class trout fishery. Although the house we just purchased is in desperate need of a new roof, I'm thinking a canoe would be a much wiser investment at this point. Stay tuned for my wife's reaction. But come hell or high water, or both, I'm going to have me a 70-fish day on the majestic Cumberland.

FICTION

I have tried to be a fisherman because
I like reading about it so much.

—Noah Adams, *Saint Croix Notes*

WHITE MILLS
CHRISTIAN CHURCH

ELvs BAss 226
fishing with STEWART BROS 90
40 ACRES + No mule 104
EXCEPT from NAT COUTER 216
SPECIAl INCDENT 220
INTo The Woops 255
Big Boy 263
HiS FiRST, BEST COUNTRY 282
SPiRiT DEER 285
CHAPTER Rich HISTORY 187
HuNTERS HoRN 209

"Building with faith"

HARRIETTE ARNOW

An Excerpt from *Hunter's Horn* (1949)

LATE NOVEMBER's gentle misty rains made a fog across the hills and brought a grayness and a stillness to the bright noisy leaves. The good hunting weather, the dog food, eggs, fresh milk, and scraps of meat from a just killed pig all gave new life to Zing. This fall, as on other falls, he was the pride and the wonder of Little Smokey Creek country.

Stretched on boards in the middle room upstairs were one red and two gray fox skins; and no man, not even Blare Tiller who was forever claiming an injustice done him or somebody else, disputed Zing's right to them. Always the first to give tongue and be off among a dozen hounds clamoring in anger and bewilderment over a puzzle of crosses and backtracks in a half-cold scent, he was likewise the first to hole the fox or bring it down.

On nights when there was no fox hunting, he would sometimes slip away, and hours later Milly would awaken to his soft whine. She would get out of bed and go to the chopping block where Nunn skinned all the game Zing caught. Once in two weeks' time there was a fat possum, and twice a big coon, dead but never much mangled, with the skin good enough to save and the meat good enough to eat. Lee Roy would come too, and no matter how wet or cold it might be, the two of them would skin the animal by lantern light and praise Zing for his smart ways and thank him for the meat.

Both Milly and Lee Roy liked better the nights when Zing was a tree dog than when he was a foxhound. On fox-hunting nights Nunn would come home, cursing Zing and every other hound in the country with ugly bitter oaths that made Milly pull the covers over her head and hope that Aunt Marthie Jane wasn't listening. Night after night and never a scent of King Devil. He was still in the country. One of the Townsends on the other side of Bear Creek had seen him walking down the road past his barn, walking along and taking his time like somebody going to church, the Townsend had said; and big as a full-grown sheep he had looked to be.

And every day for almost a month something had taken one of Nancy Ballew's big fat White Rock hens. They'd hear one short, smothered-down squawk, sometimes not even any cackling from the others; he slipped up so slyly nothing saw him, not even the hen he killed. Nancy and John and the two boys and the white feist dog would go running but never find a thing, often not so much as a feather. Sometimes the hen squawked in the woods above the house and sometimes down by the barn, and once right in the yard, not fifty feet from where the feist dog was sleeping; and sometimes she never squawked at all. Nancy would count her hens, and there'd be another missing—even the guineas were going.

It was enough to make a body believe that red fox was kin of the witches, John said one day while he and his neighbors squatted by the road in front of Samuel's store and waited for the mail.

"He'd never come that close to Zing," Nunn said with pride.

John watched a long shaving curl up from the piece of yellow poplar he was whittling and shook his head. "But Zing'ull never git him, though. He's like me; he's gitten old. It'll take a young hound to git King Devil—if he's ever got."

Jaw Buster Anderson eased his back against an apple tree. "But take a young hound now; why, he'd be old fore he could begin to learn all King Devil's tricks, an Zing, he knows em."

Willie Cooksey, who disliked Nunn—mostly people said because Preacher Jim had never thought much of the Cooksey generation—nodded and grinned. "But looks like it's taken perfessor fox hunter here a right smart spell to live up to his brags. It's goen on five year now, ain't it, Nunn, since you run that first race on King Devil, an you was goen to have that red fox hide come Christmas?"

"I ain't fergitten," Nunn said slowly and evenly. "Less'n that red fox is a witch er a devil a flyen through th air, I'll be gitten his hide one a these days. Zing's jist now a learnen how he runs."

"Aye, Lord, Nunn," John spoke kindly, "everybody makes brags that sooner er later he has to swaller. I recollect onct—was fore I jined th church an settled down more'n forty year ago—I bragged that a team of mine could pull a heapen wagonload a coal up Little Smokey Creek hill in muddy weather, an I tore my wagon up an beat my mules an made em pull till blood run frum in under their tails—an I never got that coal hauled till nigh on to spring when th hill dried up. That King Devil'ull never be took by mortal hound to my mind, an you'd better be at your farmen."

"Oh, I recken I can fox-hunt a little an still keep frum starven out," Nunn answered shortly, and remembered he had meant to start that very afternoon making shakes to mend the big barn roof that was leaking on the corn and fodder, and that Milly had been quarreling fit to kill because there was a puddle big enough to swim a hog in Betsey's stall in the old grist mill. John, now, wouldn't tolerate a leaky roof. He always kept a stack of seasoned shakes handy in case a wind blew off one or he found a leaky spot.

"Aye, Lord, I used to think they was nothen so pretty as good hound-dog music," the old man said, and added almost defiantly, "If'n th weather ain't too bad, I'm a comen with you all this comen Saturday night. I ain't been on a good fox race in a long spell."

"It's goen to be a shindig, all right," Jaw Buster promised.

"You'll hear some real runnen, an I'll bet you a drink a J. D. Duffey's last run that old King Devil comes out."

But four nights later, when the hounds with Zing in the lead swung hour after hour with long joyful bays down through the valleys and around the ridges, nobody remembered the bet. King Devil ran. The men squatted in tense silence on the Pilot Rock about a burned-out fire that nobody bothered to replenish, not even old John, whose rheumaticky bones ached in the damp cold.

All of the Little Smokey Valley men except Preacher Samuel were there, and others besides. Willie Cooksey with his one old worn-out hound that looked to be half cur; and Rans with none; and Newt Taylor from the other side of Bear Creek, with his two fine spotted July hounds; and Ernest Coffee from the valley, who had come to the end of the gravel in a new Chevrolet with two hounds—Trigs they were—he'd made his brags about before the race began, for he had paid a good $100 of railroad-section-gang money for them in London Town last spring.

But for hours now Ernest had said no more than Willie Cooksey. His hounds were back somewhere with the others, while Zing, followed close by Sourvine and Speed, took the lead and held it. Nunn squatted a little apart from the others, with his back sheltered from the wind by a scraggeldy pine, and listened with that strange wild pounding hope in his heart that always came when King Devil ran and Zing cried that his scent was hot. Maybe this time, this once, Zing would catch him—and it would be the end. Zing gave tongue, his bell-like cry rising up from near the head of Anderson Fork of Little Smokey, and echoing and reechoing through the valley.

Nunn could feel the anger and the eagerness in his call. King Devil would be close; Zing never gave tongue like that except when the scent was clear and hot. King Devil was an animal, flesh and blood and bone like Zing; press him hard enough and he could take no time for the devilish traps of backtracks and jumps and water runs he laid that would hold Zing up for minutes to-gether while the red devil sat resting and laughing as he listened to the troubled hounds.

Zing's voice and Sourvine's voice, with Speed's occasional bay just a little behind, grew fainter and fainter until they seemed no more than a fainter note of the thin whisperings of the wind in the stunted pines on the Pilot Rock. After a little space Nunn knew it was only the wind he heard. King Devil had taken the hard steep road up Caney Fork going north from Little Smokey Creek, and Zing, in the narrow gulch of the valley, could not be heard. But when the hounds had topped Casseye Ridge and King Devil had headed back toward the river, as he would, Nunn could hear Zing again.

He heard the Taylor hounds, followed soon by Lead and Drive, come up the creek, and after a while most of the others; but they were the stragglers and did not count, and he did not bother to unravel the tangle of sounds and learn whose hounds were still in the race and whose had slunk home or gone possum-hunting, but looked overhead at the sky, ragged with patches of stars and of cloud. At sunset it had looked like rain, but it was clearing now, with maybe frost by morning. The Big Dipper lay low in the northwest now, and when Zing first got scent of King Devil it had been well up in the sky; and now the bottom-most stars of it would fall behind the hills and swing free again before the race would end.

So many nights like this he had watched the Big Dipper and the Little Dipper and the Seven Stars and the evening stars go down, and the morning stars brighten and then pale in the sky, and he had stared at the unblinking, unmoving North Star un-til he knew the patterns of the stars from the Pilot Rock at all hours of the night and in all seasons as well as, maybe better than, he knew the fields and boundaries of his own land. Maybe this would be the last night; he was tired of the stars and the wind and the sitting in the dark—but the thought was old and familiar as the stars, and he got up and walked restlessly about the cliff edge.

"Don't be a walken in your sleep an a fallen off, man," Old John warned.

"Hell, I know this cliff better'n my own bed," Nunn answered shortly, and wished Zing would come within hearing soon.

Willie Cooksey and Ernest Coffee, whose hounds had not been heard for hours, were talking of going home. Willie lowed his old Bogle had swum the Big South Fork with a rabbit in his mouth, and was now sound asleep in the kitchen at home, and Ann Liz would be up waiting for him with the poker and the quilting frames, for whenever Willie got drunk, Bogle always went on home; but this was one night he was cold sober and away from Bogle. But Ernest was worried over his hundred-dollar hounds, and wondered and reckoned on their being lost; though Blare told him not to worry, for he'd heard them hole a possum and dig it out, and then start that new Chevrolet coupé for going back to London Town. John, in some exasperation, told them either to go home or be quiet, so a man could listen; he wanted to hear Zing come in.

But Nunn, as always, heard him first; to the other listeners it was only another noise of the wind, but Nunn knew, and bowed his head and shut his eyes and held his breath for better listening. King Devil had skirted the sloping side of Casseye Ridge where the running was hard in the rocky side-hill ground, a grown-over field thick with saw briars and sumac brush. Zing's voice came faintly, too faintly for Nunn to understand much of what he said; the fox scent, he could tell, was still hot and strong; he could hear that much, but how close he was he could not say.

Maybe close, one leap, two leaps; the running through the briars and sumac brush would be hard for the big long-haired fox, harder than for Zing. Maybe there on Casseye Ridge Zing would get him, now, this night, this very minute. He heard Jaw

Buster's short excited breathing, and the sound seemed like thunder, drowning out Zing's voice.

He gripped his hands angrily, impatiently, as if he would tear away and destroy all the sounds between him and Zing's voice out there in the darkness. Jaw Buster's breathing, the wind that had sunk to a moaning sigh in the pines, the rattle of the river over the shoals, and far away and faint, a train blowing for a tunnel past the Cumberland. It was uncommon for King Devil to run a straight race with no tricks and no foolery for so long. Maybe Zing was pressing him so hard he couldn't backtrack, for not once in the long running had Zing boogled or fumbled or given anything except the happy anger of his warcry when on the scent of the big red fox.

Nunn stood for a long while straining his ears, but when he heard Zing give tongue again he was on Kelly's Point at the end of Casseye Ridge, too far away and smothered by trees and rocks and wind for Nunn to hear much of what he said, whether the scent lay hot like fire in his nose or if King Devil were slipping ahead and the scent growing cold.

He squatted again and eased his back against the pine. All about him he heard the low talk and movement of men, but gave them little heed, his ears remembering still Zing's last call, his mind working it over, trying to read it like the writing on a piece of paper half washed away by rain.

WENDELL BERRY

An Excerpt from *Nathan Coulter*

From *Three Short Novels* (2002)

AFTER WE KILLED the first coon things were slow for a long time.
We went into the woods again and sat down. Once in a while
we'd hear the dogs, their voices flaring up as they fumbled at a
cold trail, then quiet again while we waited and talked beside the
lantern. Finally we got cold and built a fire, and Uncle Burley lay
down beside it and slept. He woke up every time one of the dogs
mouthed; but when they lost the trail and hushed he turned his
cold side to the fire and went back to sleep. I watched the flames
crawl along the sticks until they glowed red and crumbled into
the ashes, then piled on more. It was quiet. The country was dark
and filled with wind. And in the houses on the ridges behind us
and below us in the river bottoms the people were asleep.

About midnight the dogs started a hot track and ran it down
the hillside, and treed finally out in the direction of the river. We
went to them. They were treed at a white oak that was too tall
and too big around to climb. So I held the flashlight over Uncle
Burley's rifle sights and on the coon, and he shot it.

After that he said he was ready to call it a night if I was, and I
said I was. We were a long way from home, and since Jig Pendle-
ton's shanty boat was tied up just across the bottom we decided
to go and spend the rest of the night with him.

The boat was dark when we got there. We stopped at the top
of the bank and quieted the dogs.

Uncle Burley called, "Oh Jig."

"I'm coming, Lord," Jig said.

We heard him scuffling and clattering around trying to get a lamp lighted.

"It's Burley and Nathan," Uncle Burley said.

The shanty windows lighted up and Jig came out the door in his long underwear and rubber boots, carrying a lamp in his hand.

Uncle Burley laughed. "Jig, if the Lord ever comes and sees you in that outfit, He'll turn around and go back."

"Aw, no He won't, Burley. The Lord looketh on the heart." Jig stood there shivering with the wind blowing through his hair. "You all come on down."

We went down to the boat, the dogs trotting after us across the plank.

"We thought we'd spend the night with you, Jig," Uncle Burley said, "if you don't mind."

"Why, God bless you, Burley, of course you can," Jig said. He asked us if we'd like some hot coffee.

Uncle Burley said we sure would if he didn't mind fixing it. Jig built up the fire in his stove and put the coffee on to boil, and Uncle Burley and I sat down on the side of the boat to skin the coons.

When we finished the skinning we cut one of the carcasses in two and gave a half of it to each of the dogs. They ate and then curled up beside the door and licked themselves and slept. The coffee was ready by that time. We washed our hands in the river and went inside, ducking under the strings of Jig's machine.

The coffee was black and strong; we sat at the table drinking out of the thick white cups and feeling it warm us. Jig asked how our hunt had been, and Uncle Burley told him about it, Jig nodding his head as he listened and then asking exactly where the dogs had treed. When Uncle Burley named the place he'd nod his head again. "The big white oak. I know that tree. I know the one you're talking about, Burley."

Then Jig mentioned that ducks had been coming in on the slue for the last couple of days. They talked about duck hunting for a while, and Uncle Burley said we'd go to the slue early in the morning and try our luck.

Jig gave us a quilt apiece when we'd finished our coffee. We filled the stove with wood and stretched out on the floor beside it. Jig sat at the table reading the Bible for a few minutes, then he blew out the lamp, and we slept.

Uncle Burley woke me the next morning while it was still dark. The lamp was burning on the table again, and Jig was making us another pot of coffee. It seemed darker and quieter outside the windows than it had been when we went to sleep. While we drank the coffee a towboat passed down the river, its engine humming and pounding under the darkness.

Uncle Burley borrowed Jig's shotgun and a pocketful of shells.

"There ought to be plenty of ducks up there," Jig said. "I expect you'll have luck, Burley."

We led the dogs up the bank and tied them to trees so they couldn't follow us, and started up the bottom to the slue. The air was cold and brittle, the sky still full of stars. A heavy frost had fallen toward morning; the ground was white with it, and our breath hung white around our heads. When we got away from the trees that grew along the riverbank the wind hit us in the face, making our eyes water. We buttoned our collars and walked fast, hurrying the sleep out of our bones.

We got to the slue and made ourselves as comfortable as we could in a thick patch of willows near the water. Uncle Burley smoked, and we waited, hearing the roosters crow in the barns and hen houses across the bottoms. The sky brightened a little in the east; and we could make out the shape of a slue, the water turning gray as the sky turned, the air above it threaded with mist. While it was still too dark to shoot, four or five ducks came in. Their wings whistled over our heads, and we saw the splashes they made as they hit the water.

The sun came up, the day-color sliding over the tops of the hills; and we heard Gander Lloyd calling his milk cows. Then a big flock of mallards circled over our heads and came down.

Uncle Burley raised the gun and waited, and when they flew into range he shot. His shoulder jerked with the kick of the gun, and one of the ducks folded up and fell, spinning down into the shallow water in front of us. Uncle Burley grinned. "That's the way to do it," he said.

He reloaded the gun and we waited again, watching the sky. The rest of the morning the flocks came in, their wings whistling, wheeling in the sunlight down to the water. And the only thing equal to them was their death.

SAM BEVARD

A Special Incident

From the *Maysville Ledger-Independent* (May 29–June 5, 2003)

JOHN HAD BROKEN into a light sweat before he reached the ridge. Summer had strong influence in mid-September, but a front had brought mild weather, presaging fall, so he wore a long-sleeved camouflage shirt to abate the early morning chill. Day was sifting through the trees along the hilltop.

He watched the recurring struggle between darkness and light, as he had done at the start and end of so many days. Its luminescence was beginning to reach the earth in the deep woods around him. Cardinals had already saluted the new day, and it would be only moments until crows added their shrill reveille to the chorus of day-sounds. Above him, where the woods broke into a small upland meadow with scattered hickories, there was a snort and a crash. Two white forms floated away through the trees like disturbed ghosts and vanished over the ridge. "Deer," John whispered under his breath as he paused to rest and take survey of the awakening forest around him.

The year was aging and another season of growth was slipping into silence. Walnut and buckeye leaves were yellowing and falling, and mast trees were beginning to drop their fruit. It had been a good and gentle summer, unusually temperate and with timely rain. Hickories, oaks, and walnuts were packing a modest crop, which in most areas was hanging on the trees or lying on the earth undisturbed. Squirrels were scarce, thinner in numbers than he had seen in almost thirty years. The dearth of food the previous season had decimated them during a hard winter.

John sat along the meadow where he could scan the wooded bluff below him. There was no wind, and only a light fog, just enough dew to beat a regular cadence of dripping moisture drops. Behind him in the valley, sounds of awakening—cattle bawling, occasional human voices, and engines told that the settlement was getting started on a new day. He thought of Bob and Wilma, down there in their home, and he wondered if Bob recalled days when he had been able to take his gun to the woods. Bob was bad off, and according to neighborhood reports, Wilma worse, though she was able to get about and do a few household tasks. Both were well up in years, but not all that many seasons back, John had found Bob one morning, posted at a shagbark hickory, waiting for the two grays cutting in the tree to offer a shot. The two hunters and their quarry had remained in stalemate until John repositioned to a site from which he was able to snipe both squirrels. Feeling that Bob, who was very fond of fried squirrel, had "dibs" on them, John had surrendered both to the older sportsman. Now, Bob would never hunt again. He had been a lifelong outdoorsman, with a gift for catching fish and the grit to duck hunt on the river in single-digit cold.

John climbed to the ridge and left the timber. He stood taking in the sweep of the long grassy ridge to left and right. The slope to his front was thicketed, and it descended into a deep hollow, a drain that did not run directly to the creek in the main valley. Originating under a U-shaped open ridge, it flowed parallel to the valley, feeding one of the creek's larger branches. The glade below John on the hollow's left side was mostly in second growth and trashy woods. Many years of change had worked on the hills since John had last been down that hollow, but he remembered how a pretty woods grew right along its bed, and the early October morning one weekend during his college years when he had shot his limit from among scores of squirrels working the oaks and hickories. He had not planned to descend into that little vale, but a quiet urging, the woodsman's need to revisit scenes of past happiness, caused him to strike downhill and enter the brake. There was a burst of wing beats, and a grouse rocketed from a grapevine in the top of a pole-sized ash. Flushing the grouse made John's entry into this old territory worthwhile, for changing times had not been good to the woods drummer, and just seeing one of the great birds had become a rare thrill.

Soon, John reached the hollow a little more than halfway down its length, at what was its most attractive spot: the junction of a smaller right-hand drain where hickories dominated. He was glad to see that little had changed in the march of years. Neither logger's saw nor nature's storms had trespassed there. But except for the thrashing of jays, and the plop of dew, the boughs, still laden with aging leaves, were silent. A new era of deer had arrived since he had last walked there, and they had worn a trail along the left rim of the hollow, keeping the woods easy to travel despite the tangle of growth the years had added. He decided to follow the deer path up the hollow.

The farther he went up the drain, the smaller the trees became, until the upper reaches faded from mature woods and back into thicket. Yet, many medium height hickory trees, mostly bitternuts, towered over the understory along both sides. The hollow narrowed into a wide ditch, with a smooth dirt bottom. John noted that the bitternuts had shed their produce in heaps all along the bank and into the bed of the drain. "I've never seen so many bitternuts before," John mused. "But there are no cuttings, no sign that anything has been using them."

The cat-whine of a gray squirrel bark came from up the hollow, well out of range and sight. The sound brought John to alert, causing him to soften his footfalls and take care not to rattle brush as he passed. The barking was right along his intended route toward the head of the drain. After moving half-way to the sound, he paused behind a tree along an opening in the thicket, where he could see unobstructed for some distance ahead. An upper branch in a hickory whipped downward, causing a flurry of falling dewdrops, and a gray shape emerged onto an open stretch of a scaffold limb. The animal posed, still voicing a muted protest. John dialed the scope up to 5x and braced the rifle along the tree trunk, quickly acquiring his target. The crosshairs wavered, and then settled on its head. The .22's sharp crack sent the squirrel somersaulting from its perch into the brush beneath the hickory.

After retrieving the squirrel, John cut and peeled a sugar maple twig. He pierced the squirrel's hind feet and strung it on the twig for easy carrying. He was near the head of the drain and the end of the woods; just ahead, an open hillside of grass and scattered brambles lay in full sun. His hunt was over, and he was satisfied.

Though the hunt was finished, there was a long walk ahead before he would reach his truck. It would be through open ground all the way, however, up and over the glade ahead, then to the other side of the ridge, where he could walk a farm road leading down a hollow through shady woods back to the village in the creek valley. His route out would complete another of many circles, those mystic geometric forms in which men and animals move from instinct.

The sun was high by then and John felt its strength. A cooling breeze arose, fluttering in the leaves of a ridge line fencerow. Patches of pale blue mistflower dotted damp clearing edges, and splotches of goldenrod and coreopsis bloomed for the procession as the hum of crickets and jar flies intoned a funerary dirge for the dying summer. The earth and the land had reached that fine state of mellowness and comfort that wears on the spirit like an old favored coat hugs one's shoulders. John felt good, very much alive and in harmony with the flow of the universe. It was a fine thing to reconnect with one's past, to have reenacted part of an old drama on a familiar stage.

From the vantage of the ridge, John could see several spots important in his life as a roamer of wild places, and found solace in how little altered they appeared in the face of so many passing seasons. He felt sadness also over the death of the squirrel he had shot, but no guilt or regret, for he had acted in the ancient way of the hunter, true to tenets of the avocation he had chosen, or which had chosen him. By taking its life, he had obligated himself to put it to worthy use and to store its final moment in the vault of his heart.

John stood atop that ridge and mused to himself as he sensed the summer slipping away, just as life fades. "The old ones are going, and the young trace their paths," he thought. "We spar with fate until it corners us at endgame, and we know we have taken our final step on rough ground and pulled the trigger for the last time. The seasons pile up on the earth and on us in a sublime pageant, subtle and inexorable."

He found the road where it curved around the head of a hollow, leading to a gap. It ran downhill in a straight course, its upper length descending at a steep pitch. Human hands and crude tools had been its primal makers, but machinery had kept it usable in recent years. Where the road leveled, in sight of its opening at the village, John paused at water pooled in a rocky basin of the hollow. There he skinned the squirrel and buried the offal beneath loose rocks.

Soon, he was knocking at Bob and Wilma's backdoor. Several rank green tomato plants, growing in a flowerbed, crowded the door. They were bent with ripening fruit, and showed the brave effort of folks trying to cling to a hint of their lives. A youngish woman, their hired helper, came to the door.

"I've brought them a squirrel," he told her. "Can you fetch a pan? It might drip on the floor." But she seemed distressed and unsure of what to do with the dead thing in John's hand. Wilma appeared with a bowl, moving spryly for one so ill.

"I'll take care of that," she said. "Come in and speak to Bob."

From his recliner, the old hunter made a feeble wave and spoke John's name in a weak voice. "I see you have tomatoes," John said. "Could you use some beans? We have way more than we need."

"Beans would be nice," Wilma replied.

The late forenoon heat had arrived when John went to his garden to fill a sack with Missouri Wonder beans, crisp and moist from the abundant rains, and rich in flavor. They hung from their teepee poles in clusters one could pluck by handfuls. He found several cucumbers skulking in the shade of their own leaves and added them to the sack. It was only a short drive back to deliver these additional presents.

Wilma died within a week, and soon afterward, Bob had to go to a nursing home. It got back to John that their granddaughter told a neighbor that "Somebody stopped by Tuesday and gave them a squirrel and some beans. That was Wilma's last good day."

John felt a chill when he heard this. The old English bard had written long ago of the "special providence" even in the fall of a sparrow, and John figured that same providence had brought him and that squirrel together, and had helped him launch the round to its mark. John knew that if he lived to hunt for another thirty seasons, he would never make a better shot.

BILLY C. CLARK

Ely's Bass

From *Sourwood Tales* (1968)

HIS NAME WAS ELY, and he was a mender of fences. This was the trade he claimed to know the best, and he was willing to bargain with it for the right to fish for an old fish he called Joner. The day Pa bought the farm we inherited Ely, according to its prior owner, Tom Lucas. But before the summer was over we knew that Tom Lucas had been wrong. It had been Ely who inherited us.

It was a rough land that Pa bought. The surface lay hidden beneath scrub oak, bull thistle, and saw brier. Shaped like a bowl, the land tapered quickly from the house on the point, ending in a slice of hollow, cupping a small pond shaded by dropping willows. I saw nothing good about the land. But then, Pa always had a way of seeing things through his eyes that I could not see. His was a breed of stubborn people, a people that had learned to mold the steep ridges to fit the plow, fighting the hill country until the red clay earth nourished green seas of grass and, favored by a reasonable amount of rain, corn that often grew to more than six feet in height. He saw the second and third growth timber fall before the blades of a bulldozer and instead of scrub oak, cattle dotting the slopes fat and lazy in the sun.

The day Pa had stood on the point looking over the land with Tom Lucas I had let my eyes wander down the tall steep walls of earth to where, deep in the hollow, the small pond lay. The wind played with the willows, bending them to brush the surface.

"Good water supply for the cattle," Tom Lucas said, point-

226

ing toward the pond. "Spring-fed." A grin came to his face, and he rubbed his chin. "Good fishing, too, if you've a mind to wet a line. The fish go with the land—that is, except for Ely's bass."

Pa rubbed his chin and stared at Tom Lucas. "Ely's bass?" he asked.

"Big bass," Tom Lucas said, measuring the air with his hands, pulling them farther and farther apart.

Pa watched Tom Lucas's hands closely. Pa was not a fisherman, but so wide a measurement widened his eyes. "And Ely?" Pa asked.

"Reckon I can only say what Bill Tarp said to me when I bought the land from him thinking I could make a go of it. Buy the farm, and you inherit Ely."

Pa was never a man to question. He had his land. Nothing else mattered at the moment.

The first week that we had moved to the farm a strange thing happened. It was in the evening and I had walked a distance out the ridge to where a bulldozer had pushed a stand of scrub oak into a ravine. My job was to cut the limbs from the bigger oaks and stack the trunks so that the sun and wind could season them for winter heating. I had pulled a sizable oak from the heap when I heard a sound from farther out the ridge. I squinted my eyes and stared. But the bulldozer had not reached the distance of the sound and I could not see through the underbrush. The sound died along the slopes and I went back to trimming the oak. And then the sound came again. It was a low thud such as a man might make by beating against the side of a post and now and then there was a twang of metal. I bit the ax into the oak and crept out the ridge as quiet as if I were stalking a squirrel.

I had gone less than fifty yards when I saw him. He was an old man. Stoop-backed and his white hair blowing in the evening wind, he was mending a portion of the fence that a rotted limb from a giant oak had broken. He bent now to his knees, placed his hammer inside a small wooden box, picked up the box and a

long fishing rod, and turned down the slopes toward the pond. He stopped at the edge of the pond and brushed the low-hanging willows aside, stooped and fumbled inside the box. And when he raised his hand and flipped out over the water, I saw the ripples spread from the center and edge toward the bank.

During the next few days I did not mention the old man to Pa. I had little chance to. Pa was out of the house early in the mornings working alongside a bulldozer operator that he had hired to clear the land, and he seldom returned until darkness had crept over the valley. He had little time for talking. And handling the chores around the house, such as feeding the stock and getting the wood seasoned for winter, kept me busy. At least I told myself this was the reason. But actually I had a greedy motive for keeping the doings of the old man secret. Being by myself most of the time made the land a lonely place, and trying to figure out the old man with the white hair took away a great deal of the loneliness.

I soon learned his habits as far as the farm and pond were concerned. He came over the knoll each morning at daybreak and fished until the sun came up. During the heat of the day he walked the fence line, stopping here and there to strengthen a strand that had been weakened by time and weather. He returned to the pond toward evening and remained until dark. And as I crouched to watch the old man fish the pond I remembered again the words of Tom Lucas: to buy the farm is to inherit Ely. Was this Ely? It had to be.

I thought about the old man so much that I could not sleep. And so one morning I sneaked to the pond to wait for him. I watched daylight crawl down the slopes and saw the old man burst through the mist that rose from the pond and kneel beside it. I watched him take a lure from the box and tie it to the end of his line. Then he sneaked to the edge of the water as quiet as the mist and sailed the plug out across the water. It landed near the bank less than ten feet from where I crouched. He reeled slowly, squinted and saw me. He pulled his line from the water and walked to where I squatted. With one hand on his hip he stared at me and said nothing. The wind played with his white hair and his heavy eyebrows shaded eyes that seemed to be staring through me. And still he did not speak. I took a deep breath and said:

"Are—are you Ely?"

"I am," he said, and then jerked a stare at a splash in the water from the far bank. He studied the ripples closely, then looked at me again. "Tom Lucas's kin?"

"No," I said.

He rubbed his chin. "Friends visiting, maybe?" he asked.

"No," I said. "My name is Bob Anders. My Pa bought this farm from Mr. Lucas."

"Eh!" he grunted. "Tom Lucas sell out?"

"Yes," I said.

The old man walked to where he had laid his wooden box and picked it up. He took the plug from the end of the line and turned up the slope.

"It's all right," I hollered after the old man. "Pa will let you fish here."

He turned and stared at me. "Young man, I ain't a man to take privileges without earning them!" And he walked farther up the slope.

"But Pa don't care if you catch the big bass," I hollered.

He turned quickly. "What bass?" he asked.

"The big bass," I said, moving my hands as far apart as they would go. And seeing the old man frown his eyes, and thinking maybe the short length of my arms had caused me to do injustice to the fish, I added: "And then some."

A grin came to the corner of his mouth and disappeared quickly.

"Your pa home?" he asked.

"Yes," I answered.

He turned up the slope toward the house.

"Can I come with you?" I asked.

"Young man," he answered, "I am the trespasser."

Pa stood in the front yard stretching his arms into the morning air, shuffling his feet, uneasy, waiting for the bulldozer operator to report to work. He turned his head quickly as the old man walked into the yard. The old man wasted no time. He stopped in front of Pa, set his fishing gear on the ground, and placed his hands on his hips and sized Pa up. "Knowed Tom Lucas wouldn't last," he grumbled. "Tell he was a lowland farmer the day I seen him. Know'd the hills would whup him." He looked Pa over again. Then he stretched out his hand. "Ely Tate," he said. "I've come to bargain."

"George Anders," Pa said, seeming still off balance under the stare of the old man. Yet I thought I caught a slight grin on Pa's face. "What are you bargaining for?" Pa asked.

"A fish," the old man said.

"A fish?" Pa rubbed his chin.

The old man stood silent, a frown on his face. I thought he might be disgusted that Pa had not heard of the great fish and so to save Pa embarrassment I stood behind the old man and stretched my hands apart to measure the fish, hoping to remind Pa of the day Tom Lucas had spoken of it. And when no expression came from Pa's face I said, "And then some!"

"Oh yes," Pa said, rubbing his chin. "I believe I heard Tom Lucas say something about a big bass that was the granddaddy of the pond."

"I come to bargain for him," Ely said.

"Well," Pa said, "I see no reason why you can't just go right on fishing for him."

Ely scratched his head and frowned his face in disgust. "Let me tell you something, young man," he said. "You just don't take a fish like old Joner over there without earning him!"

"Well," Pa said, "I'm not much of a fisherman, but if you been after that fish as long as Tom Lucas said you have, I'd say to catch him would be earning enough."

"What's between me and that fish, is between just me and that fish," the old man said. "I've come to bargain."

"Then what is your bargain?" Pa asked.

"I'd like to work for the right to fish the pond," the old man said, "until the fish is caught."

"What kind of work?" Pa asked. "I'm not a man to tell another what he can best do."

"Well," the old man said. "Mr. Tarp, he owned the place before Tom Lucas, judged me to be good at mending fences. Tom Lucas found me decent at the same."

"It's an honest trade," Pa said. "And it would be most welcome around here." And they sealed the bargain with a shake of the hand.

The old man picked up his gear and started out the ridge. I followed him for a ways hoping that he would turn again toward the pond. But farther out he stopped and grinned. "Old Joner is through feeding for the day. He feeds of the mornings and of the evenings, sprawls out in the cool of the pond when the sun is high." The grin left his face and he frowned at me. "You'd best start earning your keep here at the farm. Your pa needs your help. The land is rough." And seeing the frown come to my face, he softened his own. "And then some," he said, and his laugh drifted behind him through the underbrush.

Each morning now after my chores I sat under the willows at the pond and waited for the old man. Each morning he came down the path, opened the wooden box and tied a plug on his line. The wooden box was full of lures, and he had carved them all himself. They looked so real that each time he opened the box I expected them to jump out and start running through the weeds. Each morning he started at one end, walking and casting until he had circled the pond. Some mornings after a cast

I would watch the line zip through the water and the rod bend. The old man would brace himself, his eyes growing wide. But after a few turns of the reel the smile would leave his face, and he would bring the smaller fish to the bank.

I hated to see the sun come over the ridge. Morning became short, and day began to seem longer. During the heat of the day I thought of the old man and sometimes I got to worrying that maybe the sun wouldn't set or that he might grow tired of fishing for the great bass and leave. But always, just when I was feeling the lowest, I would cock my ear to the sound that came from along the fence line somewhere out the ridge, and I knew that the old man would be watching the sun and still earning the right to fish the pond.

One evening he told me more about the great bass. "It was an evening about like this," he said. "The line didn't zip like when some of the smaller fish take it. It just sorta eased out into the pond. I thought it might be a small bass that had hold of a plug bigger than his mouth would let him swallow. I was fishing with the best plug I had ever made. It was a plug that had took enough years of thinking to gray my hair. And enough casting for the right weight to stretch a line over the moon. And enough fine carving to bring calluses the size of acorns. I gave the line a twitch, just a little twitch. It felt like I had hooked a steer.

"I reckon I fought that fish all over the pond, giving and taking line. And then he stopped. There was more fight to him just gliding through the water than there is to most fish. I knew when I looked at him here at the edge of the pond that he was worth all my years of whittling and then some. Biggest bass I ever seen. What I didn't know was that he was playing possum. I reached for him, thinking how I would carry him home, mount him over the fireplace and just sit and look at him. My hand touched the water and the next thing I knew I was blinded by spray. By the time my eyes cleared old Joner leaped high out of the water from the center of the pond allowing me one last look at my plug. Just seemed to have a big grin on his face. I 'lowed then and there that one day I'd take that fish, and take him right."

There were times as summer was ending that I did not get to go to the pond. Pa had brought more cattle to the farm, and I traveled with him each day to neighboring farms to buy hay to winter them. It would be the second year before we had a stand of grass on the red clay solid enough to cut. Most times we would get home before dark, and I would run to the fence and look toward the pond. And I would see the old man walking the slope to the ridge. I squinted my eyes hoping he would be carrying nothing besides his fishing gear. It was not that I didn't want the old man to catch the fish; I just wanted to be there when he did.

Autumn came and the brown leaves sailed through the air like meadowlarks and lit on the small blades of the first stand of grass on the slopes. Pa stood at the fence, his foot propped on a board. He was staring toward the pond.

"You know, Bob," he said, "it takes a lot of work and planning to make a good farm."

I looked over the land and for the first time I think I saw what Pa had seen the first day he had stood beside the fence. Much of the land was now cleared, and open to the sun and rain.

"Sometimes there are things you have to do that might not seem right at first," he said. "Things that have got to be done if you are to have a good farm." He rubbed his chin. I looked at him, not understanding. "Bob," he said, "I want you to listen close to what I have to say. After all, one day this land will belong to you. And what we do now will determine how good the land will be."

I looked at Pa. He was staring over the slope toward the hollow. "It's about the pond," he said. "The pond must be moved."

I stared toward the pond without saying a word.

"Before you say anything," he said, "I want you to hear me

out. I want you to know that I, too, have thought of Ely and the big fish, Joner. I know that the old man has worked hard for the fish. I've never had to go back on a bargain before."

"But how can he catch the bass," I asked, "if the pond isn't there?"

"I said the pond must be moved," Pa said, "not destroyed. It was bad judgment to put it where it is in the first place. The pond covers good land. It should have been built farther down the hollow, letting the water spread over the rocks where the land is practically useless for crops. There it would have served its purpose as a water supply. And it would hold the water much better than it does here."

"Can we wait until winter comes?" I said. "Maybe Ely will catch the bass by then."

"The land will be frozen too hard to work then," Pa said. "It must be done now. We'll build a dam below and allow the water from the upper pond to run down into it. Judging from the size of the level pipe through the clay dam, I would say that most all the fish can ride through it into the new pond."

"What about old Joner?" I said.

Pa frowned his face. "I'll try to settle with the old man for the work he's done."

I sat under the willows waiting for Ely to come down the slope. The sun had gone from above the ridge and I knew that darkness would come early now that autumn was here. For the first time I did not feel happy when I saw the old man coming.

He moved quickly around the pond to where I sat, a grin on his face. He knelt beside me and opened the wooden box.

"Look, Bob," he said, holding a new plug. "Old Joner is in for it now." He stared at me and squinted his eyes. "Well, now what's the matter? Don't you think it favors a bluegill minnow? Dogged if your eyes ain't become almost as particular as old Joner's. But it'll look better in the water."

I said, "Pa's going to move the pond." I said it flat out.

The old man stared. He did not speak, and I watched him place the new plug back inside the box.

"He's going to move it down the hollow into the trees and rocks," I said, pointing with my finger.

"I reckon I knowed it," he said at last. "Reckon I knowed it all the time. Knowed it the day I saw him. There is a difference in your pa and the others that owned the land. The pond is in the wrong place, and I knew that the eyes of a good farmer would catch it. Reckon I was hoping that it might take him a little longer. Even a little time is precious to an old man."

"What can we do?" I said, frowning.

He set his lips. "Wipe the frowns from our faces first of all," he said. "It would shame a great fish such as old Joner to think there was two quitters trying to outfox him."

I set my lips, trying to look as stubborn as Ely.

"That's more like it," he said. "Now let's bargain."

Pa must have suspected the old man would be coming once he got word of the pond. He was standing in the yard as if he were waiting. He stretched out his hand as the old man walked up.

"I guess," Pa said, "you wouldn't consider pay for the work you've done?"

"Reckon I wouldn't," Ely said, scratching his head. "But there might be another way."

"Name it," Pa said.

"When you drain the pond most of the smaller fish can get through the pipe. But not old Joner. And if a man was to wait beside the pond until the water was low enough to show his fins, he might step in the water and grab him. I've come to bargain for that right."

Dad stretched out his hand. "The fish is yours."

"Shucks, Mr. Anders, you just don't take a fish like old Joner without working for him."

A smile came to Pa's face.

"All right," he said. "What is it you want to do?"

"Help drain the pond and build the other dam," the old man said.

The dam was built lower in the trees, the old man working in the dust behind the bulldozer. And after the lower dam was built the valve was opened on the upper dam. Ely stood beside the pond watching the water gush through the pipe. The pond waters eased through the pipe and he kept a watchful eye. Here and there smaller fish jumped, and then, caught in the current, were sucked through the pipe. Everything was going along just as we had planned for it to go.

And then it happened. From the edge of the pond there came a great splash and a large fish leaped high into the air. He leaped again and again and each time he fell back into the water there was less of it to cover him until at last he landed in the soft mud and could not wiggle loose. Ely splashed through the water and muck and stood over him, his eyes wide. He straddled him, ran his fingers through his gills and pulled the fish from the water.

"Reckon," he said, looking at Pa, "I'm obliged to you."

He turned up the slope, carrying the huge fish and stopping now and then to look back to where the new pond filled deeper in the hollow. I could see his lips move as if he were talking to the fish but I couldn't hear him. The old man was leaving for good. No more mending fences. There was nothing more to earn. I rubbed my eyes and stared after him. I squinted. Something was wrong. He was coming back. And then I felt Pa's hand on my shoulder.

"I'll be doggone," he said, "I'll be doggone."

The old man walked past us to the edge of the new pond. Here he knelt and looked at the great bass. He held the fish so close to the water that his tail splashed in it. And then he moved his hand out and the next thing I knew the old bass was breaking water from the center of the new pond. Ely got to his feet and walked toward us.

"That weren't no way to take a fish like Joner," he said. And he walked away.

Pa shook his head. "Sure hate to see the old fellow go. Best fence mender I ever saw."

The sun was still above the ridge as we went toward the house. But the day was growing late. As I walked through the field I thought of the old man and my eyes watered. I rubbed them to keep Pa from seeing and started to scoot under the fence. But then I stopped. Pa stopped too. He stared at me and a smile as large as the one he had the first day he looked over his land came to his face. From out the ridge there drifted a sound. It was such as a man might make if he were pounding against the side of a post. Pa looked down at me. His expression made me feel good all over.

"Feel like bargaining, son?" he said. "You're part owner of the land, you know."

I grinned back at Pa. "I could use a good fence mender," I said. And I stood beside the fence waiting for the old man to come to strike his bargain for the right to fish the new pond, a bargain that was sure to include me as a partner.

BILLY C. CLARK

Fur in the Hickory

From *Sourwood Tales* (1968)

"YOU CAN TALK about that new repeating rifle of yours all you want," the old man said to the boy as they made their way up the slope of the hill toward the ridge where the shagbark hickories grew. "It's your gun and only natural that you ought to have some feeling for it. But me? When I go for squirrel I aim to put meat on the table. You don't see me carrying a repeating rifle, either. I take my old musket. Been with me a long time. Went through the war together. Brought a brag once from General Morgan himself." The old man stroked the barrel of the musket and jerked it into firing position. "Yep, when I lay an eye down the sights, I want to know there's fur under the hickory. It's the eye, too, Jacob. Remember that. The eye is one of the reasons you see so many fellows carrying them repeating rifles now days. Afraid one shot won't do it. Don't trust their eye or their gun. So they go to repeaters to cut down the odds."

The weeds along the path were wet from a light rain, and the old man, walking in front, took up some of the rain with his britches legs and the pants made a low whistling noise. Daylight was beginning to break over the ridge, and no wind was stirring. The trees were taking shape. Birds were stirring in the tree limbs along the path and as they moved in the wet branches the boy cocked his ears, thinking that the noise might be a squirrel jumping through the trees, traveling to the hickories on the ridge. It was a good way to locate squirrels, listening for the sprays of water made by squirrels hitting the limbs. The old man had taught him this.

On the ridge the old man stepped ever so lightly. He stopped under a shagbark hickory. Daylight was shifting fast now through the limbs of the trees. The old man stopped and picked up a half-chewed nut. He held it close to his face.

"Sampling," he said, pushing the nut into a pocket. "Too low on the ridge yet." And he looked off to where the ridge peaked. He glanced again at the new repeating rifle the boy carried.

"Times have changed," he said, walking stoop-shouldered. "When I was a boy your age I'd have been laughed out of the mountains for carrying a gun like that. If you had to shoot more than once at the same target you went back to practicing. And squirrels! If you hit a squirrel with a bullet, you didn't dare take him home. Bark 'em, that's what we did. Hit the tree right under the squirrel's chin and knocked the wind from 'im. Not a scratch on the squirrel. Everyone carried a musket and no one hit a squirrel." The old man leaned against the side of a black oak and took a deep breath. "Wasn't that we couldn't get a repeater, either. City fellows came around all the time trying to sell guns like the one you tote. But when you made a brag then in the hills, you had to prove it. And no man ever came that could match his gun against a musket. I ain't wanting to brag, but I never got beat."

The old man picked out a black oak on the ridge and sat down at its foot. Less than fifty feet away stood a large shagbark. The boy sat down beside him and stared at the leafless limbs of the hickory.

"If I'd a had to use a repeating rifle, I probably would've quit long ago," the old man said, placing the musket across his lap and stroking the long barrel. "They didn't call me Barkem Tilson for nothing, you know. But you got too many Sunday hunters now. Highfalutin outfits, and just move in and blow the tops out of the trees. But not me. When I shoot, there's just one ball.

When I look down the barrel, there's business coming out the other end."

The light broke now and shone on the old man's long gray hair and beard. Sweat caused by the long walk up the mountain ran down the wrinkles of his face. He took a piece of homemade twist from his pocket, balled it in his hands, and stuck it in his jaw.

"Can't rightly expect a fellow to do much shooting today, though, I reckon," he said. "The world's moving too fast for them. And they don't have to depend on their guns like we did. Not even in wars like they have today. I mean they get back miles away and bang away at one another. Never see the man that fired the gun. But with General Morgan you had to look the enemy in the eye. Just bring them repeating guns in here today and blow a squirrel beyond recognition. Most times don't even bother to skin it out. Just hang it on a fence somewhere and let the crows have it. Just wanted to kill it, not eat it. Want to take the spite of the whole world out on as little a thing as a squirrel. We never done that. What we killed we ate. What we couldn't eat we let grow until we got hungry again. Not many of the fellows today would carry a gun heavy as a musket. You just ask your ma. She can tell you I always kept meat on the table when she was growing up. You got to get close to your gun, Jacob. Treat it like a woman. But you're a little young yet to know about that."

The boy placed the repeating rifle across his knee, in the same position that the old man had placed the musket.

"Listen!" the old man said, just above a whisper. A light spray of rain fell and made a noise hitting the brown, autumn leaves on the ground. The spray was too even to have been caused by the wind and too heavy to have been caused by a bird. The boy looked toward the shagbark. He saw the bushy, gray tail of the squirrel blowing in the morning wind that had begun to work in the tops of the trees. The old man had the musket to his shoulder. His hands were unsteady as he tried to level the long barrel of the musket. He squinted his eye, opened it, and looked once more down the long barrel. Then the sound of the gun echoed through the woods, and a few birds took wing.

The boy watched the gray squirrel slide behind a limb and disappear. The old man lowered the musket, rubbed his eyes, and wiped the sweat from his face.

"Knocked the wind from that gray," he said. "Thought your old grandpa was just blowing to the wind, didn't you? Too old to be traipsing the mountains, your ma said. Shaw. I saw that ball nip the bark right under his chin. Go pick him up, Jacob. I'll reload. Be careful you don't scratch the barrel of that new repeating rifle of yours against one of them saplings on the way. You'd best waited for the musket to be yours." And the old man chuckled so hard that the boy saw his teeth.

The boy walked under the hickory. He stirred the dead leaves. He didn't know what he should do. He couldn't tell the old man that he had seen the squirrel slide behind a limb and then cross out. He watched the old man as he slid the rod down the musket barrel. The old man was still grinning. Finally, the boy walked back to the oak and stood in front of the old man.

"Didn't find a mark on the squirrel, did you?" the old man said, looking up and grinning.

"I couldn't find the squirrel," the boy said. "Maybe he crawled under the dead leaves on the ground and hid. Those leaves are heavy and a squirrel will do that."

"Don't I know that!" the old man said. "I taught it to you. But it didn't happen that way with this squirrel. Now if you can't see a squirrel stretched out on the ground how do you ever expect to see one in a tree? You got to use your eyes, boy."

The old man got to his feet, frown on his face. He walked over under the shagbark, the musket swinging limp in his hand. He kicked at the leaves, scattering them over the ground in heaps. Then he put his hand on a young sapling and shook it. The boy knew that the old man was testing to see if the squirrel was still in the shagbark. If the squirrel was there the movement and noise from the sapling would cause him to move and be detected. But the boy knew no squirrel would move. The squirrel was gone. The old man had missed.

"I think I'll go on out the ridge and sit a spell," the boy said.

The old man didn't answer. He was staring into the shagbark.

The boy walked along the ridge, picked a good spot, and sat down. And he thought of the old man. How sad he had looked. How he had kept his eyes off him while he looked for the squirrel. And he remembered his mother telling that he should watch after the old man. He was pretty feeble. Shouldn't be going so high on the mountain at his age. But that he would keep right on going so long as there was breath to him. The boy worried. He got up and sneaked back out the ridge to check on the old man.

He saw that the old man was back sitting beneath the oak. The musket was across his lap and his head was bent on his chest. He was asleep.

On his way back out the ridge the boy heard a spray of water hit the ground. He froze and turned his head slowly. The big gray squirrel ran along the limb of an oak and stopped in the fork of the tree. The boy raised his rifle slowly. He took a deep breath and tried to remember all that the old man had told him. He aimed under the squirrel's chin. He squeezed the trigger and the squirrel fell. The boy picked him up and looked quickly for signs of a mark. But there was no mark on the squirrel. The boy had barked his first squirrel and he felt proud and happy. He tucked the squirrel under his belt.

The old man was still under the oak with his head dropped. The boy sneaked under the shagbark and placed the squirrel in open sight. Then he sneaked away and hid behind a tree. He bent, picked up a rock, and threw it under the shagbark. The old man jumped at the noise. He looked around. And then his eyes rested on the shagbark and he rose to his feet. He saw the squirrel before he was under the tree. He grinned, looked around, picked the squirrel up, and examined it. Then he tucked it under his belt and walked back to the oak and sat down.

The boy waited a while longer before he walked to the oak.

"I heard a shot," the old man said. "Did you get him?"

"I thought I had him, Grandpa," the boy said. "But I must have shot just as he jumped."

The old man rose again to his feet. The bushy tail of the big gray stuck from his belt. The boy looked at the squirrel.

"I didn't hear you shoot again, Grandpa," he said.

"Didn't shoot again," the old man said, grinning.

"Then you found the squirrel under the shagbark!" the boy said.

"Found him?" the old man said. "Never was lost. Right there under the tree all the time. Just wanted to see if you had learned to use your eyes. Well, don't worry. You got a long way to go, but you'll make a hunter."

The old man scanned the tops of the trees. The wind was heavy now. The woods were noisy.

"Wind's too strong to hunt more now," the old man said. "Maybe I'll give you the chance to try that repeating gun of yours again in the morning. Or maybe you'll be wanting to borrow my musket."

The old man laughed as he walked down the ridge and the musket swung back and forth in his arms.

"I'd like that, Grandpa," the boy said.

GAYLORD COOPER

The Great Ohio River
Catfish Hunting Expedition

From *Down the River: A Collection of Ohio Valley Fiction & Poetry* (1991)

IT ALL STARTED when we all were fishing at the river on a Saturday night. All our poles had been fixed and set up and our
lines were out in the current waiting for the fish to bite. I was
in charge of two of the poles and I was just sitting there enjoying the river. It was so smooth and calm that it looked like a big
lake. Now when I said "all" I meant Larry, Jack, Rog, and me.
We'd been fishing together ever since any of us had been big
enough to drag a fishing pole behind us. And too, when I said
"river" I meant the Ohio River. Now here abouts in this part of
Kentucky when you said "river" why everybody knew what you
meant. Not Big Sandy, Little Sandy, or ever Tygart Creek. River
simply meant the Ohio River. Same way with "fishin." Everybody knew what that meant also. If you said you were goin fishin,
why everybody around here would know you were going catfish
fishing. If you were going bass fishing or crappie fishing or perch
fishing, why you said so. But just plain fishin meant you were going for catfish. When we, Larry, Jack, Rog, and me, said we were
going to the river to fish, everybody knew that we were going to
the Ohio River to try to catch a mess of catfish. Simple.

It was a warm and clear night and we were getting set to do
some serious fishing in the river. I was watching some poles and
Larry was watching a couple of poles and reading the Greenup

County weekly newspaper. Rog and Jack was up the bank gathering some driftwood for the fire we had just built.

All at once Larry jumped up and started hollering and going on something awful. I jumped up and ran over to him, and Jack and Rog came running, throwing driftwood every which way. We thought that Larry might have gotten snake bit or that our school had won a ball game. There was more chance of Larry getting snake bit than that, though. We all gathered round wanting to know what the big fuss was all about.

What all the fuss turned out to be was a fishing contest sponsored by the newspaper. Whoever brought the biggest catfish to the courthouse square in Greenup, the county seat, before six o'clock on Memorial Day would get their picture in the paper and a brand new hundred dollar bill. Larry explained to us that Memorial Day meant Decoration Day. The county judge and the outdoor writer for the newspaper, a local hardware store clerk who liked to hunt and fish, would weigh the fish brought in. The newspaper was the one giving the money away. Wow, none of us had ever seen a used hundred dollar bill, let alone a new one. Right then and there on the riverbank we planned the Great Ohio River Catfish Huntin Expedition.

We figured that nobody knew as much about the river and catfish as we did. We started making plans on how to spend our part of the money that Larry said would come to twenty-five dollars apiece. That was a lot of money. You had to bale an awful lot of hay to get anything like it. Larry told us all not to go countin our chickens before they hatched. Huh. A lot he knew. I wasn't countin no chickens and I sure wasn't aiming to buy any. A new rifle maybe, but no chickens. Rog said that they had plenty of chickens at home and would sell Larry all he wanted. Cheap. Larry explained what he meant.

That night on the riverbank by a good driftwood fire we set about planning the great expedition and assigning jobs. Rog would be our tactical specialist. None of us had the foggiest idea what that was, but according to Rog's brother, who was in the army, expeditions had to have one, so Rog was ours. Larry was in charge of equipment. Our reels were OK, but we would have to have new line if we were going after the really big catfish. We all gave him some of our hard-earned money to buy it. Jack would get our bait. With catfish, especially with GREAT catfish, you needed the right bait. Not just anything would do. Jack said he knew what was needed. Me? I was to be our expedition's transportation man. I would try to talk Daddy into taking us and our world's biggest catfish to Greenup on Decoration Day. We were all set. The assignments were made, all the plans were worked out, and we knew that money was as good as ours.

A week later the Great Ohio River Catfish Huntin Expedition met in my barn. I reported that Daddy said he would take us and our fish to Greenup. He'd offered to take us in the car but I told him that as big a catfish as we would be taking wouldn't fit in the trunk of a car. He agreed to take us in the truck.

Larry had brought a bag from the local hardware store. He had gotten us the best line on the market. It was triple X, strong as steel, sixty-pound-test catgut. That disturbed me somewhat and I said so. I had a couple of cats and I liked them real well. It bothered me to think that there were factories all over the country killing cats just for their guts to make fishing line. It was all right, Larry explained, they just called it catgut but it had nothing to do with cats or guts at all. I felt better after that.

Rog had found out what a tactical specialist was. That was one who looked over the ground that you were to travel, wherever you were going, and found you the best way to get there. We all knew where we were going, and we all knew how to get there, so we didn't need a tactical specialist, but Rog didn't have anything else to do so we let him plan the route.

Jack was late as usual. He had rounded up the bait we'd need to catch a really big catfish. He'd talked his granny out of a jar of her really old pickled corn. Now just any old thing won't do to catch catfish. You take an old bass or perch, why you can catch them on just about anything, but catfish are different. Jack unscrewed the canning ring from the quart jar and pried the lid off with his knife. The old cat I was pettin suddenly stuck her tail in the air, sniffed a couple times, and ran out of the barn squealing. There wasn't a dry eye in the house. Our eyes were watering, our noses were burning, and we could hardly keep from gagging. It smelled something like a dead polecat that had been left in the summer sun for a week. It was great. We were tickled to death over his good fortune.

The big day had finally arrived. We got all our chores done early so we could get down on the riverbank long before dark. We walked out of the hollow where we all lived and down to the highway that led to Greenup. With any luck we'd be on our way up that highway tomorrow before six o'clock. It was a quiet evening and the night looked like it might be a little cool. Good weather for a fire and catfish. We crossed the C & O railroad tracks and started down a steep path toward the river. Off to our left as we started down was an old worn rock wall. We'd been told that it was all that was left of a big lime kiln. And that it was full of snakes too and for us to stay away from it. It was starting to get dark already under the big maple trees growing on the upper part of the bank. We had to stop often where the nettle grew real thick

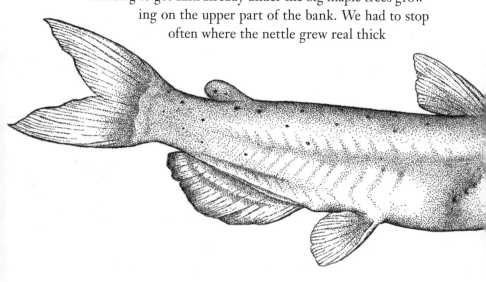

and scratch our legs real good. Finally we came out of the shadows and onto the sand and rock bank of the river itself. It was smooth and glassy and with no hint of the treacherous currents it had under the surface.

It held no hint of the giant catfish that lurked beneath it either. We had all heard tales of these big fish and had even seen a few taken from the river. We knew they were there—it was just a matter of catching them. We turned down the bank and followed the river.

We finally came to the place that we'd staked out. It was in a large shallow curve of the river. The current had cut into the bank over the years and had left a back eddy of water with various currents swirling in and out of the curve. Just the place a big catfish would love. The lapping water had smoothed the bank over the years and left this part of the river with a mud bottom. Catfish heaven. We didn't come down this far often without one of our daddys being with us, but this time they thought we were old enough and with the seriousness of our mission, they said to go ahead.

We got to our destination just before dark. We all hurried and gathered driftwood and had a good fire going when the darkness creeped out of the dark trees and settled on the river. We put our lines out and fixed our poles so the catfish wouldn't steal them. They were sneaky creatures. You'd set there and they'd play with your line ever so careful and then when you weren't looking, WHAM! You'd lose your pole, line, and everything. You had to watch careful like. The slight current of the river picked up the bait and sinkers, each in turn as we cast out and gently tugged at them till they settled on the bottom. Here we would catch the big one.

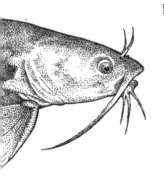

Jack, while up in the bushes, came across a rope tied to a tree. We were always looking for things we could use at home so he traced it down the bank, hoping it would be long enough to use. To all our surprise it let down the bank and out into the river. Jack was ready to pull it in but Larry said he'd better not because it might be somebody's trotline. We thought about that and Rog said he'd never seen a trotline that big. We decided to go ahead and pull it in. If it were a trotline then we'd put it back and not bother it. Our dads would skin us alive if we bothered someone else's property.

We all pulled on the rope and it felt like something was on it all right. We finally got it into the bank and was puzzled to find several gallon glass jugs tied at the end of the rope. All the jugs were about three quarters full of something that looked like water. Now none of us had ever heard of someone putting water in glass jugs and throwing them out in the water.

I guess I was the one that came up with the answer. Moonshine. It had to be moonshine. We all started looking at the jugs with new respect. None of us had ever seen it before. We'd heard talk from some of the older boys, but we'd never tried any. It still looked like water. It just wasn't too impressive at all. It being the devil's drink and all, that's what Mama called it. We were disappointed. Rog and Jack said they didn't think it was moonshine at all and that I didn't know what I was talking about. We argued some and then Larry said we should all take a drink. That'd prove it.

I know I was the one that said it was moonshine, but I wasn't too certain of that. I said it might be poison. I was voted down on that one. All said it was dumb to think that anybody would put some kind of poison in jugs and throw them out in the river. That didn't make good sense.

Larry untied one of the jugs and unscrewed the lid. It smelled like a cross between coal oil and soured hog slop. We all held our noses, but if this was moonshine then it was supposed to be awful good, at least that's what the older boys kept telling us. I don't know who took the first drink, but we passed the jug around quickly and took a good slug.

The reaction was both immediate and profound. Jack started making funny noises and jumping up and down and flapping his arms like he was trying to fly. Rog just stood there with a glassy look to his eyes. He looked like somebody who had been pole-axed and couldn't fall. Larry started to run for the bushes but only made it halfway up the bank when all his supper came up. I just stood there shocked. I was numb all over. I couldn't breathe and the burning was awful. Any minute I expected flames to start coming out of my ears and nose. I knew right then and there that I was dead. Somebody had set a trap by putting poison out in those jugs just to kill nosey kids. I looked toward the river and it kind of wavered, like heat coming off a tin barn roof in summer. I expected everything to go dark any time. It would be awful, I thought, when Daddy would come huntin us and find us all dead from drinking poison.

Things didn't go dark and the wavering passed. I still felt like someone had built a fire in my belly, but I was beginning to think I wouldn't die anyway. In fact a warm feeling was starting to come over me. We quickly put the cap back on the jug and Larry waded out into the water and lowered the jugs in the current. The line slowly tightened as the jugs settled to the bottom.

Jack went to put more wood on the fire and almost fell into it. I don't know why, but this struck everybody as being funny and we all just rolled around the riverbank laughing. We finally settled down and decided we'd better do some fishing.

The moon had been down for a while and all was real quiet. I'd had a couple of bites but hadn't caught anything. Suddenly Rog jumped up screaming. He'd dozed off and dreamed that a big catfish had come out of the river and poured poison down his throat from a clear gallon jug. We finally got him quieted down.

While this was going on I noticed that I had some action on the pole farthest from the fire. The line would slowly tighten and then go slack again. Tighten and slack. Tighten and slack. I held my breath. This was a big catfish for sure. I picked up the pole as gently as I could. The fish took off.

All the tension that had been building in my muscles exploded. I jerked the pole straight up and over my head. The tip of the pole came up and then stopped—hard. I had my fish hooked. I screamed at the other guys and they all came to help. Everyone was talking and giving me advice all at once. I reeled in some line and set the drag on the reel. I reeled in some more. I started to take in some more line when the fish took off for the middle of the river. I brought my rod up to try to stop him. It broke in half and line started coming off the reel so fast that the reel started to smoke. I stood there helpless as the last inch of line came off the spool. I braced myself for the sharp twang of a broken line. It held. The triple X, strong as steel catgut line held. Larry had done a good job.

The line held but the fish jerked me off my feet and pulled me toward the river. I wasn't about to let go of what was left of my fishing rod. Rog and Jack grabbed for the line and Larry grabbed my leg. This stopped my headlong slide toward the river, but I was sure skinned up. My knee hurt real bad where it had hit a rock and my shoulders felt like they'd been pulled from their sockets, but I still had my fish.

All of us grabbed the line and started hauling the fish toward the bank. We got it in close and into the shallows. It was an awesome fish.

When we got it in close enough to the bank and into the firelight, we could see that this fish was bigger than we had ever dreamed. It was probably as long as Larry was tall, and he was the tallest of us all. Its head looked like a corn scoop. It was enormous. I could see now that we didn't have it hooked very well. Every minute that the fish splashed and wallowed in the shallow water just off bank the closer we came to losing it. I waded into the water to try to pull it in.

It knocked me down and I swallowed a bunch of river water. By this time it seemed as if everyone was in the water. Somebody had gotten a piece of driftwood and was swinging at the giant catfish. I got hit once or twice with the driftwood and climbed back up on the bank. All this commotion was making me sick and dizzy again.

After a lot of splashing and grunting and groaning we finally tired out the great fish. It moved quietly in the water just off the bank. We had our fish and all we had to do was get him to Greenup before six o'clock.

We watched the sun come up over the trees on the Ohio side of the river. There were little wisps of fog lifting from the river and it was so still you could hear the sounds carrying across the river. A dog barked and somewhere across the river we heard a rooster crow. It was a beautiful calm morning. I was a little saddened. We had this great fish but I realized as the sun came up that he wouldn't be out there in the river come sundown. I looked at the fish and thought to myself, he wouldn't be there anymore for us or any boys to dream about while sitting by a driftwood fire and listening to the mysterious splashes in the river out in the darkness. We'd heard our dads and uncles talk about the great fish of the Ohio River and mourn their passing. It wasn't fair.

I looked at the other boys and it looked like they were thinking something like that themselves. I was a little surprised. I thought I was the only dumb one. I took out my pocketknife and slowly bent over to cut the line. No one said anything to try to stop me. I cut the line.

The big fish was free. It backed off the bank a little ways and stopped. It was almost as if it were saying, "You boys sure about what you're doing? You won fair and square and a hundred dollars is a lot of money."

The big catfish turned suddenly, throwing water all the way up on the bank. He was gone. Out in the river channel where the big ones hide. We turned and collected our poles and lines and started up the bank. Larry turned and said, "So long big fish, we'll see you next time."

None of us felt too good. Rog and Jack had to stop a couple of times and sit down until their dizziness passed. It wasn't a total loss, though. We'd got to try moonshine and we did catch the great Ohio River catfish. Nothing could take that away from us. I'd make my twenty-five dollars this summer. The hard way, working in hay. It was sure turning out to be a nice day.

RON ELLIS

Into the Woods (An Excerpt)

From *Cogan's Woods* (2001)

"DID YOU SEE HIM?" Dad said. The bird had exploded at our feet from the base of one of those cedars. "That's a pheasant for you. All jumpy and nervous." There was great excitement in his voice, a kind of passion I had not heard before, not even for the squirrels.

The bird, this pheasant, did not have a white collar around its neck and there were no bright colors on its head. It did not look like any pheasant I had ever seen on the covers of *Field & Stream* or *Sports Afield*.

"You sure that was a pheasant?" I asked.

"Not a ringneck pheasant," Dad said, "but a grouse. People up here call them pheasants."

"They're fast, whatever they are."

"I've never been able to hit one of those old brown birds. They're up and gone before I can get my gun on them. Lots of guys around Persimmon Gap have, though. My dad killed a few over the years, mostly when he stumbled onto one when quail hunting down near the river in some of those old brushy draws. I always wanted to shoot one for myself so that I could look at it real close when it was still warm and lifelike."

"I'm not sure I could hit one. But I'd like to try," I said.

"There's plenty of them in this country. We'll hunt them together here someday."

In time, I would learn to love to hunt those old brown birds.

Years later this would be the place I came to with Dad, when I had decided to become a serious grouse hunter, to make good on that promise. It was the day before Christmas Eve. We had hunted hard all day without much luck. Lady, my sweet little persimmon and white Brittany with the smiling eyes, had found a bird or two, but we had not been in position to shoot. By late afternoon, we reached the saddle in the ridge above the cedar thicket that sheltered the old road.

"I think I'll stay up here and poke around for a while," Dad said. "You and Lady go on down the road there and see if you can find a bird or two. Just down the hill is where you saw your first pheasant. Remember?"

"Couldn't forget that bird," I said. "It was the first time I heard you call them pheasants."

"I still like calling them pheasants. Guess I always will," he said. "You come back up here and get me on your way out and we'll make our way back up to the car and stop and see Sherm and Stony before dark." He moved on down the ridge and sat on a big rock.

"Are you sure you wouldn't rather hunt?" I said.

"I'm sure. And be careful. You know these woods about as well as I do by now. Still, you have to be careful. I'll be fine here. I have some remembering to do."

I left him sitting up there on that rock, the corduroy collar of his faded canvas hunting coat turned up against the wind. He was smoking a cigar and looking off toward the river, the hills across it barely visible in the dusky evening air, the barrel of his Ithaca pump gun resting back against his left shoulder. He looked content sitting there, smoking and alone with his thoughts. I wondered how many times he had done just that, at that exact spot.

I spent the next two hours looking for birds. On a flat below where Dad sat on that rock, the ground is composed of soft gray clay, mixed with chips of gray-green slate that litter its surface. The cedars grow well in that poor ground, and just beyond, toward the river, there is an overgrown pasture, a place where we had seen birds in years past. Lady searched the edges and came up with a scent that worried her. She drifted with it and worked and worked until she decided to point. I whispered to her as I moved to flank her, fully expecting a grouse to blow up in front of me before I could get set for a shot. The spongy ground sucked at my boots on every step and when I stepped into the cover, a pair of woodcock corkscrewed up through the cedars and the second-growth hardwoods. And then two more flushed and still another pair, until a total of 12 birds had floated up out of that cover. I lowered my gun, the woodcock season was long closed, and watched in awe at what had to be a legendary "fall" of woodcock, a magical occurrence I had only read about until that evening.

"Not this time," I said to Lady. She looked at me with concern, cocking her head this way and that, as if trying to understand my words, my intentions here, and then the sparkles in her amber eyes danced and I knew she understood. "Hunt 'em up, girl," I said. "Find me a grouse now."

Close to the bottom of the hill, I found and killed over Lady's next point my first Belden County "pheasant" not more than 100 feet from the spot where Dad and I had flushed that first one so many years ago. Lady found the dead bird and I dressed it alongside the old road and hung the entrails in the branches of a big cedar to keep them away from her. I placed the bird in my hunting coat and picked up the shell I had used to kill it, a green Remington number 8 shot, and sniffed at the still-warm scent of the burnt powder. Now I loved these woods for yet another reason. "Too many to count," I said to the woods. "Too many to count." And then I called Lady and headed up the steep hillside to meet Dad. Before I reached the saddle in the ridge, it began to snow. The flakes drifted slowly by, as if in a dream, falling steadily. The woods were becoming covered in white. Nothing stirred. I climbed on.

At the top, just a step over the crest of the ridge, on a narrow shelf of ground that allowed me to look out over a thicket of ancient cedars, I stopped to catch my breath and to see if I could discover which way Dad had gone. I had not been there long before I saw him below me, coming up out of the cedars, the old trees a bluish-green tint in the fading light of the evening, their soft limbs bending with the slowly accumulating snow. Dad was on a game trail that passed through the middle of the cedars, and headed straight toward me. A crow, the color of the shiny onyx ring Dad had worn for years, and which he bought with his first railroad paycheck at the age of 17, lifted off from somewhere near Dad and flew directly over my head. As it passed above me, it pulled up its ash-gray feet, tucked them into the blackness of its belly, its wings slowly flapping, and traveled noiselessly through the heavy winter sky, and then disappeared in the falling snow, headed into the heart of the Grove.

"Stay up there so you can see down into here," he said. "Call Lady and just stand there and watch."

"You got a bird down there?" I asked.

"No bird, just a surprise."

With his shotgun cradled in his left arm, Dad started back down the path, snow building on the shoulders of his hunting coat and the curled brim of his faded green Jones cap. The light was dim and it was quiet enough that I could hear the click of his Zippo lighter as he walked away from me. I saw a flame move toward a cedar to his right and then a little flame flickered within the webby green darkness of the cedar limbs, and in seconds there were several more tiny flames flickering there. Then Dad moved to his left and more tiny flames appeared in the tree limbs on that side of the trail. Before he was done, he had passed down through those cedars and lit a hundred or more white candles that he had placed in the branches on both sides of the trail while I was off hunting. The entire thicket was illuminated with white candlelight and there was more snow coming down, with

the whole place looking very much like the inside of one of those glass balls you shake to make it snow and then settle down on a Currier & Ives Christmas scene. And there was Dad standing at the far end of the lighted tunnel with a big smile on his face.

"Merry Christmas, son," he yelled. And then he walked back through the candlelit cedar trees and stood next to me on the ridge in the gathering dark.

"I always wanted to do this up here, all of my life," he said.

"This place has always felt more like Christmas to me than any place I've ever been. There's just something about the way the hills roll and the way the light comes in here in the evening. It gets all stained with the color of these cedars.

"The first time I came up here was with my father. I was young and we were out looking for a lost rabbit dog that belonged to a friend of his. The dog got to running a fox and ran out of the country. We were at this exact spot when Dad told me to stay put and listen for the dog while he cut through the cedars and went out to the point over there to listen for it." He looked off toward that place, as if looking again for his father standing out there alone. He waved his hand over the spot before going on with the story.

"Well, while I was standing here looking and listening, I didn't see or hear that hound, but coming up through these cedars on this same trail was a big buck. There weren't many deer in this part of the country then, or now, but the old men told stories about this one big buck that was said to haunt this piece of ground. Well, he came out of the cedars, just down there," he said, pointing to the spot. "His rack was draped with all this shredded greenery, like he'd been rooting around on the ground, and there was this crown of that bright green moss that grows under cedars up here, mixed with what looked like some mistletoe riding on top of his rack. He looked every bit the picture of Christmas." He paused to light his cigar, blew a thick puff of smoke into the sky, and then continued.

"That old buck stood there for some time so I got a good look at him. He was staring at me and I was too afraid to move, afraid he'd run off before I got a good look at him. Finally he pawed at the ground, snorted in my direction, and then run off, up toward Sherm and Stony's place, with his long white tail held straight up in the air as he cleared the deadfalls up on that flat of second-growth timber. When he reached the edge of the woods near the pasture, he stopped. He was silhouetted against the sky, the light just about like it is now, and he shook that big rack from side to side and then run off across the pasture. I never saw him again, and I never told my Dad I'd seen that deer. I'm not sure he would have believed me anyway. Before we left that night, I made sure to go down there and look for tracks. I found them right where he had stood and then run off, so I know he really was there. You believe me, don't you, son?" His eyes were clear and there was a good bit of grin on his face as he puffed on the cigar and shook some snow off the collar of his coat.

"Why wouldn't I?" I said.

"I knew you would. You've always been a believer. I'm glad I waited until now to tell you that story and to light up those trees. Merry Christmas, son," he said.

"Merry Christmas, Dad," I whispered, "and thanks for the story."

I showed him the pheasant and shared the story of its killing. He patted me on the shoulder, talked to Lady, and reached into his pocket and gave me a blue Peters .410 shell, a paper one, with a note rolled up inside of it. I fished out the tiny tube of paper, lit my lighter, held the flame above it, and read: *August 13, 1963. Ron killed two gray squirrels and a fox squirrel today with the Sears .410. This was his "good luck" shell. I killed two grays and a fox squirrel out on the point. The weather was wet and foggy. Ron saw his first pheasant. A good day, one to remember.*

"I thought since you're a pheasant hunter now you'd like to know when you saw your first one," Dad said. "I thought it was a good Christmas present to give out here in the woods."

"I have a shell for you, too," I said. I reached into my pocket and gave him the green Remington 20-gauge shell I had used to kill the grouse. "There's no note in it, yet." He sniffed at the green paper hull, and then rubbed it between his thumb and index finger as he had always done, like he was trying to get all of the experience out of the shell, connecting with it as deeply as possible.

"Make a note to put in it," he said. "Write down the best details so you can remember how it was, when you were happiest. You'll always be glad you did." He pulled his collar up and adjusted his carry of the shotgun. I glanced at his face and saw his eyes were red, and there was a glisten to them. "The wind's picking up," he said. "Cold, too. All of this weather's got my eyes to watering. We'd better get on back to the car."

We stood there a few minutes longer, reluctant to leave, and watched the tiny flames flickering in all that dark green of the cedars, until the last one had died out. We eased down the steep slope of the ridge and slipped out along the trail. As we passed among the cedars, one more candle, one we had not seen, hissed and gave up its final light to the snow and to the quiet coming of another Christmas in the hills.

WILLIAM E. ELLIS

Big Boy (An Excerpt)

From *River Bends and Meanders* (1992)

"MR. SMITH, how're you, today?" Rufus Brown said, trying not to let on about his great secret.

"Why, I'm right fine, how're you?"

"Right fine myself, I got a proposition for you."

"Wha's that, Rufus?"

"Come out to my wagon and look in my barrel. I got somethin' that ought to be worth a look-see."

Smith and Rufus ambled out to the wagon where the tight-lipped children were about to burst with their secret.

Rufus motioned to the barrel, and Smith slowly pulled himself up on the wagon. Cas turned back the canvas, and Smith peered down into the barrel. His mouth dropped open and he swung toward Rufus, who stood on the ground.

"Lordy, I ain't never seen such a fish. Where'd you catch it, Rufus?"

"The Kentucky River below Boonesbura," Rufus replied laconically. "If'n you let me use your big trough, I'll cut you in on the show-off of Big Boy."

"Big Boy, is that what you call him?"

"Yep."

"Done. Let's shoo this crowd away and make 'em pay to take a look at Big Boy, and I'll split it with you."

"But then I get everything for the sellin' the cat?"

"Right, I might even put in a bid myself."

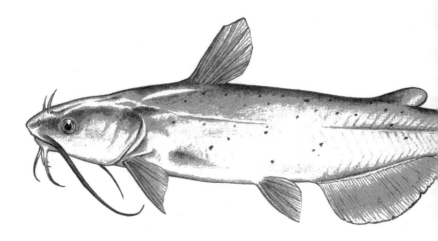

Smith and Rufus pulled a light wagon out of the livery stable that acted as a shield between the trough, Brown's wagon, and the crowd. Some of the men jostled each other as Smith swung the wagon around, but they said nothing.

Smith, Rufus, and Cas carefully worked the barrel to the back of the wagon. They slowly tipped the barrel toward the large wooden water trough and with a mighty splash the monster catfish plunged into the larger container. Cas was given the task of refilling the trough with fresh water.

A couple of mule-traders saw the flash of the fish's underbelly and ran over to the trough. "Were that a catfish? If'n it was, it must be the biggest ever caught in the Kentucky River. Is that w'ere it come from?" they said.

"That's right. Go tell that gang over there that they can see the biggest catfish ever caught in the Kentucky River. It must weigh a hunnert pounds, if'n it weighs an ounce," Smith replied.

Within minutes men, women, and children were lined up in single file that stretched back toward the courthouse. Two wagons were pulled close together so that only a single line of customers could file through to the trough. Mrs. Brown was given the task of taking up the precious coins that represented a

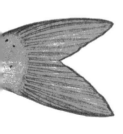

sacrifice for most of the Court Day crowd. Rufus and Smith stood on each end of the trough moving the crowd along. Big Boy obligingly surfaced occasionally, fixing his big black eyes on a lucky customer. Bets were made by a few of those inclined toward gambling as to the weight, length, and distance between the eyes of the monster catfish.

Cas and the children were given the task of running up the streets to drum up trade. "Come see the biggest catfish ever caught in the Kentucky River. The biggest in the world," Cas yelled as he circled the courthouse. Before long a line extended all the way up Main Street to the Post Office.

Rufus worried that Big Boy would die, and he or Cas periodically dipped water buckets from nearby rain barrels and threw them into the trough. With each bucketful of fresh water Big Boy became more visible, appearing to revive slightly.

"Make way for Perfesser Trundlesworth," someone said. Trundlesworth, the best-dressed man in the crowd and professor of biology and anatomy at the college up on the hill, slowly edged his way to the trough. He didn't pay ten cents.

"What's this balderdash I hear about a big catfish?" he said as he adjusted the spectacles on his nose. After what seemed like hours, he peered down into the water. He walked around the trough, stepped off distances, raised his arms as if mentally weighing the fish, and took off his hat.

"This may be the biggest fish ever caught in the Kentucky River or any other river for that matter, in my considered opinion. Who caught this catfish, more specifically *Ictalurus punctatus* in the Latin?"

Rufus pushed through the crowd that had gathered uninvited around the professor. "Where's your ten cents, perfesser?" he asked.

"My good man, I will not only give you a dime, I will give you ten dollars of good money for this fish, what do you say to that?" the professor said with a flourish of his right hand.

Rufus removed his straw hat, scratched the back of his head, and turned toward Smith. "I allow as how he's worth at least thirty dollars. They's enough fish there to feed this multitude, just like it say in the Bible."

"I don't intend to feed anyone with this fish. I want to send it to the icehouse, encapsulate it in dry ice, and thenceforth ship it to the Smithsonian Institution in Washington, District of Columbia. This fish is of great historical significance and scientific importance and must be preserved at all costs. Do you understand, my good man?"

"I don't know nothin' about that. I just want thirty dollars for my catfish, Big Boy," Rufus thoughtfully replied.

The professor pondered for a moment and then made a counteroffer: "Firstly, the fish is probably a female rather than a male so the name Big Boy is ludicrous. Secondly, I will have to confer with my superiors about the sum you request. Please do nothing until I return. Do you promise?"

Rufus rolled his eyes toward his wife and then nodded his head slowly.

"A correct decision, my good man. I shall return within the hour."

As the professor rushed off through the crowd, people again began viewing the fish, often jostling each other for a closer look. Whenever the line slowed Rufus and Smith pushed the crowd along. After viewing the fish, the county judge called in the sheriff and two deputies to keep the crowd under control. Cas was dispatched by Smith to the nearest bank where several pounds of coins were converted to greenbacks. Smith placed the money in a black money belt that he had under his denim coat.

Several people eyed the bulging belt, but Smith's imposing stature and reputation for being a no-nonsense Baptist deacon negated the threat of loss or theft.

"That catfish is gonna die, I just know it," Rufus whispered to Smith.

"Son, it don't worry me none. We done made over forty dollars," Smith replied with a smile on his face. "That's twenty apiece, don't you know." Not a few in the crowd remarked that they had never seen him smile before.

The crowd swelled. Big Boy occasionally rose to the surface, and grown men and children alike gave out squeals of glee.

"Look at the size of that booger. I ain't never seen the likes of this in all my ninety-one years," a frail elderly man exclaimed, holding on to the shoulders of two strapping great-grandsons.

A ten-year-old boy dipped his hands into the trough, hoping to catch the tail of the fish. His mother boxed his ears for his efforts as if he had desecrated the sanctity of a Sunday worship service.

Blacks and whites, men and women, boys and girls, they all filed past the trough. Dozens slapped Rufus on the back. He was offered drinks from bottles of store-bought whiskey stealthily concealed under coats. At least one local lady was rumored to have offered him her bed.

As the afternoon wore on, viewing of the catfish became the most important event since the last hanging behind the courthouse. Many people who could afford the tariff came through the line more than once. Children cried when their parents refused to pay the price of admission. Many people realized for the first time in their lives that they were poor when they couldn't tell their neighbors that they had viewed the fish more than once. The fourteen-year-old son of a prominent local businessman made enemies for a lifetime after he rushed about telling the crowd that he had viewed the catfish twenty times. His political career foundered twenty years later because of the memories many local citizens had of him as an impudent youngster who had flaunted his wealth on the day of the big catfish.

In the course of the viewing, two fistfights marred an otherwise festive event. Deputies rushed several men off to the nearby jail. All of the culprits were drunk, or they would never have violated the occasion. One woman fainted when the catfish splashed its tail as she bent over the trough. Several ladies loosened her shirtwaist and bodice, but only the ministrations of a local physician finally revived her. Actually, the dose of smelling salts that he thrust under her nose would have brought most anyone back to life who was worth saving.

Hour after hour the crowd passed by. Local buyers of fish made their offers to Rufus, but he kept his own counsel. Smith pushed several of the bidders away whom he declared were "no count." The partners in this enterprise figured to make all they could from the fish in the trough and then sell it off to the highest bidder. Cas kept freshening the water in the trough until viewers sloughed through six-inch-deep mud surrounding the viewing area. None complained. The professor from the college up on the hill did not reappear.

By midafternoon, the crowd began to thin out. In order to keep the crowd interested, Smith convinced Rufus to reduce the price of admission to five cents, and soon the crowd again backed up past the courthouse. After about an hour this ploy also faltered, and Cas thought of another way to keep up the crowd's interest.

As shadows lengthened on Main Street, Cas appeared with a hand-lettered sign painted on the back of an old political poster with William Jennings Bryan's picture on the front. In tall black letters the sign read: "GUESS THE WEIGHT OF BIG BOY. TEN CENTS A CHANCE. TEN DOLLARS TO THE WINNER."

More money came in. Smith continued to fill his money belt until it would hold no more. Just before the bank across the street closed, he deposited more than one hundred dollars into his account with the permission of Rufus. Both partners in this enterprise conferred and decided that if the fish did not die before seven o'clock they would kill Big Boy and auction it off to the highest bidder, weighing the fish on the scales at the nearby feed store. They collected over thirty dollars from customers who tried to guess the weight of the fish. Guesses were written in a black ledger book, and no duplicates were permitted. Estimates ranged from twenty-three to ninety-four pounds.

Big Boy refused to die. Every time Cas splashed bucketfuls of water into the trough, the fish revived and rose to the surface for a moment before again settling on the bottom. Six o'clock, and still the crowd came. But now darkness gathered after a brilliant autumn afternoon, and shadows settled over the trough.

More and more wagons and buggies headed out of town. Most of these people would be at work at sunup the next day milking cows, harvesting the corn crop, or doing some other unending farmer's task. Though it had been an abundant crop year, some would soon be forced out by the falling prices for tobacco, their major cash crop. Today had been a brief respite from their toil. A few ladies had bought a bit of cloth for a new dress, a few men had traded knives, mules. Almost everyone had met with friends and traded gossip. One man had been sentenced to life imprisonment in the state penitentiary at Frankfort for killing his wife's lover. Perhaps he alone of all the people in town this Court Day had not seen the biggest catfish ever caught in the Kentucky River.

Smith nudged Rufus as the crowd got thinner and thinner. "He ain't gonna live much longer, I imagine," he whispered, "hit's time to get rid of him."

Rufus slowly turned his head toward Smith. "You gotta chaw? I been so excited all day, I ain't even took time for a chaw."

Smith reached into the back pocket of his overalls and pulled out a twist of hand-rolled "long-green" tobacco. Rufus cut off about three inches of the pungent tobacco with his pocketknife and thrust it into his mouth. He chewed for a moment.

"Time to sell Big Boy," Rufus shouted, surprising himself with his loud, self-confident voice. "We gonna let you bid for Big Boy by the pound, and then we gonna weigh him. Then we gonna give the ten dollars to the best guesser."

A small group of about fifteen men crowded near the trough. Rufus climbed onto the nearest wagon and asked for bids. "Ten cents a pound, twelve, fifteen, sixteen, eighteen, twenty-one," were bid by various members of the entourage, then the crowd fell silent.

"Come on now," Smith chimed in, "who wants the honor of ownin' the biggest fish ever caught in the Kentucky River?"

"I do," shouted a portly man from the rear of the crowd, "I do, and I raise the bid to thirty cents cash money."

"Any more bids?" shouted Rufus, realizing that he would soon lose control over the biggest event of his lifetime.

No one in the crowd made a bid, although there was a hum of quiet murmuring in the audience.

"He's gone if'n they's no more bids," Smith said.

"I bid thirty-three cents and will go higher, if necessary," shouted Professor Trundlesworth as he walked up to the wagon. "This animal belongs in the Smithsonian Institution."

"Man, if you think you can get him out of the county without putrifyin', you're welcome to him," shouted the previous high bidder as he pushed through the crowd to his waiting buggy.

Rufus looked upon the professor's bid as a bit of folly. "You sure you got the money?"

"I will give a check upon the credit of the college for the catfish if my bid is accepted," the professor said slowly.

"Hold it," Smith interrupted, "this here's a cash sale. If'n you ain't got the cash, you can't buy no fish."

The man in the buggy raised up out of his seat. "I'll give you thirty-five cents a pound, and let's get off'n this foolishness." The professor, visibly shaken, had no choice but to walk disconsolately from the crowd. Alas, the biggest catfish ever caught in the Kentucky River was not to be found among the stuffed animals in the old castle of the Smithsonian Institution in Washington, District of Columbia.

"Sold." The word surprised Rufus, but it had definitely come from his mouth.

"Done. Weigh Big Boy so's I can take 'im to Lexington for the market tomorrow."

Rufus looked into the trough. Cas, Smith, and Beth gathered around him. "You gonna stick him, Pa?" Cas whispered.

"If 'n I have to," was all that Rufus could say.

Just then the miraculous happened. A big bubble of air rose to the surface of the trough. Slowly Big Boy floated to the surface on his back. The light underbelly contrasted with the dark water. He, or she, was dead.

The smaller Brown children also gathered around the trough. "Bye-bye, Big Boy," the baby said. No one else said anything, only staring at the monster fish.

"Get him weighed, if 'n you want your money," the man in the buggy shouted, "I gotta get to Lexington, right now."

Smith, Rufus, and Cas gently placed their arms under the fish and carried it over to the scales. No Methodist parishioner had ever been more gently and solemnly carried to the grave.

Big Boy's head and tail fell off the sides of the scale. Rufus carefully lifted these extremities back onto the scale surface. Smith began to place weights on the top of the ancient mechanism made in New York City. He shouted out the weights as they piled on. "Thirty pounds, 35, 40, 45, 50, 55, 60, 65, 70, 75, 80, 85, 90 pounds. Lordy mercy, I ain't never seen such a fish," he said, "and I done run out of weights."

"You sure you ain't filled that fish full of buckshot?" said the man in the buggy.

"Nawh sir, that's his true weight," Rufus said slowly, casting a look of warning at the stranger.

"Go get more weights," shouted someone in the crowd. Cas

immediately was dispatched to another livery stable. In a few minutes he was back with an armful of weights, all exactly one pound each. He handed them individually to Smith, who placed them on the mechanism.

"Ninety-one, 92," he said, and then the small crowd picked up the count. "Ninety-three, 94, 95, 96, 97, 98, 99," they shouted, and still the scale indicator was not balanced. "More," "More," "I bet he weighs a hunnert pounds," came the cries.

Smith placed one more weight on the scale and it balanced perfectly. The biggest catfish ever caught in the Kentucky River weighed exactly 100 pounds.

Although it was now dark, the gaslights on the courthouse square and the moon, which was already up above the buildings, illuminated the remaining joyous crowd. The man in the buggy paid Rufus thirty-five dollars in cash. He and four other men unceremoniously dumped Big Boy into the back of the buggy. The last Rufus saw of the fish was a spasm of its tail as the buggy pulled up the hill toward Lexington.

With thirty-five dollars in cash and sixty-five dollars from the viewing of the fish, Rufus had a hundred dollars—more than he had ever seen before, or would ever see again at one time. All of the children, except for Cas, were now fast asleep in one bed in a nearby rooming house. Another bed waited for Rufus and Beth. Cas volunteered to sleep in the livery stable. Smith went about the crowd advertising his business and inviting everyone back the next day to have their livestock properly taken care of at his establishment. The mayor, the county judge, and several other politicians made short speeches in the gaslighted atmosphere. They all lauded Rufus as the epitome of Kentucky manhood and Big Boy as proof of the purity of the waters of the Kentucky River. Great things were sure to happen, they said, in a community blessed with such advantages.

I wish I could end this tale on a happier note. It would be a better story if I could tell you that the catfish escaped from the man in the buggy; that he or she flopped off the back of that vehicle as it crossed the bridge over the river. But that did not happen. By early morning, the fish had been cut into large chunks of catfish steaks. Every square inch of flesh worth eating was stripped from that magnificent animal. By nightfall many Lexingtonians had feasted on the biggest catfish ever caught in the Kentucky River. By the end of the next day his or her bones had been sucked dry and devoured by a multitude of cats and a few rats.

The Brown family rode back home the next day, but not until after Beth had purchased a new Household sewing machine and a supply of buttons, ribbon, thread, and several yards of cloth. She had a busy wintertime ahead of her. Cas took his young lady to the pie supper on Friday night and retold the story of the catfish numerous times to admiring classmates. He spilled hot cocoa on his new white shirt.

No one's life changed much. Rufus achieved some measure of local fame and had his picture taken a few days after Court Day for publication in a Lexington paper. However, it was never printed, being bumped by more urgent news about the Harlan County coal mine disaster.

Rufus continued to work from sunup to sundown, and to run his trotlines on the Kentucky River. But he never caught another catfish that weighed near as much as Big Boy.

CAROLINE GORDON

An Excerpt from
Aleck Maury, Sportsman (1934)

IT WAS WHILE I was training Gy that I made another acquisition
— the best gun I ever had. That, too, came to me from Pat Henry.
I found it in Sid More's gunshop, standing in a corner with two
other breech-loaders. I saw the rosewood stock first and I picked
it up just for the pleasure of handling it. Sid was in his corner,
working, his back to me. I stood there and examined the gun.
It was fourteen gauge, thirty inches long, and weighed six and
three quarters pounds. My first reaction was pleasure in its lightness. You could hold it in your hand and shoot it like a pistol.
Next I examined the platinum ventholes. Then I saw the beautiful contrivances to carry caps in.

"Where'd you get this Greener, Sid?" I asked.

Without turning around he replied that it belonged to Colonel Henry. He had bought one of the new breech-loaders and had
told him to sell the Greener. He didn't know what Pat was thinking about. The Greener was a better gun any day. He added that
it had been made in London to Pat's order and had cost a hundred and fifty dollars in gold.

I set the gun down in its corner. We talked for a few minutes
about other matters, then I went back and picked it up again.

"I'll give you twenty dollars for it," I said.

Sid squared around, pushed up his spectacles, and stared first
at me and then at the gun.

"He told me to get whatever I could for it," he said slowly, then grinned. "You better take it, Professor. You'll never get a better gun."

I walked out of the shop carrying the Greener. I had eleven miles to drive but I got home that afternoon—in December it was, the last of the season—early enough to take the gun out. I carried a cut-off powder flask and a double shot pouch, cut off. I found I could load that gun, walking along, both barrels, almost as fast as any man could break a breech-loader and load it. I flushed two coveys that afternoon on the edge of the woods and I bagged nine birds. I've never seen birds cleaner shot. We found later that you could always tell whether a bird had been shot with the Greener or a breech-loader. There was always more shot in the bodies of the birds killed with the breech-loader than with the Greener.

I acquired the Greener in the days before smokeless powder came in, but I found later that it shot smokeless powder perfectly. I didn't have to clean it but once a season either. At the beginning of the season when the birds were young I'd get them usually in the head or wing. Three out of five birds would tower. As the season progressed I changed to No. 8 and wound up with three drachms of powder and an ounce of No. 7 shot. Three times in my life, using that Greener I've killed twenty-six birds out of twenty-four shots.

I must anticipate my story to tell of its fate. I shot it for ten or fifteen years before a hole came in the right-hand barrel—a man naturally shoots the right-hand barrel oftener than the left. Sid put a beautiful patch on the hole for me. The gun was as good as new—I might have gone on shooting it as long as I was able to carry a gun—but one day I was fool enough to lend it to my brother-in-law, a fine fellow and a good farmer but a poor shot. He set the gun down in the cellar near a cask of vinegar. Some drops of vinegar fell on that beautiful barrel. . . . He brought it back to me rusted. I took it out in the garden and buried it. Even to this day melancholy steals over me when I think of its fate. I could not ask better of life than to be walking again over the fields that lie between the Tink woods and Merry Point house, the Greener resting in the crook of my arm, Gy quartering the field ahead of me.

GEORGE ELLA LYON

An Excerpt from
Gina. Jamie. Father. Bear. (2002)

MABRY TAUGHT ME to ride a bike, to whistle, to program the
VCR. He made up great pretend games for when we drove to see
Grandma Pierce: "M & G, Sole Survivors from Mars" was one of
them. He designed our treehouse, including a PVC pipe firepole,
and carved our names on the rail.

In fact, he was the world's best big brother till Mom said she
was leaving, till the word came down like a cosmic axe and split
everything apart. Maybe if Mom had stayed single and just
moved to Cleveland Heights, or at least someplace in Ohio where
we could go on easy visits, but no, she waited three months and
married Whit and moved to North Carolina, his home territory.
We go there twice a year, sometime during Christmas break and
sometime over the summer.

It's never just a visit, though. Oh, no. Whit says it's "an in-
tegrative family time." This means we work together (and I accidentally put flour instead of powdered milk in the quiche mix
in the bakery at 4 A.M.), we play together (freezing our bones in
a pool fed by mountain springs), and we hike together. Hiking
is the best, because we do see neat stuff sometimes. But it's also
the worst. It takes forever. Like last time, right before school
started.

"How much farther?" I asked, leaning into the steep path,
huffing under the weight of jeans and hiking boots and a day-
pack of food and water. And from the front of the line, Whit

proclaimed, "Just till we get there. You'll hear it before you see it."

"I hate this," I muttered to Mabry, who was right in front of me.

"Don't whine," he hissed.

"I'm not whining!" I said, disgusted. "We've been in these woods for hours and I just want to know how far to the stupid waterfall."

As if on cue, Whit declared, "You're going to love it."

Oh, right, I thought. That's what Mom told us about you.

"Are you okay, Gina?" This was my mother, who was last in our staggering line. Marissa, Whit's eight-year-old, was in between us.

Before I could answer, Mabry put in, "What about me? I've given my skin to maintain the insect population."

"I want to see!" Marissa cried in her high little voice. She's always afraid she'll be left out.

"He's kidding, Tadpole," Whit told her, his voice pitched below the crunch of stick and leaves.

So I never answered Mom's question about being okay. Did she really want to know? I wondered. If she cared, would she have left us? Would she have married this Happy Hiker and taken off? But it was too hot—yes, it's hot in the woods in August, I don't care how far up you are—and I was too sweaty and itchy to go on with my wondering. I trudged on. At least I still had my world. Well, that world minus Mom.

The path turned, and I could hear the rushing water.

"Man, I'd like to be in that," Mabry said.

Whit topped the rise in front of us. "There it is!" he sang out.

Mabry sprinted the rest of the way. "Cool," he said.

I didn't hurry. Water is water. But, well, okay, when I got there, this was something. It had two drop-offs, like giant steps that the water poured down, and the air in between was white with spray.

"Great Bear Falls," Whit said. "Or, as folks here say, Big Dipper and Little Dipper."

Sometimes Whit included himself in "folks here," though Mom said he'd lived away from these mountains now as long as he'd spent growing up in them.

He went on, "Not so long ago, when the First People lived in these mountains (Whit means Indians. That's the way he talks.) they knew that Spirit connects all things"—I made my hand like a telephone and held it away from my ear to show Mabry how bored I was, but he was looking at Whit, listening. Sheesh!

"And they knew that the bears they hunted, bears who themselves hunted in these woods and fished in these waters, were related to the Great Bear in the Sky."

"The Big Dipper!" Mabry said, excited. This is why teachers love him.

"Yes!" Whit said. "So our names for the falls came from that vision."

"Daddy," Marissa broke in, "you mean Indians lived on this mountain?"

"They sure did."

"How do you know?"

If I'd asked a question that way, Dad would have told me not to be a smart-aleck, but Whit just said, "Well, honey, wherever people live, they leave things behind, like tools and weapons and pottery, and other folks find them."

"And bones," Mabry added.

"You mean dead people?"

Marissa asked. Her little eyebrows and her whole face squinched up. She was that interested.

"Yes. Human bones and animal bones, too," her daddy told her. "From the creatures they hunted."

"Like bears," Mabry said.

"We are thinking!" Whit said, too happy. He has this "we" thing, always trying to turn Mabry and me into his family. But you can't make a family like you make an army. You can't just draft kids. And anyway, we had a family until he came along.

"So bears would be in the water and Indians would shoot them dead," Marissa declared, crouching down at the edge of the stream and pulling back an invisible string on her invisible bow.

"No, no," Whit said, earnest again. "The First People didn't hunt bears like that. They waited till spring for someone to dream where a bear's den was—you know bears sleep through the winter. Then a hunting party would go to that spot and call the bear, saying, 'Grandfather, come out!' and then—" Whit didn't notice that his daughter had quit listening. She was pulling on Mom's arm.

"Whit," Mom interrupted, "that's fascinating, but these kids are hungry. Why don't we put out our picnic and eat while we listen?"

"All right," Whit said, looking confused. He took a blue tarp from his pack and spread it on the least slopey bit of ground near the falls. I was just about to sit down when he commanded, "Tick check!" and we had to line up for the once-over.

Then we sat down to assorted sandwiches made at the bakery: cream cheese, olive, and nut (yuk!); soybean and herb spread (double yuk!); and turkey and Havarti (the ones in my pack). As I handed some to Mom, she looked at my hand.

"You're still wearing Mother's ring," she said.

"Um-hmm," I said. Like it meant anything.

"I've always wondered where it came from," she said, taking

out a plastic bag of carrot and celery sticks and sliding it across the tarp to Whit.

"You told me it was Grandma Pierce's," I said.

"That's right, Gina!" Mom looked so pleased that it made me sad and mad at once. She'd given me the ring as a birthday present right after she and Dad split up. I didn't want it then or now, and I didn't want to be remembering. "It was Mother's wedding ring," Mom continued. "But my father had found it in a pawn shop somewhere. They were too poor to afford a new ring . . . ."

Mabry broke in. "She just wears that ring because she can't get it off," he said. "She was pitching for me bare-handed. I hit a pop fly and she caught the ball. Broke her finger."

Go, Mabe, I thought. Mom looked away.

Later, on the flight home, Mabry pointed out that the woods make Whit lecture more and they make Mom sappy.

"Sappy," he said, hooting. "It's a pun. Get it?"

JIM WAYNE MILLER

An Excerpt from
His First, Best Country (1993)

STANDING ON THE BRIDGE over Newfound Creek, looking down into the dark water slipping under the bridge, Jennings realized he'd stopped the car and walked onto the bridge out of old habit. There'd been an old bridge here years ago, a wooden bridge, and it was to that bridge they'd come in late winter and early spring to watch for the arrival of redhorse, a fish that ran up the creeks like salmon. He stared into the pool below, occasionally shaking his head, remembering those days, and the men and boys he ran with.

He'd lived for woods and waters in those days, he and his buddies, passionate hunters and fishermen. He recalled now how their rifles had cracked on the ridges and in the hollows, how they would come off the slopes knee-deep and noisy in red and yellow leaves, guns in the crooks of their arms, the tails of gray squirrels flying from every pocket. He could remember now the feel of a still-warm squirrel's body against his thigh, limp as after love. He recollected how they'd come home from a hunt, just before daylight, riding the fenders of a jeep or pickup full of hounds, their rifle butts resting on their thighs, ready for the fox or possum or coon whose eyes glowed in the headlights. It seemed to him now they'd been bloodthirsty mountain boys. For even the pockets of their hunting clothes drank up the cooling blood of squirrels and rabbits, pheasants and partridges stuffed into them. Instead of money, they'd carried dried blood in their pockets.

But it seemed to him now, remembering, that what they'd really thirsted for was not blood but miracles. For when the rabbit bounded out of a clump of broomsage, or when the squirrel sat in his sights, tail jerking, or when the pheasant roared up at his feet and flew, twisting and turning through the timber, it was the awe that sowed itself like melting frost along his bones, and bloomed, ice crystals in his stomach—it was that awe that drew him into the woods again and again.

The woods had been a faith they lived by, every bird or animal that swung into their sights a revelation. Killing them was just their clumsy, ignorant way of trying to hold a wonder in their hands. The miracle that was a squirrel or pheasant, its perfect, sleek wildness, had never failed to amaze him, awe him into a more perfect worship of the woods.

Unable to say it, still he'd known that certain things were beautiful. And he guessed the men and boys he hunted with felt the same way. They'd mistaken the shine of a steel trap, the aura of the clean kill, the brilliant fish leaping on a line, moonlight on a blue gun barrel, the eyes of a coon, caught in a flashlight's beam, glowing like banked fire—they mistook that light for the shine around the lives of animals, the brilliance of their strength and speed and suppleness. All the time they'd been trying to hold fire in their hands; they'd been trying to reach out, wanting to touch, to draw a wonder close and hold it still, the better to be amazed.

That was why—for they hadn't really been bloodthirsty—that was why they'd let their hands grow guns, steel traps, and hooks. He thought he understood now that back then they'd been like children making shadows on a wall: they'd held their hands before the light of their lives, and shaped them into shadowheads of hounds, and loosed them, frothy-mouthed, into the woods.

But every time they'd tried to hold in their hands the wonder that was the life of something wild, they'd had to watch the wonder fade, grow dim and lusterless, breathed out in bloody bubbles through the nose. They had to feel the last heartbeats flutter inside the soft rib cage; they had to see the brilliant fish, speckled, streaked, barred, go pale on their stringer. Birds and animals brought in the jaws of hounds fell at their feet, wet and rumpled, like bedraggled stuffed toys. The eyes of partridges and pheasants clouded over; the shine of their life, like sunlight leaving a field of broomsage, like fur that glistened and shone when muscles rippled underneath, left forever.

They'd been lethal believers, living to be amazed. Still, their death-dealing touch had given glimpses, even as the shine faded from the life of some bird or fish or animal. Glimpses. Maybe that was why they'd killed again and again. They'd killed for imperfect fleeting glimpses, for the opportunity to come so close to something amazing and beautiful.

FREDRICK PFISTER

Spirit Deer

From *Sporting Classics* (September–October 2004)

HE APPEARED LIKE an apparition. Like most deer sightings, one moment the meadow is empty, the next, ghostlike, a deer materializes. At first, I distrusted what my eyes told me was a big buck. Like a textbook case of early blur, I clearly saw deer. But the pieces did not fit. Maybe black bear was the solution. I squinted to isolate the image. It was a buck and as I watched he lifted his head, curled his lips back, and scented the evening air. His antlers, polished to an ivory white, were in stark contrast to his coal-black body. They swept up and out like an alabaster crown atop a wondrous natural rarity.

He was a melanistic deer, a genetic misprint or a harbinger of future events, depending on your science. And he was beautiful. Black-coated and totally devoid of any classic markings of a whitetail, he stood in elegance, framed by the bleached broomsedge. I raised the scope and panned the rest of the field for other deer. Nothing. I glanced back at the place where the black-haired buck had been standing. Nothing. He had vanished as quietly as he had arrived.

Seldom does anyone knock at my door. In the foothills of the Cumberland Mountains, total strangers don't approach isolated cabins on dead-end drives. Curious to know who my unexpected visitor might be, I opened the door to find Charley Tipton standing on the front porch.

"Come in, Charley. What brings you to my neck of the woods? Is everything all right?"

Charley Tipton crossed the threshold and quickly, imperceptibly surveyed the layout of the room. Fireplace, gun cabinet, writing desk, small kitchen, fresh bittersweet, back door. It is the habit of Charley's people to establish where they are, who they are with, and how many exits there are when in unfamiliar surroundings. In the Southeast, full-blooded Cherokees like Charley had generations of reasons to display caution. Although he and I were always friendly toward each other, his ancestors' teachings were universal. In his eighty-five years they had never failed him.

"I have come to ask that you not kill the black deer," Charley announced as he turned toward me and the open front door.

He had on faded blue jeans that shined at the knees from the carpentry work that had been his occasional trade. Up top, he wore a navy-blue wool jacket, button missing, elbow fabric thin, to fend off the cool night air, and beneath that, a new red flannel shirt. Charley had dressed up for this visit.

Although he was a slight man, his hands were huge. It looked like he could pick up a dozen black walnuts with each mitt. But they looked like hands you could trust. They were not long, boney, slender digits that nervously fingered everything in their reach. His hands hung still at his side, patiently waiting to be called to work.

Charley Tipton's face was pure Cherokee. He had big ears, a big nose, and a ruddy complexion. At the farmer's market, he smiled often, showing ivory teeth. He wore thick gray-rimmed glasses. All the Cherokee men wore glasses. The ones that did not, couldn't see.

Charley glanced at a muddy arrowhead that I had found in the soybean field that morning. I had laid it on my desk, intending to clean it later. Charley returned his eyes to me, waiting my reply.

"Come on in and sit down. I'm making coffee," I said.

I reached down and picked up the arrowhead.

"Do you think this is Cherokee?" I asked, handing it to my guest.

"No," Charley said. "Much older. This was made by the Ancient Ones. My people found many of these when they first began hunting here. This point is so old we don't even have any stories about its makers."

He laid the stone down and looked toward me, obviously wanting to revive his original quest.

I was caught in an awkward situation. I really wanted to pursue the melanese deer. I had planned my hunt carefully, after thoroughly scouting the trails and sign. I had positioned my stand strategically. It was simply a matter of spending enough time in the woods. And now, Charley Tipton was asking me to give up what could possibly be the finest buck of my hunting career.

"How did you know that I'd seen the black deer again this year?" I asked, trying to postpone any answer.

"Joseph said that you told him about the deer when you were buying peaches at the fruit stand," he replied.

"The word really gets out when you've found a good buck," I said while forcing an awkward laugh.

I regained my sincerity.

"Is this buck one that you personally want to shoot?" I asked. "Or does it have some 'good luck' status among the Cherokee, like the white buffalo does with the Sioux?"

"The black-coated deer is very powerful to my people," Charley said. "I believe that it is unwise to upset the spiritual balance that we have at this time."

"Charley, I have hunted all over this country. Elk in Montana, antelope in Wyoming, and bighorns in Alberta. But I have never experienced such a magnificent animal as this melanistic deer. Somehow, he has silently crept into my life.

"Have you seen him?" I asked Charley.

"No, I have not," he answered. "But two of our young men saw him feeding in the persimmon grove. My people have talked much about this and we have decided to ask you to leave this deer alone. It is our wish that he lives."

I knew at that moment that I would no longer pursue the melanese buck. But I wasn't sure why. I only knew that this deer touched the lives of a people in a way much like it had touched mine. As I sat in silence, Charley quietly spoke.

"Many years ago, when I was very young, I was allowed to join the older men on a hunt in the river bottoms of the South Fork. In those days we slept in hide tents. We hunted until dark and we gathered much meat for the coming winter. On the seventh day I saw a black-coated buck running with two does in the border swamp. It was the most beautiful deer that I had ever seen. He was black like a raven and moved as quietly as the wind. I wanted to shoot this deer. But that night, the black deer came to me in a dream and he asked that I do not kill him like my father's father had killed him. He said that some things should not be possessed by man. He told me that terrible things happen when a man tries to own more than he needs. It leaves the man hungry and he is never satisfied. After my dream I saw the black deer many times in the river bottom. I could see him when many others could not. He and I became like brothers."

Charley concluded by simply stating: "They tell me that European white men do not have these dreams."

And with that, he stood up and left my house without saying thanks and without saying good-bye. Charley Tipton was not good at small talk. He came, he stated his business, and he left. The rest was up to me.

CHARLEY TIPTON DIED in August of the following summer. I heard the news from Joseph at the fruit stand. He said that Charley's daughter was looking for me and that I could find her at the house next to Charley's workshop on Clear Creek.

Dawn was a big woman with braided black hair and a round face. We had never met, but she knew who I was as soon as I climbed out of the pickup.

She reached into a drawer by the sink and produced what appeared to be a small packet, which she laid on the kitchen table. I picked up the pouch and recognized that it was made from coal-black deerhair and that it was very, very old. It was about four inches square and had a top flap to keep its contents from spilling. The talisman had an exquisite strap, decorated in a geometric pattern of quillwork that was the finest I had ever seen. The strap was predominantly black, flattened quills decorated with white quills arranged in a very primitive way to portray deer antlers. The quillwork was beautiful and complemented the black hair of the bag in its simplicity and elegance.

Opening the flap I poured two objects out from the inner hidings of the pouch. I was astounded! They were moonstones. Egg-sized and calcified, they are occasionally found in the intestines of whitetails. With odd geometric patterns etched into their surface, they sometimes resemble lumps of white coral. And they are said to hold great mystery and power to anyone fortunate enough to possess them. These moonstones were considered even more mysterious and powerful since they came from a black-coated deer.

They had been a gift to Charley, and now they were his gift to me.

I THANKED DAWN and gave her a bag of Joseph's peaches as a gesture of appreciation. Leaving the kitchen I stepped out onto the gray, weathered boards of the side porch. Burlap bags of black walnuts leaned clumsily against the railing. There was the buzz of cicadas in the treeline. The first cool breeze proved the ending of summer. Indian summer was sneaking in.

As the screen door shut behind me, Dawn called out from within.

"My people wish that you have pleasant dreams."

JESSE STUART

Our Wiff and Daniel Boone

From *Come Gentle Spring* (1969)

"I WAS BORN at the wrong time," Wiff Hendrix said in Pudd Bently's General Store and Post Office. "I wish I'd been born the same year Daniel Boone was born. Wish I could have come into the Kentucky wilderness with Boone, and with a longrifle, a powderhorn, and a bullet mold. But maybe I am Daniel Boone. You know, I could be."

When we gathered in Pudd's store on late afternoons after our work was done, Wiff would always be the first one there. All Wiff wanted to talk about was his hunting. He wanted us to believe he was the greatest hunter in Greenwood County, Kentucky, and the United States. We had heard him tell hunting stories we couldn't believe.

"Why would you want to be born when Daniel Boone was born?" Big Aaron Howard asked him. "If you'd been born then, you'd be dead now. Right now you are alive and talking to us!"

Wiff was sitting upon the counter with his long legs hanging over. He always liked to be the center of attraction and do the talking. He worked in the shops for Big Western Railway Company. He always wore pin-striped overalls, a jacket and a cap to match, and a red bandanna around his neck. When he took off the red bandanna, he wore a blue work shirt and a black bow tie. We wondered why he went dressed like one of Big Western's engineers who pulled the throttle of a long freighter. He might have fooled others but he didn't fool us. We knew he was a laborer at the shops. He had a sharp face, a long nose, and sharp black eyes that squinted like they were sighting over a gun barrel.

"Well, I'd like to have been Daniel Boone who had plenty of game to hunt," he said. "There's not enough game left in this country to hold me, the Daniel Boone of today. I might be the greatest hunter in all America."

"Self-bragging is half scandal," Little Ed Howard said. Little Ed was Big Aaron's brother. "Who eats all the wild game you kill?"

"Of course, Effie and I can't," he said. "You know my wife works at the Deering Shoe Factory in Dartsmouth. She's had wild meat until she's tired of it. We give some of it away. Sometimes when I'm in the woods killing squirrels, I load my hunting

coat until it's too heavy to carry. I enjoy hunting so much I go on killing and just leave the squirrels lay. I let the poor hunters who never get a shot when they hunt with me pick up the game I kill and claim the rabbits and the squirrels if they want them. They don't claim them in front of me but they go home and tell they've killed them. But old Wiff's the sure-shot Daniel Boone on the cottontail when one jumps up and starts bouncing over the field."

"No wonder we've not got any wild game left in these hills anymore," Penny Shelton said. "No wonder everybody is posting his land. You've caused this, Wiff! You just work enough days in hunting season to hold your rights at the Big Western shops. So you kill game and leave it lay!"

Penny Shelton was my cousin, over six feet tall and weighed two hundred pounds, and with shoulders as broad as a pantry door. He cut and hauled timber to a sawmill. He was not afraid of Wiff Hendrix or anyone else. And when he spoke he looked Wiff straight in the eye.

"It's because of your hunting in and out of season that everybody around here is posting his land," Penny said. "That's why my father posted his five hundred acres!"

"And it's why my father posted our three hundred acres," I said.

"It's why Pa posted our two hundred fifty acres," Big Aaron Howard said.

Big Aaron and Little Ed Howard and I worked on our fathers' farms. The Howards raised strawberries and we raised corn and tobacco.

"There's not a groundhog left for miles around," Big Aaron said. "We hardly see a rabbit anymore. We never hear squirrels barking where they used to den in the hollow beeches."

"You won't be bothered with old Wiff's hunting around here anymore," Wiff said. "I know you posted your land because of me. I don't feel bad about it. You can tell your fathers and mothers I don't. And you can tell them Wiff Hendrix won't fool with this little game here any longer! Tell them Wiff is going for bigger game!"

"Where are you going, Wiff?" I asked.

"Going to the Peninsula in Upper Michigan," he said. "I'm going after the deer!"

"You know there's a limit to what you kill up there," I said.

"Oh, yes, I know that," he said. "I'll bag my two bucks, bag a few for the other fellows too if they'll let me. I like to hunt and to kill. I like to see that rabbit tumble over after I shoot. I like to see that little squirrel tumble from the tree after the crack of my gun. And it will be the biggest thrill in my life to see that buck fall after the crack of my rifle! It's hard to stop Daniel Boone, Kentucky's long hunter."

"I've often wondered how it feels to be shot," Cousin Penny said. "And every time I pick up a rabbit or a squirrel, I can't keep from feeling how that rabbit or squirrel I hold in my hand felt when I shot it. I guess I'm a bit touchy about killing."

When Cousin Penny said this I never heard a man laugh like Wiff. He laughed louder than old man Martin White used to laugh when he got his afternoon *Dartsmouth Daily* and read the funnies. Pudd, who had been waiting on a few customers, stopped in his tracks while Wiff laughed. Wiff went up high with his laughter, then down to catch his breath, and then he went high again. It was like the waves on Big River rising and falling when winter storm winds blew up the river.

"You ever hear a man talk like that?" Wiff said at the end of a spasm of laughter. Then he laughed again. "A big man like Penny Shelton talking like that! What are we coming to in this county? Will we be a land of chickenhearted men? Daniel Boone thinks we are!"

"I'd think Daniel Boone killed game only when he needed food," I said.

"I don't care what Daniel Boone would think, or you either,

Wiff," Penny spoke stoutly. "I'm no more chickenhearted with people than you are. I said I wondered how it felt to be shot because I've never been shot and you haven't either. And I don't go out hunting for the pleasure of killing. I hunt for food to go on our table!"

"Boys, you're getting a little loud," Pudd said.

Pudd didn't want to offend us, for we traded at his General Store. He never joined either side in an argument at his store. Pudd was about forty, short, fat, and balding, and he always had a half-moon smile on his jolly face. He even let Wiff sit on his counter so he could be above us while he told his stories. Wiff liked his high position where he could be noticed by everybody. We sat in chairs or we stood or leaned on the counter. The General Store was our meeting place in Kensington, a village of three hundred.

"We'd better be getting home," Big Aaron said to Little Ed. "I've heard the wind blow too often in here."

"Well, friends, I'm sorry I disturbed you," Wiff said. "When you see my next hunting story it will be in the paper. Old Wiff standing beside his car with a buck strapped on each side. I'll be standing right beside them with my trusty rifle. Game around here anymore is peanuts to me. This Daniel Boone might even outshoot the old Daniel Boone."

When Big Aaron, Little Ed, Penny, and I left the store, Wiff was still sitting on the counter with his legs dangling down. He was waiting for another one of Pudd's customers to tell a hunting story. I don't know what was going through the others' minds as we walked silently away from the store but I know what went through mine. I was thinking about the lists of wild game Wiff had posted on the front of Pudd's General Store.

After squirrel season last year, this was before there was a limit, Wiff had posted five hundred thirteen squirrels killed. He had his name printed in block letters below this. According to his posters on the storefront, he had killed sixty-one groundhogs, five hundred ten rabbits, one hundred sixteen possums, twenty raccoons, four hundred eighty-two quails, seventy-three doves, thirty-five grouse, and sixteen pheasants. In December, just before Christmas, he posted his total, itemizing each animal and bird and adding the numbers to a total of eighteen hundred twenty-four. Below the figures in block letters he had printed: WILD GAME KILLED BY WIFF HENDRIX.

This was when everybody near Kensington began to post their land. Whether Wiff told the truth or not, everyone knew he stayed in the woods, in season and out, every day he didn't have to work at the shops for Big Western to hold his "rights." And this was the year Wiff had boasted that he would go over the two-thousand mark.

"I'm glad Wiff is going to the Upper Peninsula to hunt for big game," Big Aaron said, breaking our silence.

"Maybe there'll be something left for us to hunt," Little Ed said. "Pa said he was sure Wiff had been slipping past the signs and hunting on our posted land."

"You'd better never let me catch him hunting on us," Penny said. "He's not like he was at Walnut Grove when we went to school together. He just brags about killing all the time. Something has come over him. I believe he thinks he's Daniel Boone."

"I don't believe Daniel Boone would have cared for old Wiff," I said. "Daniel Boone didn't waste his powder and lead just going through the forest killing wild animals. He killed for food."

Now this was the end of squirrel season when Wiff sat on the counter and bragged to us about going for bigger game. He never made his two thousand animals and birds. At least we didn't see any posters. But we did read in the *Dartsmouth Daily* where Wiff Hendrix had gone to Michigan to hunt deer. Two weeks later we saw a picture in the *Dartsmouth Daily* of Wiff standing beside his car with a buck strapped on either side. There was a long write-up in the paper about him. I just saw his picture. I wouldn't read the article. I knew I'd hear all about his Michigan hunt and so would everybody else who would listen at Pudd Bently's store. We knew Wiff would be there, sitting on the counter high above everybody else, looking down and bragging about his hunting with his words coming faster than the wind blows up Big River in winter.

Wiff bought a hundred copies of the *Dartsmouth Daily*, so Pudd told Penny Shelton, who told Big Aaron, Little Ed, and me. He clipped the write-up and picture and sent the clippings to his friends. Pudd said he posted the letters at his General Store and Post Office. He said he sold Wiff one hundred stamps, the biggest stamp sale Pudd ever had from a customer. I went to the store once when Wiff was on the counter telling Mort Flannery and Elija Birdsong about his kill in Michigan on the first day.

"I could have killed fifty," he said. "I helped a dozen men get their bag limit on the second day."

I'd heard enough of this and I got out of the store as soon as I could.

It was just before Christmas when I was in the General Store and Post Office when old Wiff walked in where there were a lot of Christmas shoppers. He had known the right time to catch the crowd, the Saturday before Christmas. Wiff made everybody stop, even me, to take a look at him. He was carrying a rifle over his shoulder and he was wearing a buckskin outfit just like the kind Daniel Boone had worn in his picture in our old Kentucky history book. From his buckskin cap he had a coon's tail hanging down his back. There were little fringes on his buckskin jacket and up and down the seams of his buckskin pant legs just exactly like the clothes Daniel Boone wore in his portrait in the history book.

"Daniel Boone," a small boy said, looking up at Wiff Hendrix. "Mama, here's Daniel Boone!"

"Just how tall are you now, Wiff?" I asked. "You're over six feet four now! You're higher than the ceiling. But you do look like Daniel Boone in your buckskin suit. Say, who made that suit for you?"

"I had to get a tanner first to tan the hides," he said. "Then I got a tailor in Dartsmouth to make the suit. Think it becomes me?"

"You look like Daniel Boone," I said. "Only you're much taller than Daniel was."

What I said pleased Wiff Hendrix. With all the little boys looking up at him and following him as he paced up and down the store, their mothers and others looking on admiringly, Wiff Hendrix had his moment of glory. Some few had read the number of wild animals he had killed when he posted these after each season on Pudd's storefront and fewer had read his December totals posted there. Now they knew he was a great deer hunter and he was leaving their posted farms alone. And they were happy he was going to Michigan and hunt for bigger game.

Wiff went over the dirt walks in Kensington wearing his buckskin suit with its fringes and his buckskin cap with the raccoon's tail down his back. He went to visit his neighbors in his suit. He was the most talked-of man in Kensington, where there was a junction of four roads and people came in from over Greenwood County to trade. News of his new suit and his being a great deer hunter spread all over western Greenwood County. When he wore his buckskin suit, we never saw his wife, Little Effie, with him. But he had made his brags to Penny Shelton, to the Howard brothers, and to me that he and Effie would not have children but would both work and save their money until the day they had enough to move on to the North Woods of Canada where he would find a hunters' paradise. There they would settle in a cabin so he could hunt until the end of his days.

Since Wiff and I didn't go to the same church, I heard Wiff did go one Sunday to his church of Prophecy wearing his buckskin suit. I heard Effie wasn't with him that Sunday. This might have just been a rumor but it was talked all over Kensington.

The Howard brothers heard it too. They went to the Free Will Church, while Penny and I went to the Baptist. We heard this talk about Wiff at our Baptist church. There was always talk about Wiff Hendrix, what a great hunter he was and how old Wiff might be the new Daniel Boone of America. Here was this great man in our midst in Kensington. Some even called him the Second Coming of Daniel Boone. There were some people, the Tuttles, Sharps, and Birdsongs, who believed in reincarnation, and they believed old Wiff was Daniel Boone returned to earth again. And when Elija Birdsong told me in Pudd's store he was going to the Upper Peninsula with Wiff Hendrix who was the reincarnated Daniel Boone, I told him that Daniel Boone had grown six inches in his grave because the old Daniel was five ten and the new Daniel was six four. Well, that cooled old Elija off and silenced him.

Everybody on the farms in all directions from Kensington were happy not to see any more Wiff Hendrix posters on the store. Everybody was happy that he was a man of his word, that he had quit hunting the small game, and that he had gone to Michigan for bigger game. Wiff had become a better worker at Big Western's shops too. He never missed a day. And he boasted how he was saving money, putting it in two different banks so if one busted he'd have money in the other, saving for the day when he could retire with enough money to find a hunting paradise in Canada's North Woods. His wife, Little Effie, was still working every day in Deering's Shoe Factory over in Dartsmouth, where she left early in a small bus and crossed on the ferry over Big River. She was working for Wiff's later years in a cabin in the North Woods in his hunters' paradise.

The second autumn Elija Birdsong went with Wiff to the Upper Peninsula. When they returned they had their limit, all right. They had two bucks strapped on each side of the car. They must have made a pretty picture driving along the highway from the Upper Peninsula to Kensington. People meeting them must have stopped their cars to see Wiff's weighted car pass. This time it was Wiff and Elija in a picture together in the *Dartsmouth Daily*. Wiff was dressed in his buckskin suit and cap with his rifle across his shoulder. Elija Birdsong certainly looked less colorful standing there with Wiff in an ordinary hunting suit. Later we learned at Pudd's store that Wiff had hunted in his buckskin suit in Michigan.

One late afternoon when Penny and I went to Pudd's store to get groceries and ask for mail, Elija Birdsong was in the store telling about their hunt in Michigan. He was telling about all the wild woods up there and what a hunters' paradise it was and how Wiff was the Daniel Boone, the experienced hunter of the Kentucky wilderness.

"Well, if you believe old Wiff's really Daniel Boone reincarnated, who do you believe you are?" Penny asked.

There wasn't anybody in the store except Pudd, and he stopped dead in his tracks with a big half-moon smile on his jolly fat face when Penny popped this question to Elija.

"Well, I know who I am," he shot the answer right at Cousin Penny. "You remember McGary at the Battle of Blue Licks, don't you? Remember when they tracked the Indians to the Licking River! I, Colonel McGary, took off my hat and waved it and I said, 'You who are not cowards follow me.' And that's when I didn't take warning, fell in the river with seventy comrades around me."

"That massacre was the greatest slaughter in our state's history," Penny said. Then he winked at Pudd. "You were brave, all right, McGary, but you got a lot of the best men in Kentucky killed! Do you remember how it felt to be shot?"

"No, after my long sleep I forgot the pangs of death," he said. "I don't know whether I was shot by a rifle or hit by an arrow."

Old Pudd walked away holding back his laughter. I had to laugh in Elija's face. Penny laughed louder than Wiff had laughed at him when he said he wondered how the rabbit or squirrel he had killed felt when he snuffed out its life for food for the Shelton table.

"I can't understand reincarnation," Penny said between spasms of laughter.

"Well I understand it," Elija said. "It's no laughing matter! You go on laughing like this at the truth and you might be resurrected into a laughing hyena in darkest Africa when you come back into this world again!"

"I'll take my chances on that," Penny said. He didn't like what Elija had said to him. "Come on, Shan," he said, "let's get out of here before we're turned into a bull, a fox, or a dog."

"Well, you could be," Elija said to Penny and me as we left the store.

"You ever hear such crazy talk," Penny said as we walked down the steps. "What's happened to people's minds?"

"I never heard anything like it," I said. "Say, there was a picture of Colonel McGary waving his cap at the massacre of Blue Licks in our Kentucky history book. He was standing at the edge of the Licking River waving his buckskin cap and he wore a buckskin suit just like Daniel Boone wore except it had longer fringes than Boone's suit!"

"Watch old Elija," Penny said. "He got two bucks and he'll have himself a suit made with the long fringes."

We didn't have long to wait. Before December, Elija Birdsong was out wearing his buckskin suit with the long fringes. He didn't have a coon's tail attached to his cap because McGary's picture in the Kentucky history book didn't have one. But there wasn't as much talk about Elija's suit this year as there had been last year when Wiff first wore his suit to Pudd's store. Everybody had seen a man in a buckskin suit and the newness had worn off.

"Never discourage their going to Michigan to hunt big game," Penny said. "You know wildlife is coming back here again. I've seen groundhogs again this year. I saw them playing with their young. I never saw any last year. I've heard squirrels barking in the tall timber the first time in two years. And I hear quails hollering 'bob-white' in the fields again. It's a sound good to hear. Little Ed said he heard a pheasant drumming in his father's woods near their strawberry patch the other day. And he said he'd seen his first grouse in two years. Said he saw a brace going up the hill. Never discourage reincarnated Daniel Boone and Colonel McGary from going to the Upper Peninsula for bigger game. If they go there we'll get some wildlife back here."

Time passed and autumn came again. This time when Wiff and Elija went to Michigan, it was a different story. Wiff was arrested for bagging four bucks, two more than his limit, and Elija was arrested for bagging three. Their game was confiscated and they were fined two hundred dollars and costs. Little Effie and Pearlie Birdsong, Elija's wife, went over to Dartsmouth and wired them extra money to pay their fines and get home. This time they came without any deer and there was no write-up and no picture in the *Dartsmouth Daily*.

"But we promised to be good boys," Wiff told Little Ed, Big Aaron, Cousin Penny, and me in Pudd's store. "I made a mistake and I told them so. What we ought to have done was help the other fellows get their limits. But we took two cars this time. We just got greedy. I guess if we'd got by we'd've come home with seven bucks. Say, big-time hunting up there is like the old paradise in the Kentucky wilderness. We'll go back next year!"

"What if you were turned into a deer, Wiff, when you leave this world, do you think it would be any fun to be shot at?" Penny asked with a laugh. "You believe you could be turned into a deer, don't you?"

"Yes, I know I could," he said seriously. "But if I came back as a deer I would expect to be shot at. And I'd run for my life. I would do all I could to miss bullets and live as long as I could. Don't think I've not thought a lot about being a deer in my next reincarnation."

This time Cousin Penny did the laughing. I thought such words coming from old Wiff were funny. I wondered why he went to any church. I thought he just went to accompany Little Effie.

Time passed and another season came. Wiff and Elija made preparations to go. Elija now had two buckskin suits. He had one with the long fringes like Colonel McGary's and one like Daniel Boone's. He had one buckskin cap made of hide not tanned. The other was made of tanned hide. Old Wiff had four buckskin suits now. I never knew how many buckskin caps he had, tanned and untanned. I know each one had the coon's tail. And when they went back to the Upper Peninsula for their big hunt, they dressed in their early pioneer Kentucky wilderness clothes, clothes they thought they had worn nearly two hundred years ago when they had fought the Indians together at Blue Licks on the Licking River. I wondered if they had followed their Kentucky history and remembered that Daniel Boone had advised Colonel McGary not to attempt to cross the Licking River. But I didn't know what the two hunters talked about in this modern world when they could drive a car over good highways to Michigan. There'd been a lot of changes in our Kentucky and our country since they had been reincarnated. Once I asked Penny if he believed they ever discussed the Battle of Blue Licks, when old Wiff, who thought he was Boone, advised Elija, who thought he was Colonel McGary, not to cross the Licking and McGary, who was now Elija, waved his hat and called hardy Kentucky pioneer Indian fighters cowards and they followed him and seventy were slaughtered from ambush in five minutes.

Well this was the trip to Upper Michigan that ended old Wiff's hunting. When the wire came to Little Effie to come as fast as she could get there, she drew money they were saving for later years in their Canadian North Woods paradise from one of the banks. She got young Sack Middaw, the fastest driver in Kensington, to take her to Wiff. He had been mistaken for a deer and shot by a nearsighted Michigan hunter. He had seen Wiff's buckskin cap when it was in motion and had cut down on him with an automatic. How many times he'd fired were not clear in the long telegram Elija had sent Little Effie. But he said Wiff was at the point of death and for her to get there as soon as she could.

Wiff wasn't as near dead as Elija's wire had said. But Wiff's being mistaken and shot for a deer was the talk of Kensington. No one could believe that Wiff had been shot. Well, Big Aaron, Little Ed, Cousin Penny, and I, who had killed wild game in reasonable amounts for our tables, could believe this. We were good hunters too who didn't really relish killing. And we certainly never bragged about it. We knew if Wiff had worn one of his buckskin caps made from a buck's hide that had been cured but not tanned that it was the same color of a deer, and if old Wiff doddled his head and put his cap in motion some man at a distance could mistake him for a deer in woods where there were many hunters. We heard by the second wire Little Effie sent her mother that hunters had to pack Wiff ten miles to the little train that hauled him from the timber woods on a flat car for another forty miles to a little town and hospital. Now, Wiff was coming home in an ambulance.

Well, Wiff's classmates and friends who had once studied Kentucky history with him in one-room Walnut Grove School, where one teacher taught fifty classes in six hours, boyhood friends who used to hunt with him until he got on a wild killing spree and thought he was Daniel Boone, Cousin Penny, Big Aaron, Little Ed, and I were at Wiff and Little Effie's modest little frame house waiting when the ambulance with a Michigan license rolled up with Wiff on a soft bed closed in by glass. Little Effie was sitting there beside him with her hand on his head. Elija drove in behind the ambulance with Wiff's car. It was a pitiful sight. We weren't laughing at old Wiff now. We felt sorry for him. There he lay on that ambulance bed that looked like a hearse, a once big powerful man so full of life. We walked around behind the ambulance to carry Wiff on a stretcher into his home to transfer him to his own bed.

"I got two slugs in the back," he said softly when the ambulance driver released and rolled the stretcher up where we could take hold. "I'll never be able to use my right arm again. It's nearly shot off."

"We're sorry about this, Wiff," I said.

"We certainly are," Big Aaron said.

"Yeah, that nearsighted man shot me for a deer," he mumbled.

"And he never offered to pay any of Wiff's hospital and doctor bill," Little Effie said. "What's happened to us will end Wiff's dream of that happy hunters' paradise in the North Woods."

We carried Wiff into his own home. We lifted him into his own bed.

"Thank God, I'm home," he said. "No more hunting! I don't believe I'm the reincarnation of Daniel Boone either."

When he said this the young clean-shaven, well-dressed ambulance driver stood and stared at our Wiff Hendrix. Then Little Effie introduced him to us, William E. Westbrook.

"We're so glad to be back home," Little Effie said apologetically. "I forgot to introduce this kind young man to you. He's been wonderful to us."

I couldn't forget the way William Westbrook stared at old Wiff when he said he didn't believe he was the reincarnation of Daniel Boone. I thought he never knew who he had been transporting eight hundred miles in his ambulance.

"Yes, a close call, Penny," Wiff said. "And I'm not out of the woods yet. I have thought day and night about what you said about when you killed a little animal and picked it up how you wondered how it felt when its life had been snuffed out by gunshot. I remember how funny I thought it was then and how I laughed. Well, Penny, I know now. I couldn't count the times

I was hit and how many slugs I heard sing past me, for it happened so fast. If I'd got all the slugs, I'd've been brought back in a coffin."

"Forget about that evening in Pudd's store," Penny said. "Try to get well and get back to your job!"

"I can't work anymore unless Big Western gives me a snap job," he said. "I'll only have one arm. I'll never hunt again. I'll never shoot another wild animal or bird. I'm through!"

"Maybe you can hunt with one arm," Elija said. "Maybe you can go back to the little game around here."

"I said, Elija, I'd never kill again," Wiff spoke stoutly. "I know how it feels to be shot! I'm through playing Daniel Boone and you'd better stop playing Colonel McGary who got seventy men killed in five minutes. He was no hero. You are no hero. I am no hero."

William Westbrook had a puzzled look on his face.

"Fellows, we'd better be going," Big Aaron said. "Now when you need help, Little Effie, call on us."

"Yes, call on us for anything we can help you do," Penny said. "Yours and Wiff's folks are coming in."

"How did you know to meet us?" she asked.

"We heard you were coming and we've been here at your house all day waiting," Little Ed said.

"How wonderful to have friends," Wiff said. "When I get out of here I'll sit in a chair next time at Pudd's store and I'll have a different story to tell. And I won't be dressed like Daniel Boone either."

"We'll be back later, Wiff," I said. "I see plenty of company coming."

As we left the house Little Effie was writing a check to the young ambulance driver for bringing our Wiff back home.

RICHARD TAYLOR

The Meadow

From *Girty* (1977)

SHOT THIS MORNING a fine red buck. Twelve points. Having slept in some beeches, I wake to sounds of a squirrel cutting, his long incisors gnawing small bitter beechnuts somewhere close. Breakfast. Cocking and priming, quiet as I can I settle back in my robes to spy him out, my sight fixed on leaf-ends as the upper-most glow out of the half-light and burn white along the edges, trunks still steaming. And wait. A quarter hour later brother squirrel and I both sense some third presence, the feel of some interloper moving over my body like waves. Then the hush. For a moment or two everything goes stony as we listen: insects, squirrel, twitter of thrushes, even yesterday's shower mammer-ing in the branch. Then as evenly starts up again.

Some minutes pass before I see him. Thirty paces off, head bent in the browse, a fat buck grazing his way through the high grass which abounds in the clearing. This clearing, a meadow not much larger than the shade of a sizable tree, is to my right, now fortunately upwind. Peculiar the way he moves and chews, me-thodically and cautious, raising his head now and then to catch my scent, but doesn't. He is so close I can see the dark wet dew line on his forelegs, parts of him still vague in the blue film sun-light is cutting now. The antler tree sprouting out of his crown rolls in time with the working of his jaws. Fickle, he tries one delicacy, then another, gathering salads, his arched neck deftly yanking and twisting the forage from its roots. His winter coat he has not shed yet. It's matted and shaggy, the color of dry bark, parts of it stuccoed with flaky mud. I can just make out the ring of dung beneath his tail.

Careful not to spook him, I maneuver my body into a line with his, bringing my weapon to bear. I draw a gradual bead to the center of his chest just above the jointure of the forelegs, then slowly squeeze. But my aim is off. The ball strikes slightly higher, entering right of center, and penetrates the upper neck. Ordinarily this would not stop him dead though he would likely bleed to death in some thicket several miles away. Yet this time it is enough. Too late, he pitches and bounds toward the brush. The ball must have sliced his vitals, for he wavers even while his reflexes gather the muscles into flight, gaining speed only to crumple twenty or so paces away in deep clover. Mortal.

I move toward him as if under water, my ears still swarming with the shot, that high-pitched paining sound that fills my head like a hemorrhage. When I reach him, the tremors are already in his extremities, legs stiffening in awkward jerks, large buck eyes glazing. The hooves, fine and sharp as chisels, even sharper now, have that clumsy look things take on as they are separated from their functions, lose their grace. Bending closer, I find the knot of blue-stem stuck between the front teeth, still dewed. Life and death flop in my head. Life and death. I see the long jaws chewing and now still, the yellowed glint of the cuspids with their chaw of green. My hand, no longer mine, moving by some instinct of its own to my side where the knife is. The same hand pressing the blade to cut out the tongue and liver, delicacies. Both being warm yet, more live than dead, they steam. These and some fillets from the tender part of the shoulder are all I can carry. The rest I must leave for the buzzards. Times I have seen the creeks fill with carcasses, bloated does minus one steak or a tongue. Next, I strike a fire, skewering some choice on a green stick, roasting it brown and dripping. This, with the last of my parched corn, makes a passable breakfast.

Full, I stuff what's left in my pouch, remembering to cut enough sinew from the shank to re-string my moccasins. The grass nearly dry as I gather my gear to move on. The carcass already drawing its wreath of flies. Crickets fretting their thighs inside my head. Sun inching higher. Not a gesture of cloud in the sky. Neither hearing or seeing the squirrel.

POETRY

The water made a music in his ears, there were voices in it.

    —Gurney Norman, "The Ceremony"

Predator and Prey (2004)

LINDA CALDWELL

On the farm across the creek
a drama plays in the morning mist.
Dogs bay.
My dogs answer
with territorial barks.

I see a white-tailed deer taking fences
like the athlete it is.

I find my binoculars.
The deer's long gone.
A mutt and Walker hound
nose the ground, tails moving to and fro.

My neighbor, a farmer, watches, too.
From his rigid stance
I know his agenda differs from mine.
Maybe he condemns
the hunting dogs as nuisances
or considers the running deer,
a different kind of problem.

I want to hunt with only my eyes,
pull every pleasure with my senses.

Before I return to duties,
I lecture my dogs about their safe, charmed lives.
They tilt their heads and try to understand.

I never know the ending of this morning's drama,
but I think everyone turns out with their own treasure
    except
perhaps the farmer.

An earlier version appeared in the *Chaffin Journal* (2001)

Hermit's Sack Song

JAMES GASH

What was *that?*
I peep out from the covers
just as the moon peeps out from the clouds.
Owl drops into flight
from the attic window
and floats out over the Milky Way of fog
that hangs from my windowsill.
Visage of death, leaving;
visage of life, returning
she bears meat to her gurgling young.

I crawl back under to darkness
but the moon creeps through
with a bump and a creak
and I hear the dogs leap
from the wooden drumskin of porch
taking up the alarm and carrying it off
into the distance.

Nothing. No one.

The world settles, river flowing on,
then,
sleepily,
piano notes from the musty parlor below,
truncated Satie

rising conspiratorially
from recidivist raccoon,
his lure to moonlight upon ivory.

Again the curtain parts, and
I climb out, with blanket,
onto the chill of tin roof
and into the carnival night,
all the wild things wildly
performing first summer, first bloom.
Tonight, on the glittering marquee of creation,
First Whippoorwill. First Fox.
First Peeper. First Fawn. First Cricket.

Untutored. Flawless.

And First Man.
Secreted behind my gable,
hand over mouth;
poised upon the revel
that celebrates my absence.

From *Gray's Sporting Journal* (April 2004)

The Hermit on His Gate (2004)

JAMES GASH

After months of continuous weathers together,
snowed in, mudded in, flooded in,
she's gone tonight—
her absence an oboe
in my suddenly still life
as only owl bassoons
news of thaw, up and downriver.

I flounder about in my old ways.
Four miles from any real road
what *was* it I used to do?
        one life under a single light
        in one room . . .
Old bachelor recipes wrinkle as well—
        tongue is smarter now, belly snobbier;
        doesn't want everything in one pot.

So, oh me,
        it's room to room, vacantly,
        then
                house to furthest gate,
                                stalemate.

And, oh my, I the wry
        gargoyle now
        perched atop ancient gatepost

craning outwards
straining to hear
over the moon-crazed peepers.
Irretrievably forlorn. And, unbelievably,
unnoticed. Or simply irrelevant
to this sudden Mardi Gras of woodcocks
everywhere marching out from their shy thickets
to court drunkenly across the darkling plain
all about whistling and whirring
they strut themselves into bold pairs
dancing first upon the moist earth
then gyring moonwards on tandem wing
recreating
over and again, in ritual flight
the ecstatic double-helix
exhausting the night.

For Jeff (2004)

JONATHAN GREENE

Up before dawn,
strong coffee,
out turkey hunting.

All morning nothing
sighted where last week
you saw a quorum here

voting which way to go.
But that was before
the season opened.

Easy to say to yourself:
this quiet time alone
its own reward.

Though with no bird
There's nothing
to brag about or eat.

Walking Sticks

JONATHAN GREENE

Walking sticks
huddled by the front door
with infinite patience,
waiting to hike the steep hill.

Each paired to a favorite hand
that knows its shape,
cognate of an ancient history,
common destinations
and memories stored deep
in the heartwood.

From *Fault Lines* (2004)

The Buffalo

JAMES BAKER HALL

crossing the yard to the old wall
I'm drawn along a circle
through each thing a full moon
seen over a considerable area of the earth
including the vast oceans rises
and walks down the wall
and through me
in the evolving white shape of a cat
for years these stones lay afield
gathering his footsteps even the clicks
sound old and have come a long way
his fur slipping through my hands
what did my ancestor hear
upon seeing the Shawnee step into
this moonlight with a small stone taken up
and shaped to his use what did the Shawnee hear
when the gun was cocked where did the sounds go
when the buffalo were slaughtered
were they fixed in time
or were they freed
into the real world mistaken
for snapping twigs or distant
thunder or history at night
when the small creatures walk this wall
isn't it the same gravity audible
the weight of each thing settling

defining the size of its earth the dead
clicking along in the moonlight with us
great silences in between
and within each of them
the dwindling herds

From *The Mother on the Other Side of the World* (2004)

Hawkbells

JAMES BAKER HALL

hawks valued more
for their hunting
than their flight
are called birds
of the fist they
work from trees
and fence posts
in swift dashes
and twists often
close to the ground
falcons valued more
for their flight
are called birds
of the lure they
work in open fields
from a high pitch
above the quarry
diving and swooping
when you tame a bird
of prey for sport you
are said to man it
from hawk houses
and mews you work
with gloves tethers
hoods and bribes
a bird of prey
on the wrist is

a watch her
talons time
she examines you
as closely as you
her with this difference
you belled her wanting
flight always to return
to you you turned
yourself into a what
would you call it
to hood a bird
on the wrist
you must pull
the knot tight
with your teeth
a smile maybe or
threat even a kiss
whatever the promise
the bird says bird

From *The Mother on the Other Side of the World* (2004)

Down in the Counties (2004)

STEPHEN HOLT

Baled hay aloft in the moon of wild game,
my father and his father lighting out
in a '47 coupe. Heading west.
In back, Old Dinah rides
again, yellow coat rippling. Bound
for Lewis, Fleming, Mason: counties
named for men who hunted in another early
time.
      Time to share a drink or two, unload
once more long tales of other hunts
with other men, all linked like shells
in double-barreled guns. The great dog heard
and saw it all. Dying moon, lifting fog, shouts
and blasts across her daylong run, her silver
sounds into a silver sky.
          So long
since Dinah and her master followed
phantom scents across the misted, high
grass trails. My father easing closer
toward the edge, these days I roam
frozen fields alone, hounded by the hollow
wind in empty chambers.
            In this far season
scouting through the stubble, chasing words
to fill the barrel of my pen, I squeeze
my finger on the trigger. I steady my aim
to set their story straight.

Trapper at Camp Dix Bend (2004)

STEPHEN HOLT

How does he live in such an isolated
cabin, such a mackinaw wilderness
we wondered. There he'd be, every time,

up the slope on a path worn slick
as a muskrat slide, waiting, as if he knew
we were coming. He laughed to see

our paddles dig hard through a rocky
twist and drop in the current. Once
as we passed he was scarcely visible,

separated from us by mist and pelting
rain, fresh rain that filled the creek
and our canoe, and also fell on him.

Undercurrents

CHARLIE HUGHES

In the darkest time of the year
after the dogwood blossoms floated away
and the moon was a shallow crescent
drifting in the cloudy stream,
Father would get his carbide lamp and gig
down from the smoke house wall.
After the five tines were honed
to needles, he'd slip on
his felt hat and I'd file after him
through the dark pasture to the creek.
Following the wet-weather branch,
we'd wade through the sawgrass
and into the river below the riffles.
There, we'd pause on a sandy rise, listening
to the gurgling mystery. He'd fill
the lamp with carbide, and for water
dip its canister into the stream,
then flame the acrid jet with his Zippo.
Silver shadows beneath the surface
might be a leaf or mussel shell,
or the long fish we sought finning upstream
in the current. My job was to stand and wait
with the burlap bag. I'd watch his light
floating on the misty surface and see
his giant hunchback shadow in the foliage
of the riverbank. As the moon washed

endlessly through the fingers of sycamores,
I'd become weary of waiting alone.
Then I'd follow his light into the black
swirling at my knees. Water snakes
were attracted to the light.
They'd follow the beam to its source,
periscope head slicing the rippling surface.
He'd just fling them aside with his gig.
I had neither light to attract them,
nor gig for protection.
I'd wade the rocky bottom, alert
for every prick of overhanging limb,
every scrape of ankle or slither
of saw-toothed blade against bare leg,
never knowing what we might strike,
or what might strike me.

From *Shifting for Myself* (2002)

Fishing with My Father in the Middle Field Pond (2005)

LEATHA KENDRICK

A dirt bank rises from the fescue,
on the pond side, its soil thin and shaly,
scaled and red as sunset. At the edge

the mud's an uneven scribble,
a cuneiform of cleft hoof marks.
We sit on a handy log—your long legs
in their light orange coveralls,
my short ones in corduroy,
the knees nearly worn through.

Our cane poles are long and light,
our fishing line a twisted cotton
twine. It will be years before
I know monofilament. Today
I'm learning worms—earthworms
from the garden. They whip
their head-tails back and forth—

no teeth, no mouths that I can find,
no way to tell what they would say
except that air is not their element
and they want out of it. You show
me how to thread one on a hook,

how to spit on it for luck, how
to swing the line out 'til it finds
the deepest water, how to miss
hooking my fingers or my side.
And then we sit, our twin bobbers
aslant the wind, their masts

like compass pointers. We wait
for bites. Now? I ask each time
mine tips or jiggles. No, you say—
not 'til it goes under. Quiet settles.
I see new leaves, treetops,
a patch of sky waving
in the pond. A twig

with iridescent wings lands on
my line. That's luck, you say,
and before I can ponder that
you add, Look! Dragonflies.
Two armored bits of stick
whose doubled wings are veined

in rainbows, weave and dance,
join end to end, rise and sink.
It's so still I can hear their whir.
My bobber's moving. I see
a head, like a stubby rock
with pinpoint eyes and under it

a bowl of polished stone turned
upside down and floating in
the sky-filled water. See
the turtles, you say quietly,
and two pull themselves onto
a log across the way. It's clear
they like the sun. We are

disappearing where we sit.
Our lines don't really matter—
we're two bobbers in the water.

Fish Story

JIM WAYNE MILLER

By February we were growing restless.
Evenings we sorted through our tackle boxes,
making everything neat, untangling snarls
of leaders, hooks, and swivels, sharpening knives.

Our boat sat on its trailer in the garage.
We polished brass, put in a cockpit light,
tightened cleats, coiled anchor lines,
ran the motor in a barrel until it purred.

But the lake held low and muddy, full of stumps
and rocky ridgetops jutting from the chop
like the backs of dinosaurs. A week of rain
brought the creeks down muddy. Cold wind drove

the water, slopping it against red-clay
banks, stirring it to a soupy froth
of rising falling rocking driftwood rafts.
On a Saturday in March when road signs droned in wind

we took a whole trunk full of kites and fishing rods
and drove to the big field beside the school. I snapped
a flopping shark-faced kite onto a spinning
rod and let it run, shaking its head,

up into the currents of high blue sky.
Fred flew a red-eyed dragon, Jimmy a bat.
We braced the butts of our rods against our stomachs,
we pumped, we reeled. I tried the stiff salt-water

rod and reel and burned my thumb as the shark
raced off with all my monofilament.
We gave the kites their heads, then fought them down,
adjusting drags, comforting burnt thumbs

with a kiss. The kites took off toward distant trees,
made long, bull-necked runs at far-away
power lines, darted, twisted, rolled,
swooped while we ran backwards reeling up slack line.

More than once they tangled our lines high
overhead. A low-test line I used for trout
in Trammel Creek popped like a pistol shot,
then fell toward me as the shark lunged free.

We waved to him and wished him luck.—That night
blue sky kept running underneath my eyelids,
and the shark-faced kite with jagged teeth
was climbing still, trailing a length of line.

I waved again.

From *The Brier Poems* (1997)

The Faith of Fishermen

JIM WAYNE MILLER

What they see when they go down to the base of the dam
   in rubber suits, with helmets, air lines and weighted
   shoes to inspect the twenty-six gates and clear away
   debris—what they see, the divers say we wouldn't
   believe: catfish (they shake their heads remembering), catfish lying like logs around those gates, up
   close against the concrete, catfish with heads as big
   as buckets ("We don't mess with 'em!"), eighty, a
   hundred, a hundred and twenty-pounders, yellow
   eyes that glow in the underwater beam.

But we believe. The divers are our priests. Ours is the
   faith of fishermen eager for any authoritative word.
   We need to know wonders are still alive at the base
   of the steel and concrete world we've made—a
   yellow-eyed whiskered wildness, something old and
   other, akin to what we feel, powerful, cold, living in
   the dark around the gates that regulate the rivers of
   our lives.

From *The Brier Poems* (1997)

After the Hunt

JIM WAYNE MILLER

Catch up the hounds by collar and scruff,
And drop the cattle gate!
The fox has holed in Reynolds' Bluff,
The moon is low, it's late!
    He savors flame and crowds the fire,
    A stubborn leaf in frosty air,
    The wrinkled brown old hunter.

The truck's hood skims the safety rail
And veering, blunt and black,
It dogs a darting cottontail,
A hound's nose on the track.
    He nods and pitches when I brake,
    A leaf that falls when branches shake,
    The wrinkled brown old hunter.

The truck hums down to Turkey Creek;
Loose boards slap on the bridge.
The sun comes up, a first red streak,
Through white oaks on the ridge.
    He sleeps beside me on the seat,
    Dry leaf in morning's surge and heat,
    The wrinkled brown old hunter.

From *Copperhead Cane* (1964)

Spring Hunt

JIM WAYNE MILLER

The fox has holed in the bluff.
My lantern's smoking, throwing a ragged ring.
On Hanlin's slope I raise your horn to call the hounds:
He's holed! He's holed! Time to go home!—
The horn is hushed, but in the coves,
Like flies in swaying spiderwebs:
He's holed! Go home!

My lantern flutters.
Out of the south, this wind
Must blow off melons rotting on the vine,
Off pines and sandroads,
Sulphur creeks and swamps—
A wind as sweet and thick as funeral flowers.

A hound howls answer to my horn.
The lantern globe is almost black.
I snuff the flame and wait,
Under the thin blue sickle-moon.

From *Copperhead Cane* (1964)

Woodcock of the Ivory Beak

ELIZABETH MADOX ROBERTS

[Note: It was said among the pioneers that in Kentuck
would be found a woodcock whose beak was of pure ivory.]

Bough of the plane tree, where is the clear-beaked bird
That was promised? When I walked here, now, I heard
A swift cry in my own voice lifted in laughter, —absurd
Mock at a crow, —crying under the low, rough word,
Saying, "Where?" saying, "When?" saying, "Will it be,
　　here,
The woodcock of the ivory bill? Will it be? Where?"

Old winds that blew deep chaos down through the valley,
Moan-haunted, grief-tossed, shudder and shackle, rout and
　　rally.
Where? Did you toss a feather and bend a plume a cold
　　May early
Morning, when the ivory bill shone, song lifted, pearly
Clear on the rose-stippled, blue-shadowed trunk of the
　　plane tree?
Oh, woodcock of the ivory beak, I came here to see.

From *Song in the Meadow* (1940)

Hunter

JAMES STILL

He killed one hundred and thirty-one squirrels
In a single season (a man of honor who wouldn't lie,
Where one squirrel digit too many be false);
Shot one hundred and thirty-one squirrels
To see them plummet to a mounting tally;
One hundred and thirty-one flying tails,
Livers, lungs, spines, hearts penciled to a count,
Two hundred and sixty-two eyes fixed in numbered glaze;
And I said, "Pick your ears, listen! hark to me!
Should a single squirrel remain, the final one
In the forests of the world, would you gun for it,
Go for it plumb, scour universe if you could?"
And he said (spoke in honest frankness),
"I sure would."

From *From the Mountain, From the Valley* (2001)

Mountain Fox Hunt

JAMES STILL

Fox in the thorn-patch . . .

Shrill notes of a sheep's horn billow down the hills
Crusted with shadows. Fetch the long rifle from the wall,
Draw ramrod and tallow-dipped rag through the slender
  shaft,
Awakening a dulled skill. Bring out the rusty bullet mold
With a finger of lead; blow a slow fire upon the cold hearth.
Shave the lead pellets to a good roundness ere the wildcat
Chills the night with his crying.

Call up the yawning hounds from the chimney's warmth
Beneath the puncheon floor. Call up the dusty hounds
With a rasher of sow-belly and a greasy corn-pone
While fog loiters in the valleys and dark coves
Over blossoming elder and wine-red sumac,
And a swollen moon rides the sky-orchards.

Bright on the mountain the hunter's fire strips darkness
  down
From quavering poplars fluting the night;
And slouched shadows wall the glow against a taller sky
Listening through the leaf-sounds. Listening:

The hills muffle the long crying; then suddenly clear
Over razor-back ridges comes a wild freshet of barking.

Hounds flow down the slope in a narrowing sweep
And up again in brown tidal strokes.
Their voices are the wild trumpets
Catching the night air for their blasting:
Thin, high-nasal, the young hounds with soft brown eyes
Burst into a stark tenor. Thunderous and earthy,
The bass-viol music of old hounds rends the damp air.

Gaunt and anxious, the swiftening pace
Flings the dogs clamoring down the trail
Where an odd prescience guiding padded feet shall fail
And a gum-stump mark the end of a perilous way.
In the stern interval when warm blood stains the earth
And the mellow banjos of the hounds' throats are still,
A catamount cries the chilled and living day.

From *From the Mountain, From the Valley* (2001)

Alpheus Waters
September 2, 1863

JOE SURVANT

First the black oak
taller than the rest,
then back a quarter mile
to where a patch of ferns
grows round a sinkhole,
and beyond that
the swampy place
where I shot the
big fox squirrel.
Next were hickories,
or was it cedar
then hickory?

Anne was right,
I should have hunted
our familiar woods,
not these endless, monotonous flats
where every tree's the same
and the land offers up no mark.
Still, ten squirrels is
a good day's work,
if I can follow myself out.
The big, shaggy hickory
alive with squirrels
and the ground a carpet of cuttings
must be just past this thicket.

And there's the gum
where I sat and watched awhile,
or was it oak?

The sun has long since
passed from sight
and Anne must be
worrying at the coming night.
The shade of all these leaves
grows thicker.
I can no longer see
the spider webs which
hang from all the boughs.
My eyes burn from them,
and they cling to all my clothes.
My rifle has become a burden.
The lush, soggy air
is filled with the humming
of mosquitoes
and the trees are endless
in the rising night.

From *Anne & Alpheus, 1842–1882* (1996)

Falling Asleep While Hunting

JOE SURVANT

Where hickory ends
cedar begins,
a dark house
where deer stir,
uneasy in the rooms.
I enter through the hall,
the one dry ravine
where bedrock is revealed
in sheets of solid pain.
This is where the buck
hung back
letting the does
go first.
I lie on sun-warmed stone.
My gun is laid aside.
The smell of evergreen
and gentle Indian grass.
The leaves, the rock,
the tick of the briers'
dry brown clock.

Somewhere a door opens.
The buck motions,
but I do not understand.
Then he stands and sheds
his soft brown skin.

A Statement of the Case

RICHARD TAYLOR

The words sleep under a lid
of water,
drowsing near cattail feet.

Rubbed with heat
they skim to the surface
on fish scales,

break silver
through mats of green algae
into voice-giving air.

Some are trapped
in the lure of a
turtle's eye,

but a few, four-winged,
skate up
with the dragonfly.

Still others, too many,
rise to bump horns
with the sycamore:

outmatched, stuck hopelessly,
they fret and pitch
on points of white antlers.

From *Earth Bones* (1979)

Fishing at Valleyview Ferry

RICHARD TAYLOR

Flat, unbroken below the bluffs,
the river opens its hands unhindered.
The feet of birds flown north
claw dark spurs in the bank.
Above, slicing the sky
in geometrical shards, two cables
dwindle across to
where the ferry is tethered.
Higher, above the treeline, diminished cows
calmly chew the pasture into milk.
The blade of a mower spinning in shade
strikes a root-knee, hard.
As the fish bolts from the sudden hook,
we are trussed in cables with a vision of cows.

From *Bluegrass* (1975)

Bluegills

RICHARD TAYLOR

Barely visible
they blend so well,

their glossed scales
merge with light.

Bass know them only
by their telltale shadows,

blunt-tipped cigars
that nose along the bottom,

light snacks slipped from cover
to flit past bedrock,

cross sulphurous leaf
and silt mound, trembling.

From *Earth Bones* (1979)

346

Stocking the Pond

RICHARD TAYLOR

The fish we bring to stock the pond
are fingerlings,
fat batches packed in plastic bags,
migrants caged in globes of prisoned creek.

White bass and whiskered cats,
each forms a puny version
of its prospective self,
each detail carefully pencilled
fin to gills,
perfect down to pin-stripes
on the dorsal scales,
the mica eyes precise as targets.

The hatchery says
to ease them in still bagged,
to let them be
until the waters balance
chill for chill.

Impatient, quick to set them loose
and so release ourselves,
we scoop them out
handful after silver handful,
long dimes which spill their glitter,

skim past cattails
and algae clouds,
till their noses rub against
the dark shelf
they call home.

From *Earth Bones* (1979)

American Portrait: Old Style (An Excerpt)

ROBERT PENN WARREN

II

The Dark and Bloody Ground, so the teacher romantically said,
But one look out the window, and woods and ruined cornfields
    we saw:
A careless-flung corner of country, no hope and no history here.
No hope but the Pullman lights that swept
Night-fields—glass-glint from some farmhouse and flicker of
    ditches—
Or the night freight's moan on the rise where
You might catch a ride on the rods,
Just for hell, or if need had arisen.
No history either—no Harrod or Finley or Boone,
No tale how the Bluebellies broke at the Rebel yell and cold steel.

So we had to invent it all, our Bloody Ground, K and I,
And him the best shot in ten counties and could call any
    bird-note back,
But school out, not big enough for the ballgame,
And in the full tide of summer, not ready
For the twelve-gauge yet, or even a job, so what
Can you do but pick up your BBs and Benjamin,
Stick corn pone in pocket, and head out
"To Rally in the Cane-Brake and Shoot the Buffalo"—
As my grandfather's cracked old voice would sing it
From days of his own grandfather—and often enough
It was only a Plymouth Rock or maybe a fat Dominecker
That fell to the crack of the unerring Decherd.

From *Now and Then: Poems 1976–1978* (1978)   349

Heart of Autumn

ROBERT PENN WARREN

Wind finds the northwest gap, fall comes.
Today, under gray cloud-scud and over gray
Wind-flicker of forest, in perfect formation, wild geese
Head for a land of warm water, the *boom*, the lead pellet.

Some crumple in air, fall. Some stagger, recover control,
Then take the last glide for a far glint of water. None
Knows what has happened. Now, today, watching
How tirelessly *V* upon *V* arrows the season's logic,

Do I know my own story? At least, they know
When the hour comes for the great wing-beat. Sky-strider,
Star-strider—they rise, and the imperial utterance,
Which cries out for distance, quivers in the wheeling sky.

That much they know, and in their nature know
The path of pathlessness, with all the joy
Of destiny fulfilling its own name.
I have known time and distance, but not why I am here.

Path of logic, path of folly, all
The same—and I stand, my face lifted now skyward,
Hearing the high beat, my arms outstretched in the tingling
Process of transformation, and soon tough legs,

With folded feet, trail in the sounding vacuum of passage,
And my heart is impacted with a fierce impulse
To unwordable utterance—
Toward sunset, at a great height.

From *Now and Then: Poems 1976–1978* (1978)

VII: Tell Me a Story

ROBERT PENN WARREN

[A]

Long ago, in Kentucky, I, a boy, stood
By a dirt road, in first dark, and heard
The great geese hoot northward.

I could not see them, there being no moon
And the stars sparse. I heard them.

I did not know what was happening in my heart.

It was the season before the elderberry blooms,
Therefore they were going north.

The sound was passing northward.

[B]

Tell me a story.

In this century, and moment, of mania,
Tell me a story.

Make it a story of great distances, and starlight.

The name of the story will be Time,
But you must not pronounce its name.

Tell me a story of deep delight.

From *New and Selected Poems: 1923–1985* (1985)

352

APPENDICES

Buffalo, bears, elk, pigeon, deer, waterfowls, beavers,
otters, turkeys. You could never hunt your fill.
Around the salt licks the beasts trample one another
under and you can kill as fast as you can
load your weapon and fire. The pigeons black
the air with their wings and their flights are like
a thunder in the sky.

— Elizabeth Madox Roberts, *The Great Meadow*

Kentucky State Record Fish

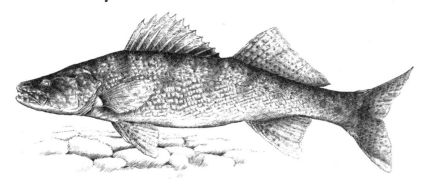

Species	Weight	Caught By	Location	Date
ANCIENT FISH				
Bowfin	15.08 lb.	Norman Moran Lexington, KY	Green River	5/31/99
Longnose gar	40 lb.	Kelsie Travis Jr. Paducah, KY	Ohio River	8/8/56
Paddlefish (spoonbill)	106 lb.	William Chumbler Calvert City, KY	Ohio River	3/23/04
Sturgeon	36 lb. 8 oz.	Barney Frazier Corbin, KY	Lake Cumberland	10/3/54
BASS, BLACK				
Coosa bass	0.15 lb.	Gerald Gallagher Louisville, KY	Martin's Fork Lake	7/4/04
Kentucky bass (spotted bass)	7 lb. 10 oz.	A. E. Sellers Louisville, KY	Nelson County	6/13/70

Species	Weight	Caught By	Location	Date
Largemouth bass	13 lb. 10.4 oz.	Dale Wilson London, KY	Wood Creek Lake	4/14/84
Smallmouth bass	8.46 lb.	Coolie Williams London, KY	Laurel River Lake	5/16/98

BASS, TEMPERATE

Species	Weight	Caught By	Location	Date
Striped bass (rockfish)	58 lb. 4 oz.	Roger Foster Somerset, KY	Beaver Creek, Lake Cumberland	12/11/85
Hybrid striped bass	20 lb. 8 oz.	Mark Wilson Louisville, KY	Barren River Lake tailwaters	4/27/91
White bass	5 lb.	Lorne Eli Dawson Springs, KY	Kentucky Lake	7/11/43
		—TIE— B. B. Hardin Mt. Eden, KY	Herrington Lake	6/3/57
Yellow bass	1 lb. 1 oz.	DeWayne West Hopkinsville, KY	Little River, Lake Barkley	3/10/91

CARP/SUCKER

Species	Weight	Caught By	Location	Date
Bighead carp	52 lb.	Donny Lee Johnson Island, KY	Green River	7/8/01
Blue sucker	4 lb. 15 oz.	Howard Hillard Livermore, KY	Green River	4/25/01
Buffalo (smallmouth)	55 lb.	Clinton Roby Waddy, KY	Kentucky Lake	3/23/00
Common carp	54 lb. 14 oz.	Ricky Vance Paris, KY	South Fork, Licking River	3/13/71
Golden redhorse	4 lb. 5 oz.	Leif Meadows Stanton, KY	Red River	4/22/98
Grass carp	55 lb. 8 oz.	Daniel Nally Springfield, KY	Private lake, Washington County	3/14/01

Species	Weight	Caught By	Location	Date
River redhorse	9 lb. 1 oz.	Denny Hatfield London, KY	Rockcastle River, Laurel County	9/20/03
White sucker	1.63 lb.	Larry S. Salachi Stanton, KY	Slate Creek, Montgomery County	3/19/98
Silver carp	9 lb. 8 oz.	Marvin Joe Southard McHenry, KY	Ohio River	8/8/04

CATFISH

Blue catfish*	104 lb.	Bruce W. Midkiff Owensboro, KY	Ohio River, Cannelton Dam tailwaters	8/28/99
Bullhead catfish	5 lb. 3 oz.	Harry Case Paris, KY	Guist Creek Lake	10/18/92
Channel catfish	32 lb.	Kyle Estep South Point, OH	Ohio River, Boyd County	5/26/04
Flathead catfish	97 lb.	Esker Carroll	Green River	6/6/56
White catfish	1.82 lb.	Charlie Crain Shelbyville, KY	Guist Creek Lake	5/3/04

DRUM

Freshwater drum	38 lb.	Larry Cardwell Morgantown, KY	Green River	6/5/80

HERRING

Skipjack herring	2 lb. 13 oz.	Greg Cary Burkesville, KY	Cumberland River	5/19/01

MOONEYE

Goldeye	2 lb. 0.64 oz.	Mark Smith Lexington, KY	Kentucky River	4/21/01

Species	Weight	Caught By	Location	Date
PERCH				
Sauger	7 lb. 7 oz.	Rastie Andrew Jamestown, KY	Lake Cumberland	4/28/83
Saugeye	6 lb. 8 oz.	Chuck Kouns South Shore, KY	Ohio River, Greenup County	2/19/98
Walleye	21 lb. 8 oz.	Abe Black Shaker Heights, OH	Lake Cumberland	10/1/58
Logperch	0.02 lb.	Amanda Webb Prestonsburg, KY	Dewey Lake	4/21/04
Yellow perch	1 lb. 4 oz.	Willie Jackson Murray, KY	Kenlake Resort, Kentucky Lake	11/17/04
PIKE				
Chain pickerel	5 lb. 6 oz.	Tommy Thompson Bardwell, KY	Forked Lake, Carlisle County	7/8/83
Grass pickerel	0.63 lb.	Gerald Gallagher Louisville, KY	Wilson Creek, Bullitt County	7/17/89
Muskellunge	44.38 lb.	Scott A. Flint Lexington, KY	Cave Run Lake	5/9/98
Northern pike	9 lb. 8 oz.	Howard F. Renfro Madisonville, KY	Strip mine lake, Muhlenberg County	10/15/81
Tiger muskie (muskellunge hybrid)	13 lb. 12 oz.	James Mollet Auxier, KY	Dewey Lake	5/5/81
SUNFISH				
Bluegill	4 lb. 3 oz.	Phil Conyers Madisonville, KY	Strip mine lake, Hopkins County	8/5/80
Crappie (white or black)	4 lb. 6 oz.	Kevin Perry Mt. Sterling, KY	Farm pond, Montgomery County	6/29/97

Species	Weight	Caught By	Location	Date
Green sunfish	1 lb. 5 oz.	Raymond Peyton Lebanon, KY	Farm pond, Marion County	6/13/00
Longear sunfish	13.28 oz.	Anthony Lynch Salyersville, KY	Strip mine pond, Magoffin County	6/23/94
Redbreast sunfish	0.88 lb.	Tim King Stearns, KY	Marsh Creek, McCreary County	9/1/97
Redear sunfish (shellcracker)	3 lb. 1 oz.	Betty Truax Finchville, KY	Farm pond, Shelby County	5/24/82
Rock bass	1 lb. 10 oz.	H. S. White Cadiz, KY	Casey Creek, Trigg County	5/26/75
Warmouth	1 lb. 6.2 oz.	Jon Hoover Louisville, KY	Private pond, Jefferson County	7/21/03

TROUT

Species	Weight	Caught By	Location	Date
Brook trout	1 lb. 5 oz.	R. James Augustus Louisville, KY	Martin's Fork of Cumberland River	8/21/82
Brown trout	21 lb.	Thomas Malone Crofton, KY	Cumberland River, Lake Cumberland tailwaters	4/30/00
Lake trout	5 lb. 5 oz.	John McDonogh Jeffersontown, KY	Cumberland River, Lake Cumberland tailwaters	4/4/83
Rainbow trout	14 lb. 6 oz.	Jim Mattingly Somerset, KY	Cumberland River, Lake Cumberland tailwaters	9/20/72

*World record—line class; catch and release.

Note: These were the records as of January 10, 2005. No listing for a species means that no record currently exists for that species.
Source: Kentucky Department of Fish and Wildlife Resources.

Kentucky's All-Time Top Ten
Boone & Crockett White-tailed Bucks*

SCORE	NAME	COUNTY
Typical		
204 2/8	R. Smith	Pendleton
191 3/8	W. Burrell	Meade
189 3/8	J. Cooper	Lewis
189 0/8	F. Kendall	Shelby
189 0/8	J. Newcomb	Pendleton
188 6/8	J. Bickett	Muhlenberg
188 5/8	B. Johnson	Lewis
188 2/8	T. Raikes	Marion
188 2/8	L. Yates	Allen
187 6/8	C. Meuth/L. Melton	Union
Nontypical		
270 5/8	C. Crawford	Henry
260 1/8	B. Brogle	Garrard
252 4/8	R. Broyles	Livingston
240 7/8	A. D. Mefford	Lewis
238 2/8	E. Rigdon	Barren
238 1/8	T. Fetters Sr.	Lewis
237 1/8	J. Fulton	Wayne
236 3/8	W. Buchanan	Union
234 1/8	J. Smith	Lewis
232 3/8	D. Hounshell	Breathitt

* Scores are based on antler length, mass, and width and rack symmetry.
Racks displaying normal antler development are generally considered typical, while those with numerous abnormal features are classified nontypical.

Source: Kentucky Department of Fish and Wildlife Resources.

CONTRIBUTORS

HARRIETTE SIMPSON ARNOW (1908–1986) was born in Wayne County, Kentucky, and graduated from the University of Louisville in 1930. She taught school in Louisville and Pulaski County, Kentucky, before moving to Cincinnati, Ohio, in 1934 to concentrate on her writing. In 1936, she published her first novel, *Mountain Path*. She married Harold Arnow in 1939, and by 1944, the Arnows had moved to Michigan. *Hunter's Horn* was published in 1949, followed by *The Dollmaker* in 1954, probably her most successful novel.

JOHN JAMES AUDUBON (1785–1851) is widely considered America's foremost naturalist and illustrator of birds. He lived and worked in Kentucky from 1807 until 1819, when he left to become a taxidermist for the Western Museum in Cincinnati, Ohio. His artistic renderings in *Birds of America*, published in four volumes

between 1827 and 1838, are considered, according to the *Kentucky Encyclopedia*, "unsurpassed in their accuracy and beauty." This work was followed by four additional books, including his well-known *Ornithological Biography* (1831–1839).

DAVE BAKER, a native of Fayette County, Kentucky, baled hay, raised tobacco, mucked horse stalls, and laid sewer lines "before wising up and getting a journalism degree from the University of Kentucky in 1985." He worked fifteen years as a reporter at daily newspapers throughout the state. He is the editor of *Kentucky Afield*, the magazine of the Kentucky Department of Fish and Wildlife Resources.

WENDELL BERRY is a poet, essayist, novelist, farmer, conservationist, and former professor of English at the University of Kentucky. He is the author of more than forty books of fiction, essays, and poetry, including, most recently, the novel *Hannah Coulter* and *Given*, a collection of new poems. His work has been honored with numerous awards, including the T. S. Eliot Award, a Lannan Foundation Award for nonfiction, the Aiken Taylor Award for poetry, and the John Hay Award of the Orion Society. He lives and farms in his native Henry County, Kentucky, with his wife, Tanya Berry.

SAM BEVARD, a native of Mason County, Kentucky, is a graduate of Morehead State University, a former teacher, and a retired Kentucky state probation and parole officer. He writes a weekly column for the *Maysville Ledger-Independent* and lives on Cabin Creek with his wife and sons.

GARNETT C. BROWN JR., a native of Louisville, Kentucky, is a retired U.S. Air Force colonel. After leaving the military, he returned to Kentucky to pursue farming and writing. He is the author of *A Death in the Family: Dealing with Grief's Slow Wisdom* and contributes a weekly column, "Open Mind," to the *Bourbon County Citizen*. His work has appeared in anthologies and in a variety of magazines, including *Kentucky Monthly* and *American Rifleman*. A graduate of the University of Kentucky, Webster University, and the National War College, he resides in Lexington, Kentucky, with his wife, Sandra.

LINDA CALDWELL lives on a Madison County, Kentucky, farm that has been in her family for over a century. Her work has been published in *Prairie Schooner, Chaffin Journal, Appalachian Heritage, Tears in the Fence*, and several regional anthologies. She is presently writing a play for the First Kentucky Women's Playwright Festival.

WALTER L. CATO JR., a native of Beaumont, Texas, grew up in Kentucky and has practiced law in Louisville since graduating from the University of Louisville School of Law in 1962. He is an avid and well-traveled hunter and fisherman, and his stories have appeared in *Southwestern Newsweek, Southwestern Weekly, Knife World*, and *Happy Hunting Ground*. He lives in Green Spring, Kentucky, with his wife, Joyce Tyrrell.

HARRY M. CAUDILL (1922–1990), a native of Long Branch, Kentucky, was a writer, attorney, professor, activist, and state legislator. After graduating from the University of Kentucky in 1948, he established a law practice in Whitesburg, where he wrote his celebrated book on the problems of Appalachia, *Night Comes to the Cumberlands* (1963). His articles have appeared in numerous magazines, including *Atlantic Monthly, Audubon, The Nation*, and the *New York Times Sunday Magazine*. His other books include *My Land Is Dying, A Darkness at Dawn*, and *The Mountain, the Miner, and the Lord*.

BILLY C. CLARK, a native of Catlettsburg, Kentucky, is the award-winning author of numerous short stories and poems and fourteen books, including *A Long Row to Hoe*, which was on *Time* magazine's list of "Best Books" in 1960; *Trail of the Hunter's Horn*, which was selected as a Crowell-Collier Classic; *The Champion of Sourwood Mountain*, a Book-of-the-Month Club selection; and *Song of the River*, which won the Friends of American Writers Award in 1957. His newest novel is *By Way of the Forked Stick* (University of Tennessee Press, 2000), and a collection of short stories, *Miss America Kissed Caleb*, was recently issued by the University Press of Kentucky. A bridge connecting Kentucky and West Virginia has been named in his honor, and a large flood-wall mural at Catlettsburg pays tribute to Clark and his works.

THOMAS D. CLARK (1903–2005) was born in Louisville, Mississippi. He completed his master's degree in history in 1929 at the University of Kentucky, where he served as a professor and department chair in history from 1931 until his retirement in 1968. The Historian Laureate for Kentucky, Clark received, at age 100, the American Historical Association Award for Scholarly Distinction. He authored or edited more than thirty books chronicling Kentucky's history, including his popular *Pills, Petticoats, and Plows: The Southern Country Store; The Greening of the South; The Southern Country Editor; Kentucky: Land of Contrast;* and *A History of Kentucky.* His most recent book, coauthored with Margaret A. Lane, is *The People's House: Governor's Mansions of Kentucky.*

SOC CLAY of South Shore, Kentucky, is a full-time freelance writer and an award-winning photojournalist whose work has appeared in most major North American outdoor publications, including *Outdoor Life, Fins & Feathers, Ohio Fisherman*, and *Fish-*

ing Facts. In 1983 he was named Kentucky poet laureate, the first outdoor writer to receive such a distinction. He is currently the fishing field editor and south regional editor for *Heartland USA Magazine,* a columnist for Cabela's *Outfitter Journal,* and outdoor editor for *America on the Road.* He was recently inducted into the National Freshwater Fishing Hall of Fame and the Outdoor Legends Hall of Fame.

GAYLORD COOPER has been writing about the Ohio River and the hills and hollows of eastern Kentucky for more than twenty years. He is working on a collection of ghost stories that he gathered in the highlands of eastern Kentucky, and he has recently become a storyteller, adapting his written material to the oral form and telling his stories in schools and state parks. He has worked for the Norfolk Southern Railroad for twenty-five years and lives in South Shore, Kentucky.

DAVID DICK grew up in Kentucky, and his wife, EULALIE "LALIE" CUMBO, is a descendant of Kentuckians who was born in New Orleans and raised in Woodville, Mississippi. In 1985, David retired from CBS News, where he was an Emmy Award–winning correspondent, and Lalie left Revlon International to return to Kentucky, where they founded Plum Lick Publishing. David is the former director of the School of Journalism at the University of Kentucky (his alma mater) and the author of ten books, the most recent being *Jesse Stuart—The Heritage (A Biography).* For the past fifteen years, David has been a columnist for *Kentucky Living* magazine, and Lalie writes a column for the Kentucky Farm Bureau's newspaper, *All Around Kentucky.* They live with their daughter, Ravy Bradford Dick, in David's ancestral home on the banks of Plum Lick Creek in eastern Bourbon County, on land purchased in 1799 by his great-great-great-grandfather Joshua.

RON ELLIS is the author of the fictionalized memoir *Cogan's Woods*. He was one of fourteen writers selected to attend the University of Montana's Environmental Writing Institute in 1998 to study with Rick Bass. His work has appeared in *Kentucky Monthly*, *Appalachian Life*, *Kentucky Afield*, and the *Journal of Kentucky Studies*. In 2004, he received a Professional Assistance Award in creative nonfiction from the Kentucky Arts Council. He lives in northern Kentucky with his wife and son.

WILLIAM E. ELLIS is a Kentucky native and a graduate of Georgetown College, Eastern Kentucky University (EKU), and the University of Kentucky. He retired from EKU in 1999 after thirty-six years of teaching at the high school, junior college, and university levels. He is EKU's university historian and emeritus professor of history.

JOE TOM ERWIN grew up on a farm in Calloway County, Kentucky, a half mile from the land settled by his great-great-grandfather in 1824. He was a marine during World War II, studied at Murray State and Indiana universities, briefly edited a weekly newspaper in Missouri, and taught high school for seven years. He was sports information director at Murray State for twenty-five years and occasionally taught journalism. He also wrote an outdoor column for the *Louisville Courier-Journal* in the 1960s and 1970s. He shares his Kentucky Lake house with Belle, a five-year-old Labrador retriever.

DICK FARMER is a native of Louisville and was raised in Paducah, Kentucky. A 1974 graduate of Morehead State University, he now manages Commonwealth NewsCall, a Kentucky-based service that produces and distributes audio news releases. Farmer has more than twenty years' experience in radio news and public relations, including seven years as news director and operations manager at Kentucky News Network. In the mid to late 1970s, he was an information specialist with the Kentucky Department of Fish and Wildlife Resources, where he produced weekly and monthly radio series, worked on the weekly television program, and contributed to *Happy Hunting Ground*.

SIDNEY SAYLOR FARR grew up in southeastern Kentucky and received a bachelor's degree from Berea College in 1980. She is the author of seven books, as well as other pieces of short fiction, poems, and articles. Farr retired in 1999 from the Archives and Special Collections Department of Hutchins Library at Berea College.

JOHN FOX JR. (1862–1919) was born in Bourbon County, Kentucky. He attended Transylvania College for two years and graduated from Harvard in 1883. He worked briefly for the *New York Sun* and *New York Times* before returning to Kentucky in 1885 due to illness. In 1890, he moved to Big Stone Gap, Virginia, where he worked for his family as a speculator. It was there that he wrote his most popular books, *The Little Shepherd of Kingdom Come* and *The Trail of the Lonesome Pine*. He remains one of Kentucky's best known and most popular authors.

W. D. "BILL" GAITHER was born and raised in the Ohio River town of Ludlow, Kentucky, where he roamed the riverbanks and nearby woods. An internationally renowned artist, he has worked in many mediums but favors bronze. His major commissions include sculptures or paintings for the Ruffed Grouse Society, Safari Club International Conservation Association, and Maruri Corporation of Seto, Japan, as well as decanters for the Austin Nichols Distillery and Old Bardstown Bourbon. His work has been exhibited in the Royal Dalton International Collection in Birmingham, England; Denver's Wildlife World Museum; and the Aichi Prefecture Ceramic Museum in Nagoya, Japan. He has also authored several books on birds and reptiles, worked as a hunting and fishing guide, and traveled extensively to fish, hunt, and study wildlife. He lives in Galveston, Texas, where he operates Gaither Studios.

GARY GARTH is a freelance writer and a regular outdoor contributor to the *Courier-Journal* and a contributing editor for *Field & Stream*. He lives in Murray, Kentucky, with his wife, Katy, and twin daughters, Rebecca and Sarah.

JAMES GASH makes his living as a farmer in rural Owen County, Kentucky, but he "poaches enough time from his chores to indulge a daily writing habit." One result, nearly completed, is a long work of fiction about the great Burley Belt farmers' strike of 1908.

JANICE HOLT GILES (1909–1979), a native of Arkansas, moved to Louisville, Kentucky, in 1941. Best known for her series of novels about the American frontier, including *Hannah Fowler* and *Run Me a River*, she is the author of twenty-four books. She lived with her husband, Henry Giles, on their farm in Adair County, Kentucky.

CAROLINE GORDON (1895–1981) was born on Merry Mount Farm in Todd County, Kentucky, near Guthrie, the home of Robert Penn Warren. In addition to her long and respected career as a novelist and short story writer, she worked as a reporter, writing teacher, book reviewer, and critic. She published nine novels, including *Penhally*; *Aleck Maury, Sportsman*; *None Shall Look Back*; and *Green Centuries*. Her short stories were collected in *The Forest of the South* and *Old Red and Other Stories*. She died in Chiapas, Mexico.

JONATHAN GREENE is the author of more than twenty books, most recently *Fault Lines* (poems) and *On the Banks of Monks*

Pond: The Thomas Merton/Jonathan Greene Correspondence. He lives on the Kentucky River with his wife, the weaver and photographer Dobree Adams.

JAMES BAKER HALL, a former poet laureate of Kentucky, is a widely sought-after ambassador of the state's exceptional literary culture. He is the winner of a Stegner fellowship in fiction at Stanford, an NEA fellowship in poetry writing, a Southern Arts fellowship in photography, and the prestigious Pushcart and O. Henry prizes. His poems have been published in the *New Yorker, Poetry,* the *Paris Review,* the *Hudson Review,* the *Sewanee Review,* and the *Kenyon Review,* among others. He has taught at Stanford, New York University, MIT, and the University of Connecticut. From 1973 to 2003, he was a professor of creative writing at the University of Kentucky.

JAMES ALEXANDER HENSHALL, MD (1836–1925), is widely known for his classic 1881 *Book of the Black Bass.* Born in Baltimore, Maryland, Henshall practiced medicine in Kentucky during the Civil War and fished for smallmouth bass in Kentucky streams, primarily Elkhorn Creek, the South Licking, and Stoner Creek. He published a supplement to his classic, *More about the Black Bass,* in 1889 and *Bass, Pike, Perch & Others* in 1903.

RICK HILL, a native of Jeffersontown, Kentucky, is a wildlife artist for the Kentucky Department of Fish and Wildlife Resources and the illustrator for its official magazine, *Kentucky Afield.* He is a largely self-taught artist, and his paintings and sculptures of fish have been featured in *Bassmaster* and *In-Fisherman* magazines, among others. In 2001, his poster "Wetland-Slough Ecosystem" won first place in a national competition sponsored by the American Association of Conservation Information, and in 2004, he won the Ohio Valley National Bank Award for "Life and Death Rhythms of the River" at the Kentucky National

Wildlife Art Exhibit. He lives in Shelby County, Kentucky, with his wife, Gina, and their children, Sarah and Clinton.

STEPHEN HOLT, from far northeastern Kentucky, teaches at Ohio University Southern. His first book of poems, *Late Mowing*, received favorable reviews from critics. In 2002, he received the James Still Award for poetry, and in 2003, his work was nominated for a Pushcart Prize. In recent years, he has served as poetry instructor at both the Appalachian Writers Workshop on the Hindman Settlement School campus and the Appalachian Writers Association Conference. His poems have appeared in numerous periodicals, including the *Cumberland Poetry Review*, *Appalachian Heritage*, *Appalachian Journal*, and the *Journal of Kentucky Studies*.

SILAS HOUSE is the author of *Clay's Quilt*, *A Parchment of Leaves*, and *The Coal Tattoo*. He has received many awards, including the Award for Special Achievement from the Fellowship of Southern Writers and the Kentucky Novel of the Year Award. He is a frequent contributor to National Public Radio's "All Things Considered" and is a professor at both Spalding University and Eastern Kentucky University. He lives in eastern Kentucky with his wife and two daughters.

HARLAN HUBBARD (1900–1988) was born in Bellevue, Kentucky, and studied for two years at the National Academy of Design in New York. He is widely known for his work as an artist and writer and for his "self-sustaining" lifestyle at Payne Hollow in Trimble County, Kentucky, where from 1952 until his death he painted, wrote, and enjoyed art, music, and food with his wife, Anna, a classically trained pianist. He is the author of *Shantyboat*, the story of a 1,385-mile river journey from northern Kentucky to the bayou country of Louisiana, and *Payne Hollow Jour-*

nal, among others. He also produced hundreds of oil paintings, watercolors, woodcuts, and sketches.

CHARLIE HUGHES grew up on a Kentucky farm. His poetry and fiction have appeared in many prominent literary magazines, including *Kansas Quarterly, Kentucky Poetry Review, International Poetry Review, Hollins Critic, Art/Life, Cumberland Poetry Review, Appalachian Heritage,* and *Cincinnati Poetry Review.* Hughes lives in Jessamine County, Kentucky, with his wife, LaVece. When he isn't engaged in literary pursuits, he is employed as an analytical chemist.

LEATHA KENDRICK has lived in Kentucky since she was three years old and grew up on a small farm in Simpson County. She is the author of two volumes of poetry, *Science in Your Own Back Yard* and *Heart Cake,* and numerous essays and book reviews. The recipient of two Al Smith fellowships from the Kentucky Arts Council (KAC) and grants from both the KAC and the Kentucky Foundation for Women, she coedited *Crossing Troublesome, Twenty-five Years of the Appalachian Writers Workshop* and wrote the script for a documentary film about the life and work of Doris Ulmann. Her poems have appeared in numerous periodicals, including *Shenandoah, Cold Mountain Review, Appalachian Journal,* and the *Louisville Review,* and in the anthologies *Listen Here: Women Writing in Appalachia, Her Words,* and *Intimate Kisses: The Poetry of Sexual Pleasure.* She and her husband, Will, live in Floyd County, where they raised three daughters.

BARBARA KINGSOLVER was born in Annapolis, Maryland, and grew up in Carlisle, Kentucky. Her stories and essays have been widely published in *Smithsonian, Paris Review, National Geographic Magazine, Audubon,* the *New York Times,* and *The Nation,* among others. She is the author of the critically acclaimed novel *The*

Bean Trees, as well as *Animal Dreams, Pigs in Heaven, High Tide in Tucson: Essays from Now and Never, The Poisonwood Bible, Prodigal Summer, Small Wonder*, and others. She divides her time between Tucson, Arizona, and a farm in southern Appalachia, which she shares with her husband and two daughters.

ART LANDER JR., a native of Louisville, Kentucky, is the outdoor columnist for the *Lexington Herald-Leader*. He began his career as a full-time writer shortly after graduating from Western Kentucky University in 1972. He was a columnist for the Kentucky Department of Fish and Wildlife Resources' *Kentucky Afield*, and his work has appeared in numerous other magazines, including *Travel, Southern Living, Outdoor Life, Field & Stream, Turkey Call*, and *Southern Outdoors*. He is the author of *A Fishing Guide to Kentucky's Major Lakes*. He lives with his wife, the folk artist Bonnie Brannin Lander, and his three children near Bethlehem, Kentucky.

GEORGE H. LUSBY, a native of Georgetown, Kentucky, spent thirty years working in the Scott County school system and has served as its judge-executive since 1990. He often writes of his love of fishing in nearby Elkhorn Creek in his column "Crawfish and Minnows" for the *Georgetown News-Graphic*. He lives with his wife, Betty, in Georgetown.

GEORGE ELLA LYON, a Harlan County native, has published more than thirty books for children and adults. Her most recent titles are *Weaving the Rainbow, Sonny's House of Spies*, and *A Kentucky Christmas*, which she edited. She holds a PhD from Indiana University. She is married to musician and writer Steve Lyon and has two sons. Lyon makes her home in Lexington and works as a freelance writer and teacher.

NICK LYONS is a former professor of English at Hunter College and the founder and publisher of Lyons Press. He is the author of several hundred essays published in the *New York Times, Harper's, Outside, Fly Fisherman, Field & Stream*, and elsewhere. He is the author of several dozen books, most of them on fly-fishing. He lives in Woodstock, New York, with his wife, the painter Mari Lyons.

BOBBIE ANN MASON was born in Mayfield, Kentucky. She is the author of *Shiloh and Other Stories*, which won the Pen/Hemingway Award; *Feather Crowns*, which was a finalist for the National Book Critics Circle Award and won the Southern Book Award, as did *Zigzagging Down a Wild Trail*; and the best-selling novel *In Country*, which was adapted for a film starring Bruce Willis. Her memoir, *Clear Springs*, was a finalist for the Pulitzer Prize, and her fiction, which has appeared in the *New Yorker, Atlantic Monthly, Paris Review*, and *Harper's*, has received the O. Henry Award and Pushcart Prize. She is writer-in-residence at the University of Kentucky and lives with her husband, Roger, in Anderson County, Kentucky.

CHAD MASON was born and raised in Muhlenberg County, Kentucky, where he grew up hunting small game with his father and grandfather. Mason is a contributing writer to *Outdoor Life*, a columnist for *Gun Dog*, and a frequent contributor to numerous other outdoor publications. His first book, *Voices on the Wind*, earned the rare "Must-Read" rating from *Today's Books*. He lives with his wife and three daughters near Des Moines, Iowa, where he divides his time between freelance writing and ministry in a small Mennonite church.

FRANK F. MATHIAS, a Maysville, Kentucky, native who was raised in nearby Carlisle, is a graduate of the University of Kentucky and professor emeritus of history at the University of Dayton, where he taught from 1963 to 1987. He is the author of *The GI Generation: A Memoir*, which was selected by the Ohioana Library Association as the best nonfiction book by an Ohio author in 2001, and *GI Jive: An Army Bandsman in World War II*. He lives in Dayton, Ohio, with his wife, Florence Duffy.

JIM WAYNE MILLER (1936–1996), a Kentucky poet laureate, was born in Leicester, North Carolina. He graduated from Berea College and Vanderbilt University and lived for more than thirty years in Bowling Green, Kentucky, with his wife and three children. He taught German and German literature at Western Kentucky University. Miller was the author of seven collections of poems, including *The Mountains Have Come Closer* and *Brier, His Book*. His first novel, *Newfound*, was named "Editor's Choice" by the American Library Association; its sequel, *His First, Best Country*, was also produced as a play. A scholar of Southern Appalachian literature, Miller edited works by James Still, Jesse Stuart, and Cratis Williams and was one of the guiding spirits behind the Appalachian Writers Workshop at Hindman Settlement School. During his life he won a number of awards, including the Thomas Wolfe Literary Award and the Appalachian Writers Association's Book of the Year and Outstanding Contribution to Appalachian Literature Awards.

JOHN E. MURPHY (1909–1982) wrote the weekly outdoor column "Afield and Astream" for the *Kentucky Post* for forty years. He also served as editor for the League of Kentucky Sportsmen and as a field representative for *Outdoor Life*. He received numerous awards during his distinguished career, including being named Kentucky's Outstanding Sportsman in 1957 and receiving the first James Henshall Award in 1963 for a series of *Kentucky Post* stories on fly-fishing.

FREDRICK C. PFISTER is an outfitter who resides in Lexington, Kentucky, where he "continues his quest for perfection in the trout fly, the side-by-side shotgun, the turkey box call, and the ultimate dry martini."

ELIZABETH MADOX ROBERTS (1881–1941) was born in Perryville, Kentucky. At age three, she moved with her family to Springfield, Kentucky, which she would forever call home. After graduating from the University of Chicago in 1921, she returned to Kentucky and concentrated on writing. Her most enduring works include the novels *The Time of Man* (1926), named a Book-of-the-Month Club selection, and *The Great Meadow* (1930), which the *New York Times Book Review* described as "the stuff of which enduring literature is made." Later in her career, she published another volume of poems titled *Song in the Meadow*. She died in the spring of 1941 and was buried in her beloved Springfield.

PAUL SAWYIER (1865–1917), an American impressionist, was born in Madison County, Ohio, and moved to Frankfort, Kentucky, at age five. Initially home-tutored in art, at age nineteen he studied under Thomas S. Noble at the Cincinnati Art Academy and four years later with William Merritt Chase in New York City, where he also observed the famous portrait painter John Singer Sargent. By 1890, Sawyier had returned to Kentucky and studied for a year in Covington under the celebrated portrait painter Frank Duveneck. From 1887 to 1917, it is estimated that Sawyier painted approximately 2,500 originals, primarily water-color scenes of Elkhorn Creek, the Kentucky River, and Frankfort. More than 300 Sawyier originals have been reproduced as limited-edition art prints.

THOMAS D. SCHIFFER has actively competed in the shooting sports for half a century, as well as serving as the director and

president of the Corps of Kentucky Longriflemen and the director, vice president, and president of the National Muzzle Loading Rifle Association. He is the black powder editor of the *Single Shot Journal* and the author of *Peters & King: The Birth &
Evolution of the Peters Cartridge Co. and the King Powder Co.* He
and his wife, Carol, live on Flintlock Farm in Boone County,
Kentucky.

DAVE "MUDCAT" SHUFFETT, the host of Kentucky Educational
Television's Emmy-winning *Kentucky Life*, served as host and
producer of *Kentucky Afield* from 1989 to 1995 before moving on
to pursue his own television series, *Outdoors with Dave Shuffett*,
which was nationally syndicated. He is a native of Greensburg,
Kentucky, and a graduate of Murray State University. He lives in
Franklin County with his wife, Diann, and their children, Miranda and Willie.

JAMES STILL (1906–2001), a poet laureate of Kentucky and the
recipient of two Guggenheim fellowships, was born in Lafay-
ette, Alabama. He came to Kentucky in 1932 and served as librarian of the Hindman Settlement School in Knott County for
six years while writing poems and short stories. He published his
first collection of poems, *Hounds on the Mountains*, in 1937; his
best-known novel, *River of Earth*, was published in 1940 and is
considered an American classic. The author of numerous other
works, he went on to publish two volumes of collected short stories, *Pattern of a Man and Other Stories* in 1976 and *The Run for
the Elbertas* in 1980, and a poetry collection, *The Wolfpen Poems*,
in 1986.

JESSE STUART (1906–1984) was a celebrated novelist, short story
writer, and poet from Greenup County, Kentucky. He was des-
ignated poet laureate of Kentucky in 1954 and was nominated

for the Pulitzer Prize in poetry in 1977. His better-known works include *Taps for Private Tussie, Man with a Bull Tongue Plow, The Thread that Runs so True,* and *Hie to the Hunters.* He was born and lived most of his life in his beloved W-Hollow in Greenup County.

JOE SURVANT, a native of Owensboro, Kentucky, has taught literature and writing at Western Kentucky University for more than thirty years. He is the author of four collections of poetry. *Anne & Alpheus, 1842–1882,* which won the Arkansas Poetry Prize, and *Rafting Rise* are the first two books of a trilogy about rural Kentucky, each set in a different century. He finished a term as Kentucky's poet laureate in April 2005.

RICHARD TAYLOR is a professor of English at Kentucky State University. He is the author of a novel, *Girty;* five collections of poetry; *Three Kentucky Tragedies;* the accompanying text for *The Palisades of the Kentucky River,* a book of photographs by Adam Jones; *The Great Crossing,* a history of Leestown and its association with the whiskey industry; and *Virginia's Western War,* a history of the Revolution in Kentucky that he coauthored with Neal O. Hammon. From 1999 to 2001, Taylor served as Kentucky's poet laureate. He and his wife live near Frankfort and own Poor Richard's Books. He is currently working on a fictionalized treatment of the Confederate guerrilla Sue Mundy.

STEPHEN M. VEST is a columnist and the publisher of *Kentucky Monthly* magazine. A native of Louisville, he and his wife, Kay, and their four children make their home in Frankfort. Prior to starting *Kentucky Monthly* in 1998, Vest was the news editor of the *Blood-Horse,* a national thoroughbred magazine, and spent more than fifteen years writing for newspapers in Kentucky, Indiana, and the Carolinas.

ROBERT PENN WARREN (1905–1989), a native of Guthrie, Kentucky, achieved international critical and popular acclaim as a poet, novelist, essayist, dramatist, literary critic, and editor. His better-known works include *Night Rider* (1939), *All the King's Men* (1946), *Audubon: A Vision* (1969), and *Now and Then: Poems 1976–1978* (1978). He was the first poet laureate of the United States and won the Pulitzer Prize three times—the only writer to win for both poetry and fiction.

JOHN WILSON served as writer and then editor of *Happy Hunting Ground* from 1973 to 1990. He earned bachelor's and master's degrees in English from the University of Florida. Wilson retired from the Kentucky Department of Fish and Wildlife Resources in 1999 and now travels the country with his fifth-wheel trailer.

STEPHEN M. WRINN is a passionate fly fisherman and the director of the University Press of Kentucky in Lexington, where he resides with his wife, Julie, and sons, Eli and Jeremiah.

PERMISSIONS

Art

Cover painting, "The Fisherman" by Paul Sawyier (1865–1917), courtesy of William H. Coffey, owner of Paul Sawyier Galleries and publisher of Sawyier art prints, Frankfort, Kentucky. Copyright by William H. Coffey.

Woodcuts by Harlan Hubbard (1900–1988) featured on the title page, with the epigraph, and on each section divider, from the collection of Claude W. Caddell, courtesy of Claude W. Caddell. Copyright by Claude W. Caddell.

Back cover painting, "Pitching Down," and pen and ink illustrations throughout by Rick Hill. Copyright by and courtesy of the Kentucky Department of Fish and Wildlife Resources.

Prologue

Excerpt from "The Adventures of Col. Daniel Boon; Containing a Narrative of the Wars of Kentucke" reprinted from *The Discovery, Settlement and present State of Kentucke* by John Filson (Wilmington, Printed by James Adams, 1784).

Essays

"Fishing in the Ohio" by John James Audubon, reprinted from *Delineations of American Scenery and Character* (Simpkin, Marshall, Hamilton, Kent, & Co., Ltd., London, 1926).

"Frog Fever" by Joe Tom Erwin. Previously published in a slightly different version in the *Louisville Courier-Journal* (Summer 1975). Copyright 1975 by Joe Tom Erwin. Used by permission of the author.

"Tickling, Noodling, etc." by Dick Farmer, from *Happy Hunting Ground* (November–December 1979). Copyright 1979 and used by permission of the Kentucky Department of Fish and Wildlife Resources.

Excerpt from "Meats: Game and Tame" by Sidney Saylor Farr, from *More than Moonshine: Appalachian Recipes and Recollections.* Copyright 1983. Reprinted by permission of the University of Pittsburgh Press.

Excerpt from "Fox-hunting in Kentucky" by John Fox Jr., from *Blue-grass and Rhododendron*, published by the University Press of Kentucky (copyright 1994). Used by permission of the University Press of Kentucky.

"Fishing with the Stewart Brothers" by W. D. "Bill" Gaither, from *The Northern Kentucky Fly Fishers', Ink.* Copyright 2004 by W. D. "Bill" Gaither. Used by permission of the author.

"Our Creek Is Full of Memories" by George Lusby, from *The Best of Crawfish and Minnows*, published by Georgetown Newspapers, Inc. (copyright 2000). Reprinted by permission of Georgetown Newspapers, Inc.

Excerpt from *Clear Springs* by Bobbie Ann Mason. Copyright 1999 by Bobbie Ann Mason. Used by permission of Random House, Inc.

Excerpt from "Inheritance" by Chad Mason, from *Voices on the Wind*. Copyright 2002 by Chad Mason. Reprinted by permission of Countrysport Press.

Excerpt from "They Call Him Lucky" by Frank F. Mathias, from *The GI Generation: A Memoir*, published by the University Press of Kentucky (copyright 2000). Used by permission of the University Press of Kentucky.

"Fly Fishing Time: Nature-Fresh, Cool;—It's September" by John E. Murphy, from the *Kentucky Post and Times Star* (September 6, 1963). Courtesy of the *Kentucky Post*.

"The Kentucky Longrifle" by Thomas D. Schiffer. Copyright 2004 by Thomas D. Schiffer. Used by permission of the author.

"The Scolding" by Dave "Mudcat" Shuffett. Copyright 2004 by Dave "Mudcat" Shuffett. Used by permission of the author.

"Chapter Added to Rich History" by Stephen M. Vest, from *Kentucky Monthly* (June 2000). Used by permission of *Kentucky Monthly*.

"Old Reels" by John Wilson, from *Happy Hunting Ground* (July 1973). Copyright 1973 and used by permission of the Kentucky Department of Fish and Wildlife Resources.

"A Connecticut Yankee in a Kentucky Trout Stream" by Stephen M. Wrinn, from *The Kentucky Fishing Journal* (August 2002). Copyright 2002 by Stephen M. Wrinn. Used by permission of the author.

Fiction

Excerpt from *Hunter's Horn* by Harriette Simpson Arnow (originally published 1949). Copyright 1997 and reprinted with permission of Michigan State University Press.

Excerpt from *Nathan Coulter* by Wendell Berry, from *Three Short Novels*. Copyright 2002 by Wendell Berry. Reprinted by permission of Counterpoint Press, a member of Perseus Books, LLC.

"A Special Incident" by Sam Bevard, from the *The Ledger-Independent* (May 20 and June 5, 2003). Reprinted by permission of *The Ledger-Independent*, Maysville, Kentucky, a Lee Enterprises publication.

"Ely's Bass" and "Fur in the Hickory" by Billy C. Clark, from *Sourwood Tales: Stories by Billy C. Clark*, published by G. P. Putnam's Sons, New York. Copyright 1968 by Billy C. Clark. Used by permission of the author.

"The Great Ohio River Catfish Hunting Expedition" by Gaylord Cooper, from *Down the River: A Collection of Ohio Valley Fiction & Poetry* (1991). Copyright 1991 by Gaylord Cooper. Used by permission of the author.

Excerpt from "Into the Woods" by Ron Ellis, from *Cogan's Woods*. Copyright 2001 by Ron Ellis. Used by permission of Pruett Publishing Company.

Excerpt from "Big Boy" by William E. Ellis, from *River Bends and Meanders: Stories, Sketches and Tales of the Kentucky*. Copyright 1992 by William E. Ellis. Used by permission of the author.

"Mountain Fox Hunt" and "Hunter" by James Still, from *From the Mountain, from the Valley: New and Selected Poems*, edited by Ted Olson and published by the University Press of Kentucky (copyright 2001). Used by permission of the University Press of Kentucky.

"Alpheus Waters, September 2, 1863," from *Anne & Alpheus, 1842–1882* (University of Arkansas Press, 1996), and "Falling Asleep While Hunting," from *The Louisville Review* (Spring 2005), by Joe Survant. Copyright by Joe Survant. Used by permission of the author.

"Fishing at Valleyview Ferry" by Richard Taylor, from *Bluegrass* (Larkspur Press, 1975). Copyright 1975 by Richard Taylor. Used by permission of the author.

"Bluegills," "Stocking the Pond," and "A Statement of the Case" by Richard Taylor, reprinted from *Earth Bones*. Used by permission of Gnomon Press.

"Tell Me a Story," from *New and Selected Poems: 1923–1985*, and "American Portrait: Old Style" and "Heart of Autumn," from *Now and Then*, by Robert Penn Warren. Copyright 1985, 1978 by Robert Penn Warren. Reprinted by permission of William Morris Agency, Inc. on behalf of the author.

Appendices

"Appendix A: Kentucky State Record Fish" and "Appendix B: Kentucky's All-Time Top Ten Boone & Crockett White-tailed Bucks," courtesy of the Kentucky Department of Fish and Wildlife Resources.